THE HAUNCH OF ˙

Picture of 'Les Mitchell holding Norman Bryant's pewter mug'. Copyright author

The Haunch of Venison

of Venison

Salisbury

AN A–Z HISTORY

Ruby Vitorino Moody

THE HOBNOB PRESS

First published in the United Kingdom in 2022

by The Hobnob Press,
8 Lock Warehouse,
Severn Road, Gloucester GL1 2GA
www.hobnobpress.co.uk

British Library Cataloguing in Publication Data
A catalogue record for this book is available from the British Library

ISBN 978-1-914407-39-0

Typeset in ITC New Baskerville 11/14 pt.
Typesetting and origination by John Chandler

Front cover: The Haunch through the Poultry Cross (photograph by Harvey Bince website: binceproductions.co.uk ; Social media: @binceproductions)

Back cover: The author on the steps to the restaurant (photograph by Spencer Mulholland)

Contents

This book is dedicated to

MARIA CHEATER POTTO
LOUISA BRADBEER POTTO
FLORENCE BRADBEER
DOROTHY BRADBEER LEMON
OLIVE BENNETT
CELIA WARD
KATE JAKEMAN
VICKY LEROY
JUSTYNA MILLER NUGENT
ANASTASIA AND ANNA SAMOILOVA

Acknowledgements

Thank you to: Les Mitchell, Frogg Moody, Helen Lederer,
And in no particular order…
D. Edward King, Alex King, Baptiste Vitorino, David Taylor, Bill Jakeman, Will Jakeman, Tony Leroy, Justyna Miller Nugent, Anastasia Samoilova, Ilya Klekovkin, Rod Poynting, Nick Spring, Ben Spring, Tim Hayter, Peter Sherlock, Kristi Summers, Ian Turner (CAMRA), Neil Beagrie, George Fleming, Elizabeth Turner, Anne Chumley, Adrian Green, Keith Blanchard, Samantha Hulass, Val Gainsford, Spencer Mulholland, Jonathon Russ of Greenfields, Matt Pike, Paul 'Nobby' Norbury, Barry Wix, Edward Stow, Albert Paz, Anthony Hamber, Alan Wherry, Gail Fawcett, Alan Crooks, Tom Corbin, chotiedarling.co.uk, Dauntseys school, Salisbury Journal.
A very big thank you to all the staff at Salisbury reference library, and at the Swindon and Wiltshire History Centre, and Salisbury Museum. Also, to all the staff at the Haunch of Venison 2022, who continue to help make it the special place that it is.

Sources

I have elected not to list each source individually, because they are mainly cited in the text:

The information found in the newspapers comes in a large majority from the *Salisbury Journal* and the articles can be found on British Newspapers Online, as can articles from Staffordshire and Essex. I have cited the year, at least, and I am confident that it is possible to find the articles using the advanced search engine. Articles which are too recent to be found online, can be consulted using the microfiche reader at Salisbury Reference Library. As I write, it is my intention to print out all the newspaper articles used, and deposit them with the Wiltshire and Swindon History Centre in Chippenham.

The History Centre in Chippenham has a large archive for the Haunch of Venison (WSA 1884), which contains leases, solicitor's letters, wills and some personal letters. The records for the Merchant's house are held in a separate box (WSA 1900). The Parish Rates books and the Easter books are in Chippenham, as are records for Salisbury Infirmary. Swayne's *Churchwarden Accounts*, 1896, are in Salisbury Reference library, as is R. G. Gorden's study, *The Inns of Salisbury*.

I have used Ancestry.com extensively when researching family histories. Ancestry is not only useful for researching family trees, but there are many wills which can be consulted free online, as well as the censuses, parish records, and army records. It is also useful for reaching out to descendants of the family concerned. I am grateful to Helen Lederer for helping me construct The Haunch of Venison Tree, which is fairly extensive and can be looked at on Ancestry, although it contains only the Bradbeer/Potto family.

Other wills can be ordered from the Gov.UK website. I have also ordered copies of a collection of death certificates, and some wedding certificates, cited in the text. These will also go to the Wiltshire and Swindon History Centre in Chippenham.

I have found a great deal of information in the archives at Salisbury Museum, which has boxes of ephemera. The source for this is Firmin Bradbeer's daughters, Mrs Dolly Lemon and Miss Marjorie Bradbeer – we must thank the foresight of Mr Bill Oglethorpe who was the solicitor and friend of Mrs Lemon and managed to pass the ephemera to the museum.

Committing oral history to paper has been an important part of this work, and I have tried to go back to the main protagonists where possible, so that they can tell their own stories, which I have tried to corroborate. Some of the longer interviews have been recorded, and can hopefully also be given to the History Centre in Chippenham.

I have consulted British history Online, and have scoured most of Salisbury local history books during the research for this book. Two which stand out are *Endless Street*, by John Chandler, which deals mainly with the Merchant's House, and Anthony Hamber's book on *The Origins of Photography in Salisbury*, in which I identified pictures of Firmin and Thomas Potto. The website 'chotiedarling.co.uk' has not only the story of Chotie and Dicker at the Haunch of Venison, but has been extremely useful for understanding Salisbury in World War II.

Timeline

Owners of the Haunch	Occupiers	Kings and Queens
1450 Provost of St Edmunds		Henry VI
Hammond family until 1685	Hammond family from 1590 at least	Elizabeth – Charles II
Powell family until c.1741	John Godfrey 1712	George I
	James Beret 1738	George II
Fawconer family until 1803	Oostis Merryweather 1784	George III
	Thomas Crewe 1791	
	Thomas Drake 1795	
	Thomas Cheater 1798	
Butcher family until 1819		
Cooper family until 1874	Maria Cheater and Firmin Potto 1832	William IV
	Firmin Potto	Victoria
Potto family until 1930	Louisa Potto	
	Alfred Bradbeer 1902	Edward VII
	Firmin Bradbeer 1903	
Simonds Brewery until 1960	Dolly Edwardes 1944	George VI
	Clifford Johnson 1949	
	Ian Roy Bennett c.1950	
Courage until 1991	Peter and Celia Ward 1967	Elizabeth II
	Bill and Kate Jakeman 1970	
	Tony and Vicky Leroy 1981	
Enerprise Inns until 2021	Justyna Miller 2006	
	Alex Marshall 2012	
	Ilya Klekovkin, Anastasia and Anna Samoilova 2015	
Stonegate in 2022		

Preface

There is a saying that old Salisbury was a city of 'Pigs, Pubs, and Parsons'. I'll change 'pigs' slightly to include the 'live' market, and Butchers Row. The Haunch of Venison sits between the Poultry Cross and St Thomas's church, and both have been integral to its history. On market days the pub would be crowded with thirsty farmers doing deals, and their customers. The picturesque Poultry market cross has meant that the Haunch has crept into paintings and photographs across the centuries.

The position of the building at the end of Butchers Row, has been important, too; it is almost certainly the reason that the pub is called the Haunch of Venison. The story of the cheating card player involves a butcher, and a smoke jack discovered in a fireplace shows that large joints of meat were roasted on the spit.

The Haunch was originally built as a church house. Later on, residents of the building worshipped at St Thomas's, married there, christened their children there, had their funerals there, and many of them, and their families were buried there. Some of them were churchwardens

The mummified hand speaks more to the proximity of the Haunch to execution sites outside Fisherton Gaol, and on the Market Square, and the omnipresent graveyard. The 17th-century apotropaic concealed objects found at the Haunch, speak to the position of the Haunch between the church (where a mummified cat was found) and the Ox Row pub's fireplace, with its apotropaic graffiti.

There are many things about the Haunch of Venison which are mysterious, and some things that we cannot know for sure. However I think that I have discovered enough information to form *my own opinion* of the history of the building which is as follows: It was built as a church house by the provost of St Edmund's church at the same time as St Thomas's Church was being rebuilt after a collapse (and the Poultry Cross was being built). It was perhaps built to house a

fraternity/chaplain paid for by the Tailors Guild, who moved from
St Edmund's to St Thomas, around 1449/50, to coincide with the
renovations at St Thomas's. It was sold to the Hammond family
around the time of the reformation, and then to the Powell family,
who sold it to the Fawconers, who sold it to the Butcher family, who
sold it to the Coopers, who sold it to Mr Potto, and the Potto family
sold it to Simonds Brewery.

Of course, it is much more complicated than that, because
different owners have sometimes leased the premises to people who
have neither lived in the Haunch building nor owned it, but have sublet it to tenants. I have not given these people an entry in the book,
but I am thinking of people like Elliott, Dodell, and Latham, who
signed a lease with James Butcher, and Sancor(?) and Thomas Brown,
who appear to have signed a lease with the Fawconers. The landlords
have changed much more frequently than the owners, but the names
of quite a few landlords have come down to us, if not always their
stories.

We would have, perhaps, known more if Courage had not
removed deeds dating from 1671 to 1755 from the file at Chippenham
for framing and display at the Haunch, and these were subsequently
lost.

I have opted not to include most of the tenants and owners of
the merchant's house, unless they lived in the side of the house which
now includes the upper restaurant room of the Haunch of Venison.
The house was a building separate from the Haunch of Venison,
and the connecting door was made only in the early-20th century.
The owners and tenants have been covered in John Chandler's book
Endless Street, and so with some interesting exceptions, I have left a lot
of them out. The records for the house can be found at the Wiltshire
& Swindon History Centre in Chippenham.

Through writing this book I have been made doubly aware of
the fleeting nature of time, and the need to capture the experiences
of Bill Jakeman, Tony Leroy, Justyna Nugent and Anastasia Samoilova
at the Haunch of Venison, so that they can tell future generations of
pub goers just what the Haunch was like 'back then'. How I would
love to know how landlords in previous centuries felt about the
Haunch, and what they served up to eat and drink, and who were
their regulars!

Sadly, it is through the stories of those later landlords and manageress that we can see only too clearly how the rise of the pub companies has threatened old buildings like the Haunch of Venison. The owners of the Haunch are not responsible for its expensive upkeep – the landlords are – and the size of the rooms limits the volume of customers possible, meaning that if landlords don't have broad shoulders, they are condemned to failure. I would love to see the Haunch of Venison under the protective wing of the National Trust, put pray that it will always stay a pub/restaurant, and never ever become a twee tearoom.

A is for Alchemy

Until 2020, a small notice on a lectern, on the north side of St Thomas's Church (directly behind the Haunch of Venison), announced that an alchemist once lived in a room above the North Porch, which was demolished in the early 19th century.

This statement seems to be based on the finding of five crucibles, graduating in size, which were found to be walled up and plastered over, in the room, when it was taken apart in 1835. It was taken that these were the bowls of an alchemist. Alchemists were trying to turn base metal into gold, discover 'the elixir of life', and find something to cure all illnesses, amongst other things. It was long thought that the elusive substance which would enable them to do these things was 'the Philosophers Stone'. Crucibles were needed to conduct experiments in alchemy.

Local Historian, Alan Crooks, is of the opinion that if an alchemist indeed lived in St Thomas's Church, then he might well have been the famous 16th-century alchemist, Simon Forman, who was born not far from Salisbury at Quidhampton in 1552. For those who are interested in Forman, much of his fascinating later history can be read online, and in print.

Simon Forman – also described as 'an astrologer, occultist and herbalist' – wrote in his diary that he was living in St Thomas's churchyard, Salisbury, at one time. Indeed, Crooks has pointed out that the Bishop of Salisbury's Deposition book states that Forman was caught fornicating with his mistress, upon the new grave of the Sheriff, Sir Giles Estcourt, buried within St Thomas's church. It was Estcourt who had been responsible for sending Forman to prison (on the south side of Fisherton Street) two years earlier, for having books on astrology and magic, within the Church.

Forman had taken to holding seances and asking the dead what the future might hold (necromancy), whilst in Salisbury. He is said to have foretold his own death, although this might have been suicide.

The Haunch of Venison stands behind St Thomas's Churchyard, and would have been an inn well known to Simon Forman (whether or not he was the tenant of St Thomas's Church). The back door of the Haunch used to be an alternative entrance to the building. Since Forman was a man known to distil Aquae Vitae (brandy), and who had been a Christmas, 'Lord of the Revels' (Lord of Misrule?) it is surely not too far of a reach to suppose that Forman would have raised a tankard or two in the Haunch, warmed his bones by the fire, and eaten some meat from the spit, before weaving his way home amongst the gravestones...

A is for Anchor Taverns

The Haunch of Venison was once an 'Anchor Tavern' at the time of landlords Ian Bennett and Bill Jakeman. 'Anchor Taverns' (created by Barclay Perkins) had become part of Simonds' hotel and catering department in 1961, and became 'Anchor Hotels and Taverns Ltd'. It was a subsidiary of Courage, Barclay and Simonds Ltd.

Its L shaped Dining Room on two levels, the old black oak Saloon Bar where barrels of beer must be rolled with nice exactitude through the Bar itself to manoeuvre them into the cellar, the 'machine' which adorns the Bar with its eighteen pewter taps once connected to the same number of casks of Sherry, Port, Gin and Rum, the delectable food and quality drinks no wonder this popular and live Tavern has established itself as a favourite with everyone who finds himself in Salisbury. For full measure there is a ghost, the Grey Lady, who walks the churchyard adjoining THE HAUNCH OF VENISON.

Salisbury itself, with its superb Cathedral and the loveliest Cathedral Close in Europe, should not be missed by any visitor from Overseas who sets foot on English soil.

An Anchor Tavern.

The oak panelling in the lower bar, described as 'black' in Anchor's publicity, was given a good clean by new landlords Bill and

Kate Jakeman when they took over the pub, as it was actually black with cigarette smoke. It is now a warm brown.

A is for Architecture

The present buildings (1-5 Minster Street) housing the Haunch of Venison pub and restaurant date from *c.*1450 (the reign of Henry VI), and form a group, together with the building on the neighbouring corner. However, it has been said that an inn dating from *c.*1320 stood near the site prior to that (Historic England. 2020). It is a Grade II listed building.

The pub was originally built as a Church House, and is referred to as such in the will of a neighbouring barber surgeon, John Wynchester, in 1458. The large restaurant room (belonging to Carters the Jewellers, downstairs) was built as a wealthy merchant's house, slightly later. A badge containing a merchant's mark can still be seen in a private area off the main dining room, and can be viewed when the spooky 'secret' 'Cloisters Bar' is opened up on Halloween, or on visits with the Civic Society.

The medieval market cross opposite the Haunch is of a similar date, and the Architect D. Edward King suggests that the Haunch of Venison should be seen in context, together with the 'Poultry Cross' as it is known. Mr King points out that links to the market cross would have originally have been much stronger, without the separation of the modern road, speeding traffic, and raised pavements. He also suggests that the Church and Commerce had much stronger links at the time. Indeed, Historian John Chandler has suggested that prior to the 1450s, the buildings on this site were most probably medieval 'shoppes', with access front and back, and King thinks that individual sites were all originally church owned land.

The Haunch of Venison appears to have become an inn sometime during the reformation, the merchant's house later being divided into two dwellings.

Edward King suggests that the other context in which the Haunch of Venison pub should be seen is to begin by looking at the buildings either side of it. This is because the façade of the Haunch has been greatly altered over the years, being rendered over, bricked in, and with the windows replaced in the 18th century. The second-floor elevation has been built up to form a parapet which conceals the lower roof and the gutter. The corner building is also timber-framed

15th century, with three stories, and it has an attic. The upper floors have been restored to expose the timber frame, with white rendered infilling. The frame has been removed at ground floor level, and replaced with cast iron columns, to provide large windows for the shop. This was common in the late 19th and early 20th centuries. The merchant's house has larger bays than the Haunch of Venison, which rise up to form two gable ends with a higher roof. It is largely unaltered, apart from the jewellers' shopfront. All the details, such as jettied floors, bay windows, bargeboards (replaced 19th century) and decor, go to demonstrate the wealth of the woollen merchant who built it.

The rear of the building is tile hung, and can be seen from the churchyard, or the alley behind the buildings.

The Haunch of Venison is a timber-framed building, which means that it was put together rather like a flat-pack. The cross frames and wall frames would have been made by master craftsmen in a carpenter's yard, or open ground, and then hoisted into place, and attached together, in a definite order, according to the prepared timber joints in the frame. The 'assembly instructions' were given by 'carpenters' marks' in the wood, and some of these can be seen carved into the frame of the Haunch lower room of the upstairs restaurant. Pegs, or 'trennels' holding the joints together, can be seen in the frame of the merchant's house upper dining room). The façade of the Haunch of Venison would have originally had exposed beams, like the buildings to either side of it.

The beams in the upper bar (the Smoking Room, or 'House of Lords'), have adze marks visible everywhere, as the beams have had their surfaces straightened, showing that they were meant to be seen. The surfaces are also keyed, to allow plaster to adhere, indicating that the room was once plastered over. Indeed, at the time of an Edwardian restoration, the then

The beam in the Haunch of Venison 'House of Commons' bar

landlord mentions in his booklet of 1909, that the beams of the lower bar ('House of Commons') were still 'decorated with paint or distemper', when a false ceiling was taken down.

The difference in height between the two bars is due to the 'Lords' being raised to accommodate a cellar beneath it, the water table being so high that the cellar could not be sunk to any depth.

The tiny bar to the right of the entrance, as you enter, is usually taken to be a 'Ladies Snug', known as the 'Horse Box'. It was formed when the lower jetty was walled in.

It is interesting to consider the damage that the heavy traffic in Minster Street has done to the frame of the Haunch of Venison, and considering the method of construction of timber-framed buildings, its survival in the modern world. In 1988, the *Salisbury Journal* claimed that the whole building had 'tilted a ¼ of an inch toward the road' (*Salisbury Journal* Oct. 13th 1988). Then landlord, Tony Leroy, speaking to the *Journal*, said that the 'floors are being pulled apart as the building slips forward' due to the building 'shuddering with each passing lorry'. Even before that, ex-landlord Bill Jakeman remembers the front of the building being lifted off, in the early 1970s. in order to insert a steel girder, because of the threat from the traffic.

The Haunch of Venison had the lower bar panelled as part of the renovations of 1906, with the panelling in the 'Lords' being 18th century. Some of the woodwork in the 'Lords' and passage way is of 17th-century origin. The panelling is usually described as 'oak' (and a former landlord, Firmin Bradbeer, mentions cherry was also used), however Rod Poynting, who works with wood, thinks that the grain shows that it is sweet chestnut; fight amongst yourselves. Beams are oak and chestnut.

The black and white marble chequered floor in the 'House of Commons' came from the Choristers part of Salisbury Cathedral, 'when the heating system was changed'. It was bought for £11.

When eating in the restaurant upstairs it should be noted that, as you pass from one part of the restaurant to the other, you are walking from one building to another. The two buildings passed into common ownership in the 18th century, the restaurant being extended in the 20th century.

The Merchant's Restaurant is the 'Great Hall' that has survived the different owners and tenants through the centuries intact. Edward King points out that the great fireplace has dressed stone, and the difference in standing between it, and the quality of the details of the Haunch of Venison proper, are readily apparent. He notes that the windows have horns dating them as late Victorian or Edwardian, although the ground floor windows are likely to be Georgian.

The floors above are no longer accessible to the public due to safety concerns, the stairs being extremely steep, and of a perilous design (although they were rented out as hotel rooms, and to lodgers, landlords and staff, until fairly recently). There is a list of them under 'R is for Rooms'.

A is for the Ancient Order of Haunchonians

I'm grateful to Keith Blanchard for sharing with me the logo of the Ancient Order of Haunchonians which he designed, together with Ken Lailey.

Les Mitchell remembers the day that the Order was created: 'there was some sort of beer festival at the Haunch, and the place was packed all the time and we couldn't get served. Well, we (*the regulars*) were fed up about that, so Keith and Ken went away and made these badges – they were only cardboard,

The Haunchonian Logo © Keith Blanchard

mind – but you couldn't tell. They were painted up, and attached to ribbons.' Keith remembers the logo printed onto T-shirts.

Les goes on, 'When we wore them, everybody just moved away and let us get served first. We didn't have to say anything. They thought that we must be something official, you see.'

B is for Bar

The bar is Edwardian, and was installed by landlord Firmin Bradbeer. The bar has ensured that the Haunch of Venison is on CAMRA's list of pubs of historic interest, because there are only a handful like it still surviving in the country.

It has a beautifully ornate wooden arch with ten little gravity-fed taps for spirits and fortified wines, and a further eight taps on the wall. According to CAMRA's website, the spirit cocks 'can be found in only four other UK pubs'. There is a date on the arch of 1910, and the name 'H. Neale, Plumber, Salisbury'.

Haunch of Venison bar then and now

The front of the bar swings open, below the rare pewter counter, to allow small barrels of beer to be delivered and manhandled into the cellar which has a short steep stair leading up to the bar. These barrels were originally delivered to the pub using a small handcart. The beer is dispensed using hand pumps mounted on the back wall – again, something which is very rare. The back counter also has original little drawers.

The lovely pewter bar counter is one of only six remaining in the entire country. In his *c.*1920 song 'The Firm Inn' Mr Firmin Bradbeer describes the bar thus: 'And her tankards <u>all</u> are shining; <u>ALL</u> her taps and counters shining;' Pewter tankards hang behind the bar, still. (The 'her' referred to would have been one of the young barmaids, Gwen Burden or Elsie Gray,).

On a cosy evening when the polished pewter and inlaid brass work is gleaming in the candle light and the soft glow of the fire, it's easy to imagine Gwen and Elsie, now long dead, rubbing and polishing away, and serving flat clear bitter in shining tankards.

B is for Bennett

Ian Roy Bennett took over the Haunch from Clifford Johnson in the early 1950s. Johnson was a 'caretaker' manager for Simonds Brewery. Bennett is still remembered by Gail Fawcett as being there in the early 1960s. He and his wife, Olive had, according to a 1956 article in the 'Hop Leaf' magazine, just the 'right type of personalities for such an outstanding house'. *Tatler* magazine described him as 'jovial'.

Ian Bennett had been born the son of the foreman of a Birmingham metal factory in 1907 but, evidently being of artistic bent, became a musician, marrying Olive whilst part of an orchestra in Scarborough, Yorkshire. By 1939 the couple had moved to the Isle of Wight, with Ian now a 'general worker' as well as still playing music.

The restaurant flourished under Mr Bennett's stewardship, and Gail can still remember beautiful fitted red carpets and matching chairs in the upstairs dining rooms. She and her sister would come in to help out on a Saturday morning: 'We would fill the salt and pepper cruets, and the mustard pots, . . . set the tables. It was Silver Service. Linen napkins and tablecloths'. Her father, Ken Fawcett, was Head Waiter, and wore a tail-coat and bow-tie – 'and it wasn't one of those on elastic; I can remember watching him tie it'.

Mr Bennett wore an evening suit, although Les Mitchell remembers him standing at the end of the bar, in the 1960s, 'dressed up to the nines – but with a pair of Wellington boots on!'

'The food and wine are of the best', said *Tatler*, in 1956. The same year, the *Hop Leaf* described the Haunch as still

Ian Roy Bennett – © Simonds family

'quite unspoilt from a traditional point of view, but it has in recent years enhanced its virtues through the excellent reputation it has won for its food, particularly its steaks and grills'.

The 'chef' was an Austrian woman named Lena Cavanagh, and she and her husband Josef lived in a caravan in Amesbury. 'She made a mean apple strudel', remembers Gail. 'I think that they were probably Jewish, and may have been wartime refugees'.

Bessie Carruthers worked in the kitchens, peeling potatoes and preparing vegetables, having taken a job as a kitchen assistant during the war years, and staying 25 years, (before retiring aged 71, when the Jakemans took over (*Salisbury Journal.* 1971), having worked also for the Wards.

Bessie Carruthers – © Salisbury Newspapers

The waitress was Muriel, and the waiter, Maurice (possibly Mcno-Lorenzo, who lived upstairs in 1971). Dorothy Fawcett (Gail's stepmother) worked in the Cloisters cocktail bar. Says Gail: She was 'a striking woman, in many ways (ouch!); Scottish, red haired, and quite tall'.

Customers for dining could enter the upstairs restaurant, without crossing the pub, via the Cloisters bar, which had one table. Ruth Phillips, the mother of historian Frogg Moody, once told this author 'The Haunch of Venison was definitely a strange place then. The restaurant was very well to do, and I would go every year, with a work colleague (She was manageress of Burtons). We would get done-up to go there, with long dresses, and get our hair dressed, but if you went in through the pub door and up the stairs that way, then it felt very odd crossing the bar, because it was quite rough'. It seems that upstairs and downstairs at the 'Haunch' have often felt like different worlds.

Downstairs was particularly busy on Market days, and the Haunch had an extension on Tuesdays until 3.30pm (the law at the time dictated that pubs must only open between 12pm and 2.30pm at lunch times).

Ian Roy Bennett was particularly famous for his inimitable way of signalling last orders of the evening to his heaving pub – He would use a 7ft length of piping, imitating a military bugle, to play the 'Last Post'. 'It never fails!' gushed the *Hop Leaf*, whilst the *Tatler* was more restrained in its admiration of Ian's 'unusual gifts'. Neither of them wondered where Ian might keep a 7ft length of piping in such a busy small space

B is for Beret

R. G. Gordon, who did a detailed study called 'The Inns of Salisbury' (available in Salisbury reference library, 2022), positively identified the following newspaper snippet, as referring to the Haunch of Venison: 'On Friday, James Beret, who kept a Brandy shop near the Poultry Cross, died raving mad.' The snippet is dated March 12th 1738.

B is for Bradbeer

Many members of the Bradbeer family were associated with the Haunch of Venison from at least 1871 until 1949, beginning with Louisa Bradbeer. she was a celebrated landlady of the Haunch of Venison under her married name, Louisa Potto. She employed her close family members, who lived and worked at the Haunch. (See Appendix 1. for a family tree of the Bradbeer family).

Louisa Bradbeer/Potto

Louisa Bradbeer's father, Francis Henry Bradbeer, was a respectable tailor, living with his family in Brown Street, Salisbury (see Appendix 2.). She was born in 1840, and was the second youngest of seven children. Her mother died when she was only four, and her father was left to bring up the children on his own. She became a dressmaker. The most interesting thing for us is when she appears on the census of 1871, as housekeeper to Firmin Potto, at the Haunch of Venison. Louisa was 30 years old, single, and living alone in the Haunch of Venison with Mr Potto, then aged 66.

There are a number of things about the situation that we can deduce: Firstly, that Salisbury nicknamed as it is now 'Smallsbury', and being much smaller then, Louisa is likely to have known Firmin Potto before she worked for him. The Bradbeers and the Pottos all worshiped in St Thomas's Church, and indeed Francis and Firmin had both been overseers to the poor for St Thomas's parish, and Francis was churchwarden. The Pottos, however, had risen financially and socially well above the Bradbeers, mostly due to Firmin's acumen, whilst Francis had been made bankrupt.

It is quite possible that Louisa had simply grown tired of dressmaking, which demanded constantly learning new styles to keep up with the dictates of fashion, and working all night by candle light to fulfil orders – even as one might develop eyesight problems. She might have been struggling to earn a living. As it was, a 'Housekeeper' was in charge of the servants and earned £20-£45 a year. This was the equivalent of up to £5, 648, in today's money, although it would go alongside board and lodging. Nevertheless, 'Housekeeper' was still 'in service'. There was no servant living in the house with them on the night of the census.

Although they probably had gas lighting downstairs in the public bars, they almost certainly sat by the fire upstairs, lit by candlelight and kerosene lamp, as the draughts whistled through the creaking building, and cold pipe tobacco lingered in the air. With no television, and no radio, they perhaps read to each other, interrupted only by the screech of an owl or a vixen screaming in the graveyard just beyond the dimpled glass in the window. As 'Housekeeper', Louisa was not working in the pub.

Two years later, on February 28th 1873, Louisa Bradbeer married Firmin Potto. He was 36 years older than her. There are a number of things that we might want to speculate about concerning Louisa and Firmin's marriage, and the first thing might be Firmin's motivations in marrying for a second time. Firmin Potto was to die just short of two years after the wedding. It states on his death certificate as a cause, 'natural decay', which is a Victorian euphemism for 'old age'. However, Firmin Potto was only 70 years old when he died, and must have had underlying health problems which were undiagnosable at the time. I suggest that his handwriting might indicate Parkinson's Disorder.

Perhaps, in his darkest night of the soul, Firmin Potto already knew that he was dying when he married Louisa Bradbeer and his love affair wasn't with her, but with the Haunch of Venison, and the successful import and wholesale business which he had built there. It is true that he might have thought to have a last-ditch attempt for a son and heir – but one did not arrive, although Louisa was only 32. It has to be said that, at this time, women would not be given a licence to run a pub, unless they were the widow of the former publican, and Mr Potto wanted to assure the continuity of the business which he had taken over from his in-laws, the Cheaters, and built up (he told this to his Potto relatives). He trusted Louisa as a capable safe pair of hands, and recognised her aptitude for running things. He wrote into his will directives for her to always see to the upkeep of the building, and to keep up the fire insurance.

The year that the wealthy, respectable, and influential Potto married Louisa, her grateful younger brother, Alfred, named his new baby son 'Firmin' Bradbeer in recognition of his eminent brother-in-law.

In February 1874, Firmin Potto bought the freehold of the Haunch of Venison. He left the Haunch to Louisa only for the remainder of her life. After Louisa's death the freehold of the Haunch was left to Firmin Potto's niece, Eliza Perry Stow Johnson. Eliza's son, Samuel Potto Johnson, later inherited the Haunch – he would state, 'it was my uncle's intention that the Haunch of Venison should always remain in our family'. The Bradbeers, then, would never own the Haunch of Venison.

It cannot be doubted that Firmin Potto spent the last year of his life inducting and instructing Louisa into the running of his wholesale business. He died in January 1875, and is buried behind the Haunch in the churchyard of St Thomas's. He left his widow the stock, and the fixtures and fittings enabling her to carry on his business.

Louisa Bradbeer – now Potto – soon made the Haunch of Venison her own Queendom, because as we have already seen, she set about giving jobs and a home to her close relatives, beginning with her sisters and nieces, and nephew. She employed two of her older sisters, who lived at the Haunch until Louisa's death.

Sarah Mary Bradbeer, who was born in 1828, was described as a tailoress in 1861, and single and living at home. By the 1881 census she had become a barmaid at the Haunch of Venison and was reported as living above the inn. She was aged 52, which considering that people aged faster in the past (and of course, women of her place in life didn't wear make-up nor dye their hair, in this era), gives a flavour of the pub with its elderly barmaid. She would not have served from behind the present type of bar, because bars like the Edwardian one, seen now, with its counter, taps, and shiny brass, came into fashion later, evolving from 'gin palaces'. Sarah would have served at the tables. Sarah was still working and living at the Haunch in 1901, aged 72, but is then on the census as 'Spirit Merchant's Assistant' to her 60-year-old employer, Louisa. It is remarkable that both Sarah's mobility and eyesight allowed her to negotiate the stairs in the Haunch. Sarah eventually retired after Louisa's death to a house at 41 St Ann Street, Salisbury, where she died in 1903. She is buried in London Road Cemetery, together with Louisa and her sister Emma under a monumental, and exceptional, Celtic Cross.

Emma Dinah Bradbeer was born in 1830. Whether she ever worked as a dressmaker or tailoress is not known, since a crucial ten years fall between the censuses. The paper trail suggests that Emma was sent to look after her paternal uncle's family in Charlton, Woolwich, London (then Kent), and was living with them in 1851, aged 20. The household consisted of the widowed Mary, aged 70, and her son Charles House Bradbeer, aged 38. Emma is listed as 'niece' to Charles, the head of the household. This begins one of the many mysteries associated with the Haunch of Venison pub. According to all the paperwork available, Mary Withers was Emma's paternal

grandmother, and Charles, her father's brother – yet Emma married Charles House Bradbeer, and all the ages and dates suggest that this was her uncle! This seems to be extremely unlikely, since such marriages were forbidden by the Church since 1560, but the couple duly had the banns read, and the marriage ceremony performed in church in 1858. The wedding certificate has a Francis Henry Bradbeer, Clothier, as the father of both; Emma's Father – as the oldest son – was named after his and Charles' father, Francis Henry. Emma and Charles married six months after the death of Mary Withers. This might be what is termed an avunculate marriage, that Mary would not approve of.

Charles House Bradbeer was a Master Tailor and Clothier who employed two men, and Emma is not listed as working during the marriage, when the couple lived in London. They had four children. Their son, Harry, died under the age of one, and two daughters, Emma, and Annie never married, but stayed with their mother all their lives. If it is true that Charles and Emma were close blood relatives, and shared 25% of their DNA, it is possible that the children suffered some sort of consanguinity problems, and were both handicapped to some degree? Remarkably their other daughter, Kate, married a relative, Henry Bradbeer and had a son, and lived to be 98. Charles died in 1881 and sometime between then and the census of 1891, Emma moved to the Haunch of Venison, living and working there as 'an assistant'. The other assistants who lived at the Haunch, were Emma's daughters, Emma and Annie; her sister Sarah, and a nephew, Francis – all working for Louisa. In 1891, Emma Dinah was still living and working at the Haunch, alongside her daughters. She was then 70, and Emma and Annie were in their 30s. Emma and her daughters were finally allowed to retire to a house at 69 London Road, Salisbury, together with her elderly brother, Charles. She died there in 1919, aged 88. Her daughters continued living at the same address (and are on the 1921 census), dying in 1932 and 1933 respectively.

However, Louisa's sisters and nieces were not the only relatives that Louisa employed. Her 16-year-old nephew, Francis – known as Frank – came up from Southampton to live and work at the Haunch of Venison. He was the second son of Louisa's youngest brother Alfred (and an elder brother of Firmin Bradbeer). Frank would stay at the Haunch over 20 years, and appears to have become the bar manager, whilst Louisa concentrated on the wholesale business.

Louisa was landlady of the old inn for 23 years, and she often appears in the pages of the *Salisbury Journal*. She could always be relied on to give prizes for the annual shooting contests of the 1st battalion Wiltshire Rifles Volunteers (as did most important tradesmen of the city, including her neighbours Mr Carter, and Mr Powney), offering typically bottles of whiskey, gin, and port. Salisbury had been one of the first cities to respond to the Volunteer movement in 1859, and the 1st battalion was raised at the White Hart Hotel the same year. Prospective members had to apply to a committee, and pay for their own uniforms, but were supplied with rifles (paid for by subscription) which remained the property of the battalion. Louisa's nephew, Francis (Frank), of the Haunch of Venison, was a member of the Wiltshire Rifles, as would be his brother Firmin Bradbeer – both captained by W. H. Jackson.

When the Reservists of 2nd Wilts battalion left for South Africa and the second Boer war in 1899, the Volunteers of the 1st battalion organised a send-off, and Mrs Potto bought them each a pipe. Although it's clear from the newspaper that tobacco was paid for from a fund begun by the *Journal*, Mrs Potto is the only person noted as presenting a gift to the departing soldiers, and it illustrates her support for the army, perhaps again through the influence of Frank, and that she had money.

Like the Pottos, and the Bradbeers, Louisa was a staunch Conservative. The Haunch of Venison provided the refreshments buffet for the annual ball of Salisbury Conservatives, at the Guildhall. In 1891 that was for 'upwards of three hundred ladies and gentlemen'. One might imagine that Louisa was in competition with other catering establishments in Salisbury, but could offer the desired quality at an advantageous price (since she was also the wholesaler for wines and spirits). Amongst those present at the ball, was Mr W. H. Jackson, solicitor. The Haunch stayed open until four am to serve conservative supporters a night cap, after the ball!

> Mrs. Louisa Potto, of the Haunch of Venison, applied for permission to sell till four o'clock in the morning on the occasion of the Conservative ball on the 6th of January.—The application was granted.—Mr. Edward Paine, of the Bell and

On August 9th, 1902, Edward VII was crowned king at Westminster Abbey, and Salisbury celebrated with a procession around the city, and the Haunch of Venison celebrated with a photograph of its own. It would be an easy error to assume that because the name of Louisa Potto was above the door, as the licence holder, that she *must* be in

Haunch of Venison 1902 – Who is the woman standing in the doorway?
© Salisbury Museum

the picture, but is she? Louisa was 62 years old at her death, but this woman doesn't have grey hair.

Although Louisa was the licence holder of the Haunch of Venison, it would be a big mistake to think of her merely as an 'Innkeeper'. As can be seen from the notice for auction printed after her death in the Bristol newspapers, Louisa was a business woman, continuing the Potto import business.

At the time of her death, in November 1902, she had choice Irish and scotch whiskies, Port, and Spanish wine coming by ship to Bristol, and of course, this was not a one off (she probably had French and German products coming into Southampton, too). Most probably, Louisa never worked physically in the Haunch of Venison in decades but was entrepreneur, manager, clerk and accountant. The woman in the picture has hoisted sleeves, and together with her lack of jewellery, and strong body, suggests that she uses elbow grease. Louisa had assistants to do the physical work in the pub.

VERY IMPORTANT SALE OF
CHOICE BRANDIES,
IRISH AND SCOTCH WHISKIES,
PORT AND TARRAGONA,
IN ALL AMOUNTING TO ABOUT 3,000 GALLONS.
Now lying at Messrs. Ford and Canning's Bonded Stores, Bristol, and being part of the Estate of the late Mrs. Louisa Potto, of Salisbury, which
MR. THOMAS PARRY has been favoured with instructions from her Executors to SELL by AUCTION, at the Grand Hotel, Bristol, on THURSDAY, July 2nd, 1903, at Two o'clock in the Afternoon.
Full Particulars in Catalogues, to be obtained of the Auctioneer, Albany-chambers.

On the afternoon of the coronation celebrations, a tea for the ladies of Salisbury was given in Victoria Park (the men having enjoyed a lunch in the Market Place, earlier). Since Louisa's sisters, and at least one niece, are not present, it would be fair to suggest that they were together in Victoria Park – with Louisa – when the photo was taken.

Alternatively, Louisa was to die only a few months after the coronation, and would have already been ill. From her death certificate, on seven November, Louisa died of 'Granular disease Kidneys' which she had had for three years, and dilation of the heart (a side effect of kidney disease) which she had had for six months.

Who might the people in the photograph be? My money is on

Louisa Bradbeer's brother Alfred to the left (he briefly became licensee of the Haunch of Venison in 1903, and was perhaps taking charge of the business during her last illness). To the right? Probably Francis Bradbeer, Alfred's son, who had been managing the establishment for his aunt. Or Firmin Bradbeer – who was in Salisbury, singing at the Cathedral that day. The mysterious woman? My money is on Emma or Annie Bradbeer, Mrs Potto's nieces, who had been living and working at the Haunch, with their (now) elderly mother, for many years. They were then in their 40s.

Incidentally, my money is also on *this* lady being the real Louisa Potto. The picture is amongst the Haunch of Venison archives at the museum. She shows a family resemblance to the Bradbeer side of the family, and is clearly a wealthy widow (she is wearing jet mourning beads), and a sophisticated dress (Louisa was a professional dressmaker). She is not Firmin's mother (a photo exists of her for comparison), and the age is correct. Furthermore, she looks related to the man to the left of the doorway, whom I speculate is her brother, Alfred.

Is this the real Louisa Potto?
© *Salisbury Museum*

Louisa died on seven November 1902, aged 62. It was Firmin Bradbeer, her nephew, who informed the authorities, and so he must have come up from Southampton to be with her. He gave his address as the 'Poor House. Southampton' (he was a teacher there), even though he had been a brewery traveller on the previous census. Louisa was buried under a monumental stone cross in London Road cemetery. The day on which I visited it, deer were grazing around it.

Francis and Firmin's brother, Charles, were executors of her will, along with a Richards cousin, and the pub licence was temporarily transferred to them, with Louisa's brother Alfred and his son, Francis, running the Inn. Alfred, a widower, and retired, then briefly took over the licence of the Haunch of Venison. Louisa left £400 each to her brothers and sisters, along with smaller bequests to other family members and god-children. The household goods were left for her elderly sister to enjoy, and were then to be sold.

Alfred Bradbeer

Alfred was born in 1838. He was the closest in age to Louisa. He left for Southampton to become a Printers Compositor, setting up the typeface for printing presses. He had to be able to set the letters back to front, so that they would print out correctly in a mirror image of the text. He would have been expected to work at speed and correct spelling and punctuation as he went along. He worked for the local newspaper. He was 23 when he married Rosanna Harrison, from Millbrook, Southampton, in 1861; she appears to have been an artistic and clever young woman, and six years older than him. Rosanna's father was a gardener, and she went into service, working as a nurse for successive medical Doctors. After Alfred and Rosanna married, they went on to have four sons. Two daughters died in infancy before Firmin, the youngest son, was born, meaning that there was a gap in

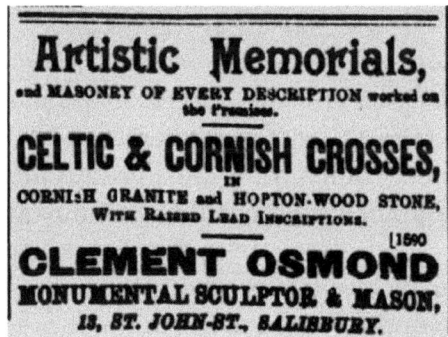

The gravestone of Louisa Potto and her sisters © Rod Poynting
Was it made by Clement Osmond?

age between Firmin and his older brothers (see Appendix 3). The family lived at 7 St Mary's Road, Southampton, and attended St Mary's Church. Alfred's second son was the Frank who moved to the Haunch of Venison as a teenager.

Francis Bradbeer

Frank was the second son, and ten years older than Firmin, and it certainly appears that he was being groomed to take over the business of the Haunch of Venison, as the successor to Aunt Louisa, who was childless. Frank spent over 20 years at the Haunch of Venison, as the assistant to Louisa Bradbeer.

Frank was Louisa Bradbeer's representative, appearing first on the census of 1881, when he was only 17. He was then living with Louisa, her elder sister, Sarah, and his cousin Emma. He was still living above the pub ten years later, but moved to Hulse Road when he married Ada Smith in 1894 and started a family, staying there until Louisa's death in 1902. From the newspaper snippets mentioning Frank, he appears to have been 'Front of House' at the Haunch of Venison, and in charge of the pub. He put 'licensed victualler' on his wedding certificate (although the licence wasn't in his name), when he married Ada near Andover, with Louisa as a witness. Ada was a blacksmith's daughter.

Frank was a committee member for 'kindred societies', when the Manchester Unity Friendly Society visited Salisbury. Toasts at the society dinner appear to be to 'The Queen', 'to the Army and Navy', and to the 'Church and Bishop'.

He was an ardent member of the Volunteers, 1st battalion, and was promoted in 1894. Incidentally, Frank served with W. H. Jackson. He was a keen marksman, and won prizes in the annual competition. Frank was referred to as 'The best shot of the Battalion of A Company', whilst a private, and was soon promoted to corporal, and then transferred to B Company as a lance-sergeant no. 1100.

It was in 1894 that Frank had to go to court, at the Guildhall, to help convict a London man, named Carter, who had come to Salisbury with the intention of passing counterfeit five-shilling coins ('crowns'). He went drinking in Salisbury and soon met up with two local men, and headed to the Haunch of Venison. Carter actually passed two counterfeit coins, one to Frank, who initially accepted it, although he was doubtful, and one to his cousin, Emily or Annie, who could not recognise Carter afterwards.

Eagle-eyed Frank was back in the news in 1897 when a bag was snatched by two men during a delivery to Carters the jewellers, the men escaping in a 'get away' horse and cart, to hide the swag in the woods. He had seen one of the men snatch the bag and run, and could identify him in court.

Frank went straight to the police again, when a drinker, a little worse for wear, dropped a glass bottle with the stopper engraved 'Southern Drug Company', and he testified in court when the toper was arrested for stealing the bottle. And Frank was clearly in charge of the Haunch a short time after, when he is mentioned as refusing admittance to a drunk.

Frank was commended by the Salisbury police for regularly helping them, and testifying in Court as a witness. This would have meant that the Haunch of Venison had a reputation as a very respectable establishment, since wrong'uns would surely not have wanted to drink in a pub where the bar manager was broadcast in the newspapers as a copper's nark!

One mystery of the Haunch of Venison, surely, is why, after waiting in the wings for two decades, did Frank decide **not** to take over the licence of the Haunch of Venison upon his aunt's death? The import business was a lucrative one, but instead Frank elected to become a postmaster, grocer, and baker (so running a grocery business in a local post office) in Netley Marsh, near Totton, with his wife and many children. The post office was then The General Post Office, and state owned. It therefore involved being responsible for government money, and employees had to be trustworthy. The very respectable Frank's friendship with police and army must surely have stood him in good stead! Frank and Ada later took over the post office in Ringwood, Hampshire, where Frank died in 1946.

Firmin Bradbeer

Firmin Bradbeer, the next landlord, knew the Haunch of Venison well from his earliest childhood, Southampton being just a short ride away from Salisbury by steam train.

We can imagine the Bradbeer family coming up for a day out, on high days and holidays, to see their extended family. It is interesting to consider what the Haunch of Venison must have seemed like to a small boy – it was small and dark and old fashioned. It had false ceilings downstairs, and the shiny bar counter and taps weren't there. It didn't have the panelling in the front room, nor the carved 'haunch' over the fireplace. It was probably white washed, although often streaked by the smoke from the fires and the clay pipes and

cigars of the customers. The
fireplace in the smoking room
was bricked up, and wood
almost black. The chequerboard
floor was there, and gas lamps
hung from the ceiling. The
place was full of old ladies in
rustling dresses, who probably
tried to freshen themselves up
by drenching themselves in
lavender water. Then there were
the maiden aunts. And brother
Frank. On market day, the place
was crammed elbow to elbow,
with gentleman farmers, and the
clank of frothing pewter tankards
and cut-glass decanters could be
heard.

Firmin Bradbeer
© *Salisbury Museum*

The Haunch, like other
pubs around the market place,
was a place where farmers did
deals, and it occasionally featured in the newspapers as the background
to agricultural disputes.

It was perhaps in childhood, that Firmin's vision of the Haunch
of Venison as a part of a romantic olde England, filled with ghosts,
was formed, as he explored the cupboards and the attics. He had a
particular connection to the old building, too, because the Bradbeer
family would never forget his namesake – old Firmin Potto. His
unusual first name bound Firmin Bradbeer to the Haunch for the
older citizens of Salisbury, too.

However, the Haunch of Venison was surely destined to be
Frank's one day, and Firmin determined to follow another brother,
Alfred into teaching. Indeed, on the 1881 census, Alfred is 17 and a
pupil teacher schoolmaster, and Firmin is aged 7, and it is logical to
assume that the inspirational Alfred practised by teaching his younger
brother. They were the only two brothers living at home.

Ten years later it was Firmin's turn to be a pupil teacher,
attending the training college in Winchester. He was now living
with brother Charles's father-in-law, retired quartermaster, Major

McIntire. His first job was as teacher for Southampton Workhouse. His reference for the job was written by the curate of Holy Trinity Church, who evidently knew the whole family well, and wrote that he was of 'eminent respectability'. Firmin, he described as 'careful, painstaking, and industrious at whatever he takes in hand'. Firmin was proud enough of the commendation to keep the letter all his life.

Firmin taught the Sunday School at Holy Trinity in 1893, and sang in the choir. He also trained the boys choir in the Workhouse, who were often commended for their 'sweet singing'. Apart from carpentry (he won third prize for wood carving and fretwork in a competition in 1899 – did Firmin carve the Haunch of Venison panel in the bar of the pub himself?), and music, another early hobby was politics, and he joined Southampton parliamentary debating society in 1895. These Victorian debating societies were very popular, and governmental roles would be assigned the participants, who would then argue topical subjects. In Southampton, Firmin's role was 'President of the Board of Trade'. A lifelong pleasure of his was reading, writing, and collecting books, and perhaps it is no surprise that another extra activity of his was as Workhouse librarian.

He evidently felt himself overworked and underpaid, since there was usually a request for overtime from Firmin, at meetings of the Board of Governors. He soon got an increase in wages at the Workhouse because of 'the most efficient manner in which he had performed his duties. He also took the children on school trips, including on the Isle of Wight steam packet. The most interesting trip though, in light of his later life as a publican, was a visit to the Temperance fete at the Crystal Palace. This was a massive annual 'fete' at which all sorts of national groups allied to the temperance movement took part. The temperance movement was actively trying to close as many pubs as they could, restrict sales of alcohol, and if possible, get men to 'take the pledge' – promise to become teetotal. As landlord of the Haunch of Venison, Firmin would write to newspapers to argue with members of the movement. He would be the Treasurer of the Salisbury Licensed Victuallers Association for over 20 years, and one time president, and made a speech at one annual dinner about the injustices which he felt the temperance movement did towards the pub trade, urging publicans to guard their own interests. He felt that publicans were 'the scapegoat for ministers of religion who fail to teach the morality they profess'. Firmin was himself a churchwarden, so it is an interesting statement. He thought it rum that religion wasn't blamed, when religious men behaved badly, and druggists weren't blamed when people became addicted to drugs. Firmin would point out that publicans didn't want drunks for customers, who were an annoyance, but honest citizens enjoying conviviality. Mr Bradbeer would go on to attack the temperance movement directly by saying 'it is argued that if they reduce licences, then they would reduce intemperance, but it is obvious that if they reduced the number of licenses, those people who drank would go into a fewer number of houses' (1913).

Perhaps it was the visit to the Temperance fete at Crystal Palace that led to Firmin Bradbeer handing in his notice at the Workhouse in 1901, and becoming a 'traveller for a brewery'! At any rate, since his aunt, brother, and two cousins ran a pub, it was not such a surprising career move as it might have been. It is very likely that Firmin already knew local publican's daughter Florence Pomeroy, and perhaps since childhood, since he grew up in St Mary's Road, whilst her father, Phillip Pomeroy ran the Bridge Tavern on New Road, now the site of a Premier Inn. She was six years younger than him. Phillip Pomeroy later ran the Northumberland Hotel, where he died. After her father's death, the Pomeroy family continued at the Northumberland, with Florence's mother, Maria, as landlady. They then ran the Bevois Castle in Bevois Street (Florence's brother was also Phillip Pomeroy). It is possible that Firmin and Florence already had the ultimate ambition to run their own establishment, and even that they had their sights on the Haunch of Venison, knowing that Frank and his family wanted to move on.

In the event, Firmin's father, Alfred, took over the licence for the Haunch of Venison, but only for a matter of months. Louisa had not been dead a year when The Salisbury Journal announced that Firmin Bradbeer had taken on the licence (albeit temporarily) in 1903. In fact, the licence would be far from temporary, since he would stay there until his death in 1948. Florence Pomeroy came up from Southampton to marry Firmin at St Thomas's church in the September of the same year, although the Rector of St Laurence, Southampton performed the ceremony. It is curious that the couple were not married in their home town, where the bride was still resident, but perhaps the bridegroom felt a particular pull to St Thomas's, with its doom painting featuring an 'ale wife', and wanted to organise celebrations in his own Inn, avoiding travel for his elderly Bradbeer relatives?

Firmin Bradbeer's grandfather's name was upon the wall when he married in St Thomas's in 1903, because he was a past churchwarden. Francis had died when Firmin was only seven.

The young couple did not move into the creaky and antiquated old building, though, preferring to rent what was then a new house on Harnham Road, which they called 'Clausentum' after the roman settlement from which grew the city of Southampton; Firmin was passionate about history. Their eldest daughter, also Florence Gertrude (but known as Dolly), was born there the following year, 1904, followed by a son, Firmin Pomeroy Bradbeer, two years later. Firmin was an enthusiastic cyclist (joining Salisbury cycle club), and one can imagine he and Florence bowling along on their light roadster bicycles through Salisbury Close – in at Harnham gate, and out at the High Street. They still kept private rooms at the Haunch (advertising for a servant, for that part of the house), but the elderly Aunt Emma and her daughters were moved to a house in London Road. Some staff for the public house also lived at the Haunch.

Firmin Continued Louisa's tradition of presenting a generous prize for the Volunteers' annual Christmas shooting contest; like his brother Francis, he enjoyed shooting and was a good marksman. He had been a member of the Volunteers in Southampton, and now joined the Wiltshire regiment.

Firmin Bradbeer was no doubt already well known in Salisbury, through his family connections, but he now set about involving himself with Salisbury life, and making the Haunch of Venison the meeting place for his prominent connections. In 1904 he attended the funeral of Samuel Fawcett with some of the most important people in the town. Fawcett was a nephew of Henry Fawcett, the blind Post Master General, whose statue stands in the market square, and he had married a Lovibond daughter, from an important brewing family. Fawcett had also been a leading member of Salisbury's volunteer fire brigade, alongside men like the Folliotts, to whom he was connected by marriage, and who were also brewers and local politicians. Firmin appears to have been present as a Freemason and a member of Elias De Derham lodge, Crane Street, Salisbury. He was wearing white gloves and carrying a sprig of white acacia, as he lined up at the gates of London Road Cemetery.

Firmin was elected to the committee of the Fisherton Conservative Working Man's Club in 1906. As a Freemason and an active supporter of the local Conservative party, we can get an idea of the society that Firmin Bradbeer kept when he became landlord of the Haunch of Venison pub. He certainly saw the income for the Haunch of Venison as coming from the Import business, and barely an edition of the *Salisbury Journal* was published, without Firmin Bradbeer taking out large – and expensive! – advertisements.

HAUNCH OF VENISON,
POULTRY CROSS,
SALISBURY.

GENUINE
IMPORTED WINES
AND
PURE SPIRITS.

FIRMIN S. BRADBEER,
WHOLESALE AND RETAIL
WINE AND SPIRIT MERCHANT.

ESTABLISHED THREE-QUARTERS
PURE   of a   PURE
POT STILL   CENTURY.   JAMAICA
IRISH WHISKY.   RUM.

SPECIALLY RECOMMENDED:—
COCKBURN'S ◆◆ PORT
(DOUBLE DIAMOND).
DELICATE FINE OLD TAWNY.
MATURED IN WOOD. FIT FOR IMMEDIATE USE
36/- PER DOZEN.
3/- PER BOTTLE.

ON DRAUGHT}
DRAWN FROM}1/3 ½-pt., 2/6 pt., 18/- per gallon.
WOOD.}

FIRMIN S. BRADBEER,
WINE MERCHANT.
TELEPHONE 24   CELLARS—CULVER-STREET.

By 1908 the Haunch of Venison had a telephone – Salisbury 24. The cellars were in Culver Street. Firmin also bottled his own beer, and one wonders if his time as a 'brewery traveller' had been a conscious preparation for his future career in Salisbury.

Firmin Bradbeer, landlord of the Haunch of Venison, was a keen cricketer, playing for South Wilts club (the club first played in 1854). His great friend Captain W. H. Jackson, can be found playing cricket alongside him for the Volunteers, in 1908. Not content with this, he also joined the South Wilts Golf Club.

Incidentally, physical sport was not the only competitive pastime which Firmin excelled at. He played chess to a high level, and was President of the Wilts County Chess Association. He played the former British Chess Champion, Blackburne, many times, and drew with him at an important contest. This was no little feat, because Blackburne was known as 'The Black Death', and was an international celebrity at the time, who, famously, could play matches blindfold.

Firmin had already renovated the Haunch of Venison in the

early days of his tenancy, imposing upon it his vision of Tudors and Cavaliers and 'romance', by exposing the beams, continuing the panelling and unblocking the inglenook fireplace in the smoking room, when he found a mummified human hand, amongst other objects. He also modernised the house, installing the fashionable new bar, lighting, telephone, fire hoods, and benches (the latter things are decorated with arts and crafts 'medieval' stylised plant motifs). Who paid for all the expensive work is not known, but the building belonged to Eliza Perry Johnson at the time, who was the Suffolk-based niece by marriage of Louisa Bradbeer (Mrs Potto). The Potto Johnsons evidently trusted the Bradbeers to continue to uphold the standing of the old Inn, and to choose how to modify it.

As an avid historian, Firmin Bradbeer wanted to research the history of the Haunch of Venison, and he evidently consulted original archives, since he knew that the building was a church house (as confirmed by the will of John Wynchester). He also must have trawled the newspapers. He subscribed to a published work on Wiltshire merchant's marks. When the restorations were finished, he wrote his research up in a booklet about the Haunch of Venison in order to relaunch the pub, and wrote letters to all the newspapers, both local and national, to promote it (Firmin Bradbeer was always an avid correspondent to newspapers and magazines!).

AN OLD SALISBURY INN.

A brochure written by Mr. Firmin S. Bradbeer and illustrated from pen and ink drawings by Mr. William Brown, describes in an attractive manner the "Haunch of Venison," one of the oldest houses in the city of Salisbury, under the title of "The Story of an Old Salisbury Inn." Built, in all probability, soon after Salisbury Cathedral, the house has a history stretching back into those spacious days when romance was the accompaniment of every-day life. In such a house one expects and finds picturesque old corners, ancient beams of oak and chestnut, and many another evidence of antiquity. Careful restoration has done much to enhance the real character of the house. The sketches which accompany the description are the work of an obviously sympathetic hand, and the brochure, as a whole, will be of value to the visitor who intends viewing the antiquities of an ancient city. The pamphlet is published at sixpence.

This advertisement appeared in the newspaper in 1909

It is the same year, 1909, that Firmin Bradbeer begins to be mentioned in connection with the Salisbury Parliament. This was a political debating society of the same type of which he had been a member of in Southampton. It gave the two bars their nicknames 'House of Commons' and 'House of Lords'.

ELECTION ADDRESSES.

T O THE BURGESSES OF ST EDMUND'S WARD.

LADIES AND GENTLEMEN,—I wish to thank you very heartily for the honour you have conferred upon me by electing me as one of your representatives in the Town Council. I am especially gratified that my return was unopposed.

I hope to be able, by attention to my duties, to be of service to the Ward and to further in every possible way the interests of the City.

I am, Ladies and Gentlemen,

Yours faithfully,

F. S. BRADBEER.

November 1st, 1910.   [2570

He certainly put his skills as an orator and a writer of political speeches to good use, since he could be found at Conservative party fundraising dinners and rallies in Salisbury, and surrounding towns, as a Speaker. Not suprisingly, he wanted a stronger Army and Navy. More surprisingly, for such a traditionalist, he wanted to reform the House of Lords – although 'moderately'. It was a logical step, therefore, that Firmin Bradbeer should be elected to Salisbury City Council, for St Edmund's Ward, in 1910.

One of Mr Bradbeer's interests as a Councillor was the 'Historic Places of Salisbury' committee, on which he served with his friend, Alderman J. A. Folliott (brewer and pub owner – including the Duke of York, in York Road). He put forward the motion in 1911, that 'descriptive tablets be fixed to public buildings, houses and places of historic interest in the city', and one supposes that he hoped to get a plaque for the Haunch of Venison, in this way, which would make it of higher standing for tourists!

Firmin Bradbeer was also involved with the London Road Allotment Committee, and it is clear that the allotments were seen as a way that the poor of the town could grow their own food and be independent of 'the rates', and it would bring out in them 'that old yeoman spirit'. Firmin opened the allotments in 1911, toasting Dr Bourne, who had lent the land, to the accompaniment of the municipal brass band.

However, Mr Bradbeer was far-seeing, and had a world view which went beyond Salisbury. At a Conservative dinner in Stoford, the same year, he said, whilst again pleading the case for a stronger Army and Navy, 'The World is in a state of what has been described as 'armed peace' and it is idle for us not to imagine there are great dangers before us'. Whilst Firmin could see World War I on the horizon, he could not have been able to predict the slow and painful descent that his own life would take. His daughter Marjorie would later speculate that all the unhappiness was due to an evil spirit in the Haunch of Venison.

It was pouring with rain when the civic procession, the councillors wearing their red robes and regalia, marched to Salisbury Cathedral on June 25th, 1911, to celebrate the beginning of the reign of George V. Hundreds of men dined in the Market place in a steady downpour. A dinner in the Market Place was the traditional way for the people of Salisbury to celebrate national occasions and, for some older people there, it was the fourth such outdoor dinner. The last one had been only in 1902, for the celebrations of Edward VII's coronation. However, in 1911 The chairs and table cloths were sodden, the food and drink swimming in water, and the bread soggy, as heavy rain persisted. Mrs Florence Bradbeer donated money towards the plum puddings. Florence was very busy, because while Firmin sat with the council, in the market Place raising a toast to the newly crowned King, Florence was one of the women in charge of organising the Ladies Tea in Victoria Park, the poor women, all 4,000 of them, had to squash up their chairs under the trees, as they couldn't sit on the grass as they might have. There were 300 helpers all together, and Florence was one of four women in charge of the organisation for St Edmund's Ward (one of the others was Mrs Folliott). The Ladies got soggy cake, rather than wet baron of beef, whilst a brass band splashed around the park.

It is interesting that it was *Mrs* Bradbeer who had donated the money for the plum puddings, because it is an inescapable fact, that whilst Mr Bradbeer was out campaigning; potificating; playing soldiers; playing cricket, golf and chess; studying archives; reading; writing; doing the accounts of the Licensed Victuallers Association (and no doubt visiting the pubs of other members), *somebody* was running the Haunch of Venison public house and restaurant. Whilst Louisa Bradbeer (Mrs Potto) had had Frank to run the pub, as well as her sisters and neices to help her, the censuses, newspaper articles, and memorabilia do not show any bar managers for Firmin Bradbeer until his daughter Dolly took on the job. It was Florence Bradbeer who ran the pub (and she was a publican's daughter), as well as the household in Harnham, whilst giving him several children. In 1911 she had given birth to their third child, Reginald, born in the house in Harnham, that January. She was, of course, expected to support him at any civic or club events to which women were invited, and to volunteer for work in his ward – as she did at George V's coronation.

Reginald died in December 1911, at only a year old. He had been suffering from vomiting and diarrhoea for three days. (He died at 'Clausentum', Harnham.) This was a common death for babies at this period who might get viral gastroentritis and suffer fever and dehydration, or ingest bacteria from the rubber teats or tubes on feeding bottles not being sterilised.

In 1911, Firmin Bradbeer signed a new lease with Samuel Potto Johnson, who had inherited the freehold of the Haunch of Venison from his mother, Eliza, six years earlier. The lease was for 28 years, and Firmin would pay Johnson £175 a year. It was managed by Fulton Solicitors, in Salisbury, who could make sure that Mr Johnson's asset was managed correctly.

The Dining room referred to in the advert for The Silver Grill is the smaller restaurant room, because the Merchant's Hall was part of the Bradbeers' living accomodation at this time, and had to be accessed by a separate entrance. It was made possible for them to move in next to the Haunch because William Holderness Carter had moved out of the merchant's house in 1911.

Firmin was churchwarden of St Thomas's church, in 1913, and had his name upon the church tower, visible from the back of the Haunch. It can still be seen inside the church. He was a member of Salisbury Diocesan Choral Society and sang in Salisbury Cathedral.

The outbreak of war meant that the import business of wine and spirits had to stop (or at least, it is never advertised again), although beer would continue to be bottled at the cellars in Culver Street.

TELEPHONE No. 24

"Haunch of Venison,"
Salisbury,
December, 1911.

SILVER GRILL.

With the idea of making this Old-Established Inn a complete house of refreshment, the Proprietor has installed a Silver Grill of the London type for the convenience of his Customers.

The Dining Room, like the other rooms in the house, shows signs of great antiquity, the house dating from the 13th Century. Its interesting features have been carefully preserved, and it will be found a comfortable room overlooking the ancient Poultry Cross and the busy little Square around it. Whilst making a speciality of the Grill, the Proprietor wishes his Patrons to understand that an extended menu can be served at short notice, and that he will be pleased to arrange Dinners or Suppers for Parties. The Dining Room is also available for Afternoon Teas.

Although "The Haunch" is a fully Licensed House, Mr. Bradbeer trusts that Visitors to the Dining Room will not consider themselves under any obligation to purchase exciseable liquors. It is his aim to make this Old Inn a Refreshment House in the fullest sense of the term, and those who desire to partake of non-alcoholic beverages will be equally welcomed.

Instructions by Post or Telephone will receive prompt attention.

The quality of the Wines & Spirits for which this Old-Established Free House has long been noted is strictly maintained.

Firmin joined up, although he was by now over 40, meaning that Florence was alone running the pub, although she was pregnant with their last child, Marjorie. The baby was born upstairs at the Haunch, since the family were obliged to give up the house in Harnham and had moved into the pub.

We can see what Firmin thought of the war because he wrote a Libretto for a patriotic operetta called '1915' for the Salisbury Operatic Society. '1915' urged young men to sign up and do their duty. The young heroine, who could not be attracted to a coward, was called Marjorie, after Firmin's young daughter, born the previous year.

The First World War meant that the restaurant closed. Obviously, rationing meant that serving food to the public was difficult for them. Strict laws were brought in which forced pubs to open only between 12.30pm and 2pm, and remain closed until 6.30pm. This was to stop all day drinking, because the government (particularly Lloyd George, Minister for Munitions), was concerned about productivity in the factories. To this end, men were encouraged not to drink on weekdays, and beer was ordered to be watered down. It became against the law to buy another man a drink ('treating'). Firmin Bradbeer joined the RFC and then the RAF, staying on an extra year .

Firmin Bradbeer had left his position as councillor for St Edmund's ward in order to join up at the beginning of World War I, but on his return to Salisbury in 1919 he stood as councillor once again – this time in St Thomas's. Things were very different after the war. Lady Edith Hulse was elected as councillor, with a majority well above his. The macho Firmin appears to have taken it very well; at least, politely. In 1927, Edith was elected Salisbury's first Lady Mayor (only the third in the country), saying, 'I stand as an Independent owing loyalty only to my country, to the city of Salisbury and the electors whose votes I solicit . The success of Lady Hulse in politics can hardly have failed to influence Dolly Bradbeer's own political ambition. A woman had trounced Daddy.

In March 1920 the newspaper stated that the Silver Grill was reopening, and that the Haunch of Venison was looking for two barmaids, one waitress, one cook and two kitchen maids. In fact, it wouldn't be a waitress who would get the job, but rather 'plus-four Tim' – a waiter!

In 1922 Firmin Bradbeer was one of the founding members of

Salisbury Rotary Club. The club President was W. H. Jackson. Firmin was present at the first meeting, held at the Cathedral Hotel on 15th December (they afterwards moved to the Red Lion). The Rotary Club of Southampton was also present, to whom Firmin proposed a toast. He was soon on the Rotary Club Council. The Rotary Club raised money for philanthropic works and had annual outings for disabled children to visit Sandbanks in a charabanc, with Christmas parties for the poorest children of the city held at the Guildhall, as well as one-off gifts for deserving causes. Wives were invited to some events, and Florence Bradbeer's name is there, along with Mrs Jackson's.

An event occurred in January 1926 which evidently haunted Firmin Bradbeer for the rest of his life: Mr W. H. Jackson died of cancer. Florence Bradbeer accompanied him to the funeral (although by then they were estranged). It seems certain that this death appeared to symbolise the end of Firmin's career as a successful man in his own eyes. Firmin Bradbeer's dying request, 22 years later, would be that he be buried close to Jackson.

In February of the same year, 1926, the Haunch held its annual dinner at Mr Martin's Sale Rooms. It was in 'remembrance of all those who have passed on in the Great War and since, that the Haunch has known'

> *Remembrance*
> I drink to that great Inn beyond the grave
> If there be none the gods have done
> > Us wrong
>
> Ere long I hope to chant a better stave
> In some great *joyous* inn beyond the grave
> And quaff the best of earth that heaven can
> > Give
> Red wine like blood, deep love of friends
> > And song
> I drink to that *great* inn beyond the grave,
> And hope to meet my golden lads ere long.
> > *Attributed to Ben Johnson*

It was in the same year, 1926, that Firmin Bradbeer wrote to Samuel Potto Johnson (The then owner of the Haunch) asking to buy the Haunch of Venison, but Johnson wrote back politely declining. Why Mr Bradbeer wanted to buy the freehold – and how he proposed to afford it – isn't clear. He had, by now, severe money problems. Although he still had 14 years to run on his lease, he wanted to sign a new long-term lease, if he couldn't buy the building. Potto Johnson again declined, citing that it would be unfair to his family, since he himself would already be 77, if he lived to see the end of the present lease.

Florence Bradbeer left him. On the 1939 register, Florence is living on 'private means' with the wealthy Greenwood family, staunch Conservative party supporters. They lived at Hightrees House in Alderbury. Florence died in Bournemouth in 1962. Marjorie Bradbeer thought that her sister, Dolly, had put a photograph of their father, Firmin, in Florence's coffin.

Why Mrs Bradbeer walked out is a bit of a mystery. The Bradbeer's youngest daughter, Marjorie, would later write to her solicitor, Bill Oglethorpe, 'I was upset to find my parents' solicitors letter concerning their separation'. She went on, 'the real reason was never disclosed. I asked my sister over the years, for she was 21 at the time, and must have known what really happened, but she would never tell me'. There are some clues as to what happened, though, and events which Marjorie probably wasn't aware of, since she was only 11 or 12, and at school.

In 1925 a publisher had placed an advertisement in a newspaper publicising a forthcoming novel (which probably never existed). According to Hansard, the result was the Authors' (Law of Libel) Protection Bill February 1926, debated by Lord Gorell on behalf of the Society of Authors. Lord Gorell stated that the pre-publicity for the novel said:

> A middle-aged man and woman have done well in life together, but chiefly through the woman's power and charm. Circumstances then bring the man, Firmin Bradbeer, back to the surroundings in which he passed his childhood. Here he reveals what has always laid dormant in him before the eyes of his wife.

The Bill was withdrawn, and re-presented in 1927 as the Law of Amendment Bill. The chief problem for the Society of Authors,

Playwrights, and Composers, was that Firmin Bradbeer attacked the *publisher* for libel, who without reference to the author, settled the claim for a small sum.

According to Hansard, again, reporting on the Law of Libel Amendment Bill being debated in the House of Lords the following year (1927) 'it was stated that the book was concerned with the adventures of two people, one of whom, 'Firmin Bradbeer, owed his success in life to his wife's charms'. The account goes on 'before the book had been published, a gentleman saying that his name was, in fact, Firmin Bradbeer, wrote and complained bitterly of this usage. He was not content with an apology, he was not content with the alteration of the name, he wanted damages. He saw a chance, because he held such a very unusual name, to extract money from the unfortunate author who had invented a name'.

Firmin should not have had damages because, it was argued in the Lords, if authors could be taken to court for using names in novels (however strange), which turned out to be the names of real people, then all authors would have to use the letters A, B, and C for their characters, or be at risk of litigants.

It would be difficult to argue that the advert and the court cases were not the trigger for the Bradbeers' separation in 1926. The text in the advert put the couple in opposition. It must have been written by an educated and literary man, with an interest in the psychology of fictional characters because 'circumstances' brought the fictional Firmin 'back to his childhood', and he reveals to his wife what has always 'laid dormant in him'. It is a fantastic blurb designed to allow the reader's imagination to run riot with all sorts of 'red top' scandalous revelations, and guaranteed to make us read on.

The advert might, or it might not, have had any fundamental truth, but it evidently would cause a blow to Firmin's reputation, despite the fact that he received damages. It also suggests that the success of the Haunch of Venison was perceived as being down to Florence, and that she perhaps confided in the publisher of the advertisement.

The legal agreement for a separation being drawn up by a solicitor would include a financial agreement, and this must have contributed to Mr Bradbeer's financial woes. Dolly Lemon (née Bradbeer) later told Mr Oglethorpe (who told me) 'what happened was not Daddy's fault'.

In 1927 Firmin got permission from Johnson to mortgage the remainder of his lease to Ind Coope (it is probable that he had wanted a new longer lease, for this reason, or even that he had wanted to buy the freehold to sell it to a brewery at a profit). He borrowed £750, repayable in less than a year, with interest. In 1928 he celebrated 'A quarter of a century. The Landlord in the chair'.

Simonds, the Reading brewery, had an office in Salisbury, and in 1930 Firmin Bradbeer managed to negotiate another mortgage – this time with Simonds until 1939 – when the lease ran out. The conditions that Mr Potto Johnson put on allowing this to happen was that Firmin Bradbeer would remain the landlord of the Haunch of Venison, for the public, even though he was now a tenant of Simonds. Although he had received a lump sum from Simonds, he now had to pay them £200 per annum, payable at £50 per quarter. Beer was now supplied by Simonds brewery.

There was then another event, which would be just as cataclysmic for Firmin Bradbeer, as Florence Bradbeer leaving. He became ill. His obituary (in 1947) would say that illness was the reason that, from being one of the most active and well-known citizens in Salisbury, Firmin Bradbeer became almost reclusive, having given up most of his pastimes, except the theatre (he wrote some plays for the Dramatic Society). His death certificate would state that he suffered both from heart disease and pulmonary tuberculosis (which was rife in Salisbury between the wars). It is sure that he also suffered from depression. Dolly Bradbeer's solicitor would later say that Dolly would insist that the root of Firmin's problems was really financial. Either way, he looked for help to his children.

Marjorie Bradbeer was around the age of 19 when this new crisis blew up. She doesn't appear to have been living at home then, since electoral rolls for the inter-war years show her living at the Orchard Hotel, Uxbridge (now the Old Orchard Hotel), a beautiful small country pub and hotel. The reason that she found a job there might be due to RAF connections, as it was very close to RAF Uxbridge base. Marjorie returned to the Haunch during World War II when she appears in the newspaper after she was fined for showing a light during the blackout. She was a shop assistant on the 1939 register, but it also has 'nurse' in the margin. She appears to have had no affection for the Haunch of Venison, although she had been born there. She would die in 2003, aged 89, having never married.

Firmin Bradbeer had hoped that his son, Firmin Pomeroy Bradbeer would work for the Haunch of Venison, but it wasn't to be. Firmin Jr. had attended the Cathedral Choristers School, and then went to Dauntsey's Agricultural School between 1921-1924. Dauntsey's is a Public School in West Lavington, Wiltshire, which at the time of Firmin Jr's attendance, gave an agriculturally based education. Its pupils were often the sons of gentlemen farmers or Army officers. Firmin Jr. did not excel at academic subjects, although he did play cricket. When he left the school aged 18, records at Dauntseys show that it was to act as 'secretary and accountant to his father' at the Haunch of Venison. His inability and particular personality, must have put extra pressure on his parent's marriage at this time leading up to their separation. Firmin Jr. was exceptionally tall (one account says 6 ft. 4 ins. as a teenager, and another 6 ft. 6 ins. later in life), and it was probably his height that led him to be accepted into Swindon constabulary. His nephew by marriage, Mr Tim Hayter, gave me the following information:

Firmin Pomeroy Bradbeer ©Tim Hayter

Firmin Pomeroy Bradbeer suffered from some sort of mental illness, although this was not diagnosed (Mr Hayter used the word 'schizophrenia' speculatively). He was a constable for his whole career, and was never promoted, in consequence, although he stayed in the police force – probably through the shortage of men, due to two world wars. When he was stationed in Swindon, he used to visit a high-class confectioner in Newport Street frequently. The sweet shop was owned by Mr Hayter's grandfather who had been a manager for Ushers in Trowbridge, and Bowley's in Swindon, and his Aunt Mabel worked behind the counter. Firmin Jr. began to pay his attentions to Mabel, much to the annoyance of her father, who couldn't stand the sight of the persistent constable. They met during World War II, but knew each other for a long time before they married in 1960. Mabel only gave in because she was 51 and feared that she would never find anybody else, but it made her family very sad, although her father was dead by then. Perhaps it was a good job, because Firmin Jr. would always say that he'd married beneath him – he appeared cultured and he spoke with a public-school accent, and he was very proud of his father's collection of 1st-edition books, which he'd inherited; he'd say 'you can look, but you can't touch'. He'd also come out with strange things like he said once that he had dug up women's brassieres in the garden, and another time that he'd found a cache of Nazi memorabilia. He took to hiding in cupboards. After he married Mabel, the couple lived together above the sweetshop, but he would become violent and hit her – once he even had his hand around her throat (Dolly reportedly told her carers that Firmin Snr would beat his children). When this occurred, Mabel would kick him out to lodgings. But she always took him back. They lived at Cosy Lodge, Lambourn, then Lockeridge. He died in a retirement home in Marlborough in 1991, and is buried in Overton Churchyard.

Backing up Tim Hayter's assertion of the younger Firmin's violent nature, the constable made the newspapers in 1937, when he appeared in court claiming to be assaulted by a gatecrasher at a wedding which he attended. Although it was the policeman who was taken at his word, it is clear from the gatecrasher's testimony that he was hoisted home to Bishopstone – where he wanted to go alone – and he was then beaten up by Mr Bradbeer who used his truncheon multiple times, including when he was helpless on the ground.

'Dolly' Bradbeer/Edwardes/Lemon

She was the Bradbeer child who did return to help her father, and it is she who would be the last of the extended Potto/Bradbeer family to hold the licence for the 'Haunch of Venison'.

Dolly was born Florence Gertrude Bradbeer in 1906, but by the time she was at Leehurst Convent School (later, La Retraite, now Leehurst Swan) she was calling herself 'Dorothy' (this is even the name on her ration book, following World War I). She would continue to be known as Dorothy or 'Dolly' to family and friends all her life, despite using Florence in her professional career.

Dolly appeared in the Salisbury Children's Peace Pageant as a nun following the Countess Ela. She appears to have had three passions in her early life, and they were dogs, politics, and the RAF. Photographs that exist of her 'off duty' seem to have dogs in them. They also tend to show her with her face turned in the same direction, and looking down.

Her shyness before photographers gives a false impression though, because 'Dolly was a good laugh. She was ever such good fun to be around'. Her social group included the young RAF men who frequented the pub, according to her sister. They probably also included young Conservatives.

Florence Gertrude Bradbeer -known as Dorothy or 'Dolly'. Dolly Bradbeer with her dog © Salisbury Museum

Dolly grew up against a background of feminist politics, since the date of her birth means that her childhood has for a background the suffragist movement, and her parents were active politically. For example, in 1908, the question of votes for women had been raised at a meeting of Salisbury Parliament (a political debating society) in the following terms:

" This House is of opinion that the time has now arrived for granting parliamentary suffrage to women on the same terms as it is, or may be, granted to men."

The PRIME MINISTER (Mr. F. S. Bradbeer) agreed with the motion, and spoke highly from personal experience, of the wonderful change wrought in Poor Law administration by the inclusion of women on Boards of Guardians. But he pointed out some feminine characteristics which he thought would be disadvantageous if the granting of the vote were followed by admitting women to Parliament.

It was made clear in the newspaper that it was difficult to say anything original, because this subject had been debated so many times at different events. Over 200 visitors packed the Central Hall in Endless Street, for the meeting, and these were nearly all women. They hissed when something was said that they didn't like, but were otherwise quiet.

It would be interesting to know the 'feminine characteristics' which Firmin had observed, which he felt would be disadvantageous in female MPs. It could be that his wife was not always compliant in deferring to his opinions! Two of the ladies present (unnamed) wrote a very intelligent review of the meeting, which lamented the levity in the men's speeches, and stressed the urgency of extending the vote to women, but which stressed women's influence as being on the side of 'temperance, peace and purity', and their interests as being motherhood, and domesticity. Surely referring to Firmin Bradbeer's speech, they remarked on the speaker who was afraid that if women were admitted to Parliament, then they would want to form an all-female political party which would have an 'insatiable desire to override male opinion'. Another point that outraged them was a speaker's contention that politicians of both sexes sitting in Westminster, would lead to wild flirtations in the House, and a female Foreign Minister would be in danger of succumbing to handsome and charming foreign ambassadors. 'At first sight, this seems almost insulting,' the ladies remark, 'until one remembers that men have occasionally fallen victims to intriguing women, and one can only claim the consolation that, in such circumstances, the women generally come off best'.

We should not forget that Firmin Bradbeer's wife (and Dolly's mother) would go on to leave him some years later, which was a very unusual thing for women to do at this time, and suggests that she was a feminist who didn't think that she was her husband's property, and who was not afraid to strike out on her own.

It should be noted that Millicent Garrett Fawcett, the feminist political pioneer, was married to Henry Fawcett (the blind politician whose statue stands in Salisbury market place, facing the site of the house where he was born). Although Millicent was an elderly widow by the time that Dolly became involved in politics, she had once been a frequent visitor to the family cottage in Cathedral Close, and was no doubt an inspiration to Salisbury feminists. Furthermore, Dolly not only had the political influence of her parents, and lively debates at the Haunch of Venison, but private girl's schools such as the one which she attended generally had debating societies also, keeping the pupils abreast of current affairs.

Between the time that Dolly left school in the early 1920s, and 1932, she was pursuing a career in politics, for the Conservative Party. Referred to by her real name 'Miss F. G. Bradbeer', upon her appointment as 'Organising secretary of the Woman's branch' in Hanley (Dolly beat 14 candidates, sent by Central Office, for this position), the *Staffordshire Sentinel* lists her progress up until 1930. 'She has had a varied political career, having served on the Central Office Staff in the Louth Division of Lincolnshire, Mitcham, Tunbridge Wells, Salisbury, Battersea (by-election), London, and Nottingham (General Election 1929).

It would have been quite extraordinary for a young woman to have the confidence to move around the country to different branches, let alone take up a career in politics, at a time when politics were still dominated by men who had paternalistic attitudes like her own father, who had grown up in the Victorian era. The National Society of Women Organisers had only been created in 1927.

CONSERVATISM IN HANLEY DIVISION.

New Organising Secretary of Women's Branch.

Miss F. G. Bradbeer has been appointed Organising Secretary of the Women's Branch of the Hanley Conservative and Unionist Association in succession to Miss D. Marson, who has left Hanley to take up a similar position in the Horncastle Division of Lincolnshire. Miss Bradbeer has had a varied political car er, having served on the Central Office Staff in the Louth Division of Lincolnshire, Mitcham, Tunbridge Wells, Salisbury, Battersea (by-election), London, and Nottingham (General Election, 1929).

Dolly's job made her a senior person within the Woman's Branch of the Hanley Conservative Association (Stoke-on-Trent) She was responsible for organising the branch and was the contact for other Conservative Association branches. She would have needed a lot of confidence and personal social skills, and would need to gather information and disseminate it, as well as keep records. She organised social events between senior Conservatives, local figures, and other organisations, and did fund-raising. Her job involved supporting the local candidate at election time, and recruiting other women to join the Conservative cause. She also did some fund raising for the Men's Branch of the Conservative Association.

Dolly organised many events such as dances and whist drives, St Patrick's Day celebrations, and an annual picnic, and she must have had a busy social life. The organisation and hosting of social events to facilitate networking and support, financial and practical, had long been a role of women interested in politics. However, Dolly also organised a 'class for canvassers' where she demonstrated, together with the local candidate, how householders should be approached in an organised house-to-house visit of the constituency, to a 'mass class' (1931). She organised a visit to the Branch by the female MP, Mrs S. A. Ward, talking about the influence of Women in Politics.

HANLEY CONSERVATIVES—Miss Higgins, Mrs. Emery, Mrs. S. A. Wood, M.P. for Cannock, Miss Bradbeer, Miss M. E. Wedgwood, O.B.E. (President), Mrs. Orr Jones (Chairman) and Captain J. Cotton (Agent) at the annual meeting last night of the Hanley Women's Branch of the Conservative and Unionist Association.

One interesting thing is Dolly's support for the Hanley Junior Imperial League (IMPS). This was for young people aged 14-25, and was the forerunner of the Young Conservatives. Whilst the word 'imperial' has negative connotations to modern ears, it signified only the IMPS desire to include young people from across the world, who belonged to what was then the British Empire. The object was to interest young people in politics, and encourage them to be involved in a practical way – hopefully signing up for the Conservative Party! Since Salisbury had a thriving IMPS, with many social events, it was perhaps through this route that Dolly began her career. She was probably also a member of the Junior Primrose League in her childhood, since her parents were members of the League, and family events included the 'Buds'.

It was the IMPS who presented Dolly with an engraved silver cigarette case in 1932, when she handed her notice in to go home to run the Haunch of Venison, and look after 'Daddy', whom her friends say she adored. She would later say that her time in Hanley had been the happiest of her life. She was evidently a woman who believed in 'Duty'.

So, Dolly came back to the Haunch, and signed a contract with Firmin to be his Manageress. She was to have no outside interests, but to concentrate solely on running the pub and restaurant.

Ironically, Samuel Potto Johnson finally **did** decide to sell the Haunch of Venison but by now Firmin Bradbeer's problems with his health and finances

Dolly Bradbeer in Hanley © Staffordshire Stentinel

meant that he did not buy it. It was put up for auction, and was bought by Simonds Brewery, although Firmin Bradbeer continued as licensee.

Dolly made a success of running the pub, gaining the restaurant a fine reputation. Peter Sherlock told this author that he remembered stories of the Haunch of Venison when Dolly was the landlady, and that she had her special group of favourite customers. On Market Day, when the pub was always heaving, and you couldn't get a seat, her favourites would enter the Haunch by the restaurant entrance and be entertained by Dolly in the Cloisters bar where she allowed her favourites to sit. The Upstairs rooms were let as an hotel.

In 1942, Mr Woolley (Woolley and Wallis, regional auctioneers) was prosecuted for overcharging on venison to

present.
    Mr. Walter Ireland, prosecuting on behalf of the Ministry of Food, said Mr. Peter Woolley sold a number of lots of venison. Lot 1, a carcass of 70lb., was sold to Miss Bradbeer, of the Haunch of Venison Hotel, Salisbury, for £7, an average of 2s per lb., or an overcharge of £1 3s 4d. Lot 4 was also sold to Miss Bradbeer, 74lbs. for £8 10s, an average of 2s 3½d per lb., or £2 6s 8d overcharge. Lot 9, sold to an R.A.F. Mess, weighed 92lbs., and was sold for £17 5s, an average of 3s 9d per lb., or an overcharge of £9 1s 8d. On the 13th

Miss Bradbeer at the Haunch – there was, of course, rationing, once more. It is interesting that the Haunch still had the wealthy clientele to enjoy Venison there, during the war, but also that Woolley's other customers for venison were the RAF.

Her solicitor, Bill Oglethorpe, said that he believed that Dolly was nursing prisoners of war at the camp which then stood at Odstock (Salisbury hospital being the Infirmary, next to the Clock Tower). Since her sister, Marjorie, was nursing part-time, whilst working as a shop assistant, this is probably correct, although unconfirmed.

It was during the war that Dolly began a romance with the tall and dashing married pilot, Jack Edwardes, who was also a comic actor, and married him in 1944, after his divorce. She was 40 years old, and Jack was only 31. It was probably as a result of this marriage that Firmin Bradbeer finally allowed Dolly to become the licensee, although he was already only receiving weekly pocket money of £6 and 15 shillings a week, with his daughter keeping the totality of the profits after charges.

Jack was soon working at the Haunch, and rapidly became known as the landlord. He announced in the press that he

Dolly Bradbeer/Edwardes
© Tim Hayter

would be standing as a Conservative candidate in the local elections, although he was not elected, and he organised the Battle of Britain Benevolent Fund for Salisbury (and sat on the National Committee). Dolly organised the Ladies Section, and Jack bought her a diamond brooch in the shape of the RAF wings.

Sadly, the marriage was short lived, like many wartime romances, and it was Dolly who moved out of the Haunch of Venison and into a House at 1 Prospect Place (near the Devizes Road Inn). Jack continued to live at the Haunch of Venison with Firmin Bradbeer. Her address is given on the notice for her divorce in the papers.

Mrs Spurr (who was nearly a hundred!) remembered the excellent food at the Silver Grill, when as a scientist she was based at Porton Down, just after the War. It was the best value in town she told this author, with a three-course meal costing two shillings. 'For that you, you got a savoury, a pie and vegetables, and a sweet. But you could have two savouries or two sweets. It was the savouries that were so good – I always remember them! We loved the Haunch of Venison, and aways ate there when we could. Otherwise, it was the County Hotel or the White Hart'.

Mrs Vera Piton (nearly the same age) had her wedding reception at the Haunch of Venison, around the same time, at the end of the war. 'The Haunch of Venison was very smart, but it was not so expensive as some other places in Salisbury'. Her young husband worked in a garage in Castle Street, 'He would always tell me if old Mr Bradbeer came in with his car, He was a bit of a celebrity in Salisbury'.

Firmin Bradbeer died in September 1947. It was Jack who was with him when he died. It was just before the Battle of Britain remembrance celebrations, and Dolly and Jack sat on steps of the Guildhall, dressed in black, separated by the mayor. The funeral service was held in St Thomas's church. Firmin was buried near W. H. Jackson in London Road cemetery, at his request, over 20 years after Jackson's death.

Dolly never worked at the Haunch again, choosing to give up the licence, and by 1949, Jack had gone, and remarried his former wife the following year. He would go on to become a national TV star.

Dolly remarried equally quickly, to wealthy Robert Lemon, who ran the Phoenix Insurance office, (next to what is now Salisbury Library, 2022), just around the corner from the Haunch of Venison. He had only been widowed six months, and was over 20 years older than her when they married. Bob Lemon was part of Dolly's social group of friends, who had congregated at the Haunch even before the War. I am grateful to Peter Sherlock, whose father, Chris, worked for Bob Lemon. Peter wrote 'my father regularly drank at the Cloister Bar at the Haunch'. His letter continues 'I have in my possession a silver tankard given to my father with the inscription 'Haunch of Venison Salisbury'. Underneath it is inscribed 'To Hunker from Dolly. April 1938". Dolly and Bob lived at Grasmere House, in what is now the Grasmere Hotel, and Mr Lemon was driven around his area in a chauffeured Rolls Royce. Mr Lemon had a passion for boxing (according to local historian, Frogg Moody, he organised boxing matches at the Guildhall). The couple moved to Park Lane (next to Victoria Park), and when her husband died in 1972, she moved to South Street, Wilton. Dolly died in a Salisbury nursing home in 1999, aged 94, and her ashes were scattered privately on Harnham Hill. Her memorabilia of the Haunch of Venison were given to Salisbury Museum and form the basis of their collection.

B is for Brewery

In 1960, Simonds (who had first gained control of the Haunch of Venison under an agreement with Mr Firmin Bradbeer, and who had later bought the building from Mr Samuel Potto Johnson) merged with Courage, and the company then became Courage, Barclay, Simonds & Co. They merged with Georges Bristol Brewery, the year after. In 1970, they shortened the name to just 'Courage Ltd', and in 1972 they were taken over by the Imperial Tobacco Group.

After having been bought and sold by the Hanson Trust (whom some have accused of being 'asset strippers') it became part of Elders 1XL (an Australian agricultural business). Elders changed its name to Fosters Brewing Group in 1990 – most famous in the UK for Foster's lager.

'Courage', was of course still known as 'Courage' to ordinary drinkers, who still enjoyed a pint of 'Courage Best' or 'Directors'.

Lord Young's Beer Orders of 1989 meant that Courage became one of the 'Big Six' brewery companies who fell foul of the Monopolies and Mergers Commission in the 1990s (the others were: Allied breweries; Bass; Grand Metropolitan; Scottish and Newcastle; and Whitbread).

There had been around 15 previous government reports and complaints from CAMRA, The Licenced Victuallers Association, the Society of Independent Brewers, the British Beer Company amongst others, that the British pub trade was a monopoly of the 'Big Six', who unfairly stopped competition, kept prices high, and removed 'choice' from customers. Together they owned three-quarters of both the beer production and pub buildings. They also had a monopoly on supplying free houses with their products by offering discounts and loans, and pricing the products of the independent brewers out of the market. The upshot of it was 'Lord Young's Beer Orders' which said that the number of pubs which could be owned by one of the breweries was 2,000 (they also had to allowed tied pubs to put on a 'guest beer'). Courage alone owned 5,100 pubs, and needed to get rid of 3,100!

The big brewers discovered that they could get around these laws by selling their pubs to non-brewing companies (property companies), who would then need to be supplied – by the big brewers. Grand Metropolitan did a deal with Courage (owned by Fosters), to stop brewing beer and running pubs, and they formed a 'Pubco' called Inntrepreneur which had 4,300 pubs, including the Haunch. Grand Metropolitan in turn sold Watney, Mann and Trumans to Courage who could then supply them (they had in fact swapped beer for pub buildings).

Others followed the lead of Courage/Grand Metropolitan, and in 1991, Enterprise Inns was formed, by buying up some former Bass pubs. In 2004, it bought the then 4,054 pubs belonging to Inntrepreneur (who had changed their name to Unique Pub Co Estate, when they had been bought by the Japanese bank, Nomura). In 2021, Enterprise Inns Group sold out its 4,000 pubs to Stonegate pub group, owner of the Slug and Lettuce, and Walkabout, chains, and it is now the biggest pubco in the UK. In this way, the Haunch of Venison passed from the Potto/Bradbeer family to Stonegate.

The large dining room has always been leased from Carters, and is a 3rd party agreement between Carters and firstly Mr Bradbeer, and then whichever brewery has owned the Haunch of Venison.

C is for CAMRA

In May 2013, the Haunch of Venison was named in a book produced by CAMRA, as one of 'Britain's Best Real Heritage Pubs', and feted as a 'national treasure'. The Author, Geoff Brandwood, came to Salisbury to sign copies of the book at the Haunch of Venison, and to present then landlord, Alex Marshall, with an award. Said Geoff, 'Our pubs have changed so much over the

Alex Marshall receiving an award from CAMRA
© *Salisbury Newspapers*

last half century, that ones with genuine historic interiors are an incredible rarity'.

Mr Brandwood was sadly only too correct; a browse of the *Hop Leaf Gazette*, the in-house magazine of Simonds Brewery, shows that pubs as ancient as the Haunch of Venison were being bulldozed to make way for supermarkets, and heritage pubs were having their interiors ripped out to be painted in fashionable colours and 'modernized'. In Salisbury, the Old George Inn (Boston Tea Party, 2022) had its ground floor removed to make the entrance to a shopping mall. The Haunch of Venison was lucky to survive intact. Alex Marshall said, as he received the award, comparing it to other Salisbury pubs, 'It's the only one with a completely untouched interior, including the original pewter bar counter, and spirit taps'.

Alex was right, because CAMRA noted on their website: 'CAMRA is only aware of four other sets of spirit cocks: at Shipman's Northampton; Queens Head 'Turners Vault', Stockport, Greater Manchester; Bull, Paisley, Scotland; and Crown, Belfast, Northern Ireland. all CAMRA Heritage Pubs.' They go on to say, 'The only way to get casks of beer into the cellar is from the public bar and while firkins (9-gallon casks) can go through the door on the left of the servery, larger ones involve removing the shelf behind the counter and opening up the bar front – very rare.'

Ian Turner, Branch Chairman, Salisbury & South Wilts CAMRA said about the Haunch: 'The Haunch, something of a local institution, was on CAMRA's radar in the late 1970s, the formative years of CAMRA. The Haunch was featured in their flagship national Good Beer Guide throughout the 1980s and into the 1990s selling predominantly Courage Best and Courage Directors premium bitter. As interest in real ale increased some additional beers were sold including John Smiths and Bass. Ownership eventually passed from long time owners Courage to the fledgling pub company Enterprise Inns which coincided with a less regular appearance in the guide. It remains a popular beer drinkers' destination to this day and the current version of Courage Best still appears as a guest beer from time to time alongside beers from breweries such as Hop Back.'

C is for Cards

When Firmin Bradbeer unblocked the fireplace in the little smoking room around 1903, he found, along with other objects, two playing

Playing cards found in the 'House of Lords' fireplace
© *Salisbury Museum*

cards, identified by Salisbury Museum as being 18th century. They were the Ten and the Queen of Clubs. The Queen is a full upright figure, who doesn't have two heads, as Court Cards have today. Mr Bradbeer speculated that the cards had fallen through slatted wood when being shuffled. He linked them to the mummified hand also found bricked up in the same area, and began the famous Salisbury legend of the cheating whist player, who had his hand cut off with a cleaver for trying to swindle a local butcher.

It is unusual to find cards that have survived such a time since they are fragile, and many were either worn out and disposed of, or were eaten by mice and rats if they fell into an inaccessible place (these ones were preserved because they were buried in ash from the fire). Nevertheless, playing cards are still found hidden in the walls of old houses, because they have a magic significance; different cards have different folk meanings in cartomancy and tarot readings. It is interesting that according to cartomancy tradition the ten of clubs is the 'card of fortune', it signifies 'financial success and material abundance'. The Queen of Clubs is 'the woman that most men would like to marry' (according to Cardarium website). She is traditionally a sincere friend to men who love her, but a dangerous rival to other women, apparently. Could the cards be apotropaic and signify 'Lady Luck', protecting the house from witches possibly coming down the chimney? Or are they a charm to bring winnings to the landlord during card games?

It is interesting that the cards were found with a '300-year-old bottle' (dated by Firmin Bradbeer after comparison with one in 'a Kensington museum'), which had three hearts imprinted upon it. It is possible that the Haunch was known as the Three Hearts at the time of the cache. The cards might also be older than the 18th century they have been estimated at.

It is worth noting that cards were valuable, and taxed, in the past, and they would be unlikely to be shuffled on something which had gaps which they could slip through by accident, nor left there if they had.

The cards were given to Salisbury Museum by Mrs Dolly Lemon (née Bradbeer) and Miss Marjorie Bradbeer.

C is for Carter, Ambrose

Ambrose Carter was a shoemaker who leased half of the merchant's house from Thomas Cooper. The rooms which he rented included the Hall, now the upper restaurant of the Haunch of Venison. According to John Chandler, this was probably divided to create a bedroom. Carter died there in 1691.

C is for Carters, the jewellers

Carters the jewellers, is one of Salisbury's oldest businesses, and has been the next-door neighbour of the Haunch of Venison since 1817. The business started as a watchmakers, and made a large round clock, which pictures show used to hang in the downstairs bar of the Haunch.

Carters is installed in the merchant's house, which has been a totally different building to the Haunch for most of its

The 'House of Commons' with the clock made by Carters © Salisbury Museum

history. The house had been divided into two houses, and Carters eventually bought both halves, reuniting them in 1877. The Carter family lived above the shop.

It was when William Holderness Carter, who owned the building, moved out of the living accommodation in 1911, that Firmin Bradbeer and his family moved in, renting it. The Bradbeers had moved from a house they called 'Clausentum', in Harnham Road. It's probably a coincidence that William Carter moved **to** Harnham Road at the same time, but tempting to speculate that they did a 'swap'. The private accommodation had a separate entrance, the other side of Carters, and now has an old sign 'the Haunch of Venison' above it (probably the neon sign, referred to as being in storage in 1930, in the Simonds inventory, now in Salisbury Museum). The larger restaurant room, with the big stone fireplace, was part of the Bradbeers living accommodation.

At some time, the restaurant was extended into the merchant's house. This is generally thought to be 1950, since the 'Pizarro' theatre bill was found in the wall of the lower restaurant 'during extension work', that year, according to the *Journal.* However, the Bradbeer ephemera given to Salisbury Museum contains a menu dating from 1927, with a photograph showing the large dining room. The Secret Bar also used to extend into another room, now private to Carters. The two rooms are not included in Firmin's contract with Simonds. .

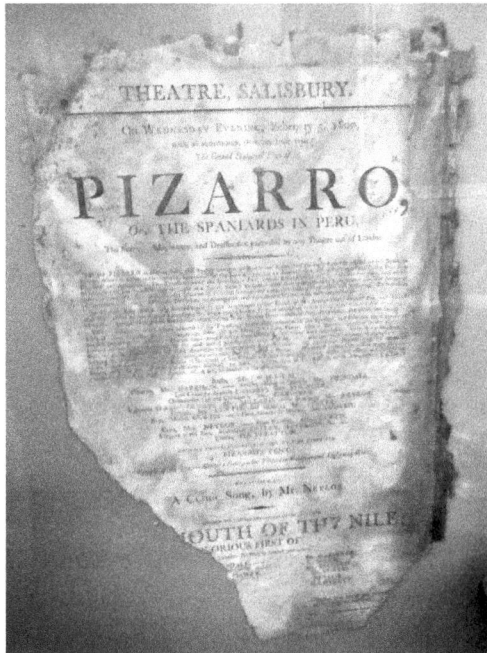

The Pizarro theatre bill © Frogg Moody

My own opinion is that the Cloisters Bar and the restaurant door opening took place after World War I. The 'Pizarro' workmen

The upstairs restaurant © Salisbury Museum

changed the height of the steps, and stripped back the wall whilst taking off wallpaper.

The merchant's house restaurant continues to be owned by Carters (2022), who have a third-party agreement with Stonegate. They use the 'merchant mark' as their logo because they own it, although it is now part of the Haunch of Venison. In this way, Carters and the Haunch of Venison are closely tied.

C is for Cellars

The cellar under the Haunch of Venison could not be sunk to any depth because of the high-water table. It is the reason that the Smoking Room (the 'House of Lords') is built higher than the lower bar – it is directly above the cellar. Because the cellar was tiny, The Haunch did not brew its own beer, but was supplied in beer and spirits by other

> *To INNKEEPERS & others.—FREE HOUSE.*
> **T**O be LET, and entered upon at Mid-summer next,—All that very desirable INN and PREMISES, called The SARACEN's HEAD, situate in the Blue-Boar-Row, Market-Place, Salisbury, directly opposite the Corn Market, for many years in the renting of Mr. Benjamin Wilks, who is retiring from business.— The Stock, &c. to be taken by the tenant at appraisement, who will have the privilege of serving the Haunch of Venison Inn, Salisbury, with Beer.——Apply to Mr. Cooper, solicitor, Salisbury ; if by letter, free of expence.

12t June, 1820. (Incidentally, Mr Cooper the solicitor would come to own the Haunch of Venison)

wholesale businesses. We know from the *Journal* that the beer came from the Saracen's Head when the Cheater family had the pub (the Saracen's Head no longer exists, but stood in Blue Boar Row).

When Firmin Potto began his own import business, also mentioned are his cellars in the High Street, in George Yard (*Salisbury Journal* 1832). Firmin Potto's brother William had cellars next to his pub, the Wheatsheaf in Fish Row, at one time (see appendices), and it is possible that these were also used by the Haunch. Rod Poynting, a local historian collecting pottery stoneware beer bottles, found the following fragment of a bottle labelled 'Firmin Potto' in Culver Street, when foundation building work was being carried out there for the car park. He thinks that this would suggest that Firmin Potto and his widow, Louisa Potto, were already using cellars in Culver Street before Firmin Bradbeer took over the Haunch's import business.

There is a very good description in Arthur Maidment's book *I Remember* of cellars rented by Louisa's nephew Firmin Bradbeer in the 1920s. These cellars were very old – possibly medieval – and took up the area of four houses – numbers 52, 50, 48 and 46 Culver Street. They had thick walls (3-4ft thick), round arches, and low ceilings. The cellars were accessed by double doors under numbers 48 and 46. The houses above the cellars were ordinary brick houses, and Maidment speculates that an important merchant's house may once have stood on the spot. Sadly, the cellars are now under Culver Street car park, although they may one day be rediscovered.

The cellars were accessed by wide stairs which had flat sections of metal either side, which could take runners which operated like a 'cliff top railway'. The 'lifts' were operated by a pinion wheel on a rack in a well

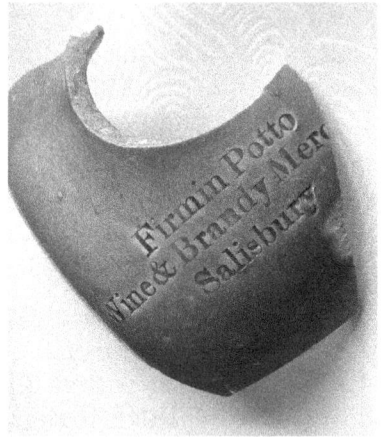

Fragment of a jug found in Culver Street © Rod Poynting

sunk into the centre of the stairs, in turn worked by cranks turned by hand. One of the lifts described by Arthur Maidment can be seen behind Bill Golding, to the right. Incidentally, his overall was of green baize. Apparently, Bill would 'puff' when cranking the lift, as it took a good deal strength to operate.

Bill Golding, right, the lift can clearly be seen behind him © Salisbury Museum

Beer was delivered to the cellar by horse drawn dray carts, in large barrels, and had to be got off the carts and onto the lifts to be cranked to the cellar. The beer was bottled each day, and delivered twice a day to the Haunch by handcart. There was also stout, and cider. Wine was bottled, and corks forced in with a corking machine, and then wrapped, and rolled in dust to look aged. Spirits were kept in small casks to sit above the gravity fed spirit taps at the Haunch bar. Bill Golding and

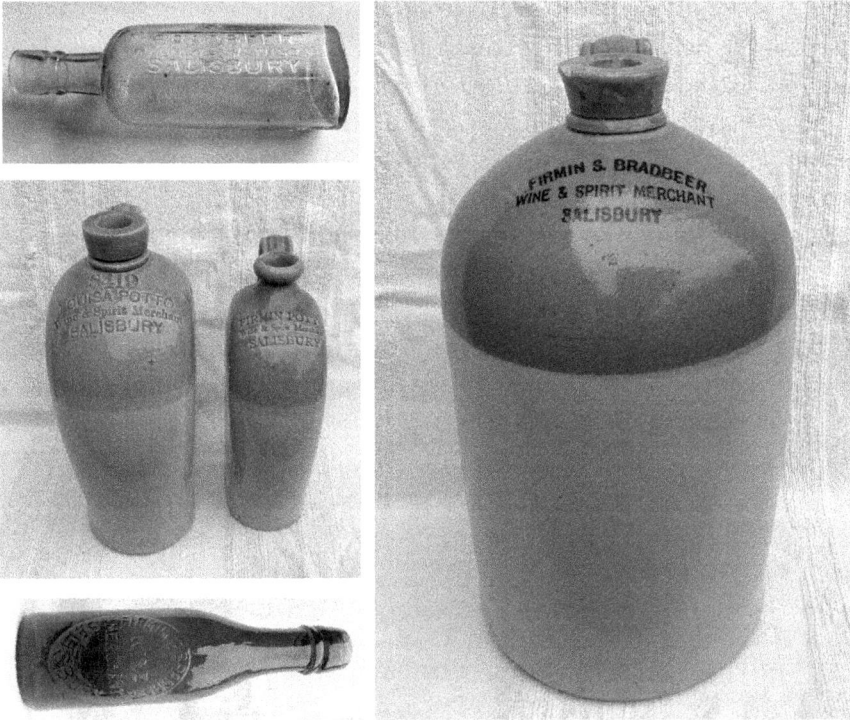

An assortment of 2 jugs and 2 bottles from the cellars of the Haunch of Venison
© Rod Poynting

Arthur Maidment are commemorated on the Culver Street mural. There was a machine with a revolving brush to clean the used bottles each day, which then had to be rinsed and dried in an oven. By 1927 Firmin Bradbeer was no longer wholesaling alcohol, but had made an arrangement with Ind Coope, and one presumes that the cellars had gone.

C is for Cheater

Thomas Cheater was the landlord of the Haunch of Venison from around 1798. Son of a butcher, He had been born in Plaitford, Romsey, Hampshire, in 1774, and married Jane Munday in Warminster in 1793. A son, John followed. By 1798, the Cheaters were in Salisbury, when Eliza was born. Eliza died at only two months old. Their daughter, Maria, was christened in St Thomas's Church in 1800. A younger brother, Charles, followed in 1802. Thomas Cheater took over the Haunch from Thomas Drake, Landlord before him.

Mr Cheater seems to have got into trouble with James W. H.
Fawconer, early on, since his solicitor wrote to him complaining
that he wasn't answering correspondence, and threatening him with
'ejectment'. Fawconer had no rights to the Haunch, which his brother
had legally sold, but he appears to have wanted to grab it, and was
embroiled in a complicated legal case.

The Haunch of Venison freehold was sold by the Fawconers in
1803, whilst Thomas Cheater was in occupation. It was bought by
James Butcher and resold to William Cooper, a solicitor of Castle
Street, for £464. The deeds mention again that the Haunch had been
in the occupation of Thomas Drake previously. (Leases and letters are
consultable at the Wiltshire & SwindonHistory Centre, Chippenham).

HAUNCH OF VENISON, SALISBURY.

TO be SOLD by AUCTION, on the Premises, by
HENRY SUTTON, on Friday the 29th day of July instant,
at four o'clock in the afternoon,—All that good accustomed
PUBLIC HOUSE, called THE HAUNCH OF VENISON,
situate in Minster-street, Salisbury, now in the occupation of
Thomas Cheater.

For further particulars, or to treat for the purchase, apply to
Messrs. Tanner and Cooper, attornies, Salisbury.   [40

A rather tragic story was in the *Salisbury Journal* in 1810. The
Haunch of Venison stands quite near to Salisbury's old prison, which
stood where the Clock Tower is now (you can still see an old cell, if
you go behind the tower). A lady who had come to see her husband
at the prison arrived just as he was being taken out in chains – he
had just been sentenced to two years for stealing some bacon. The
man had been a gentleman's servant, but had tried to open a shop,
which had failed. His wife was seven months pregnant, and the shock
of seeing her husband in chains made her go into early labour. She
was taken in by Mr and Mrs Cheater at the Haunch who 'though she
had no claim on them except her distress, and who, though she had
no money, bestow'd all possible care and attention in the premature
birth of the child; a few shillings have since been collected for her by
a lady, and the child thus untowardly born, seems likely to live'.

The Cheaters, then, were a kind family (although if this is the
same Thomas Cheater that had to make a printed apology to Mrs
Jane Stone, for bringing false charges against her in 1803, he wasn't

that kind!).

Thomas Cheater signed a lease for another seven years with the owner of the Haunch of Venison, William Cooper in 1819. (He had evidently learned to do his signature by then, which he had been unable to do on the marriage register at his wedding, when he had had to sign with an 'x'!) The yearly rent agreed was for £21. It was paid four times yearly – Michaelmas day, Saint Thomas Day, Lady Day, and Midsummer Day. The Cheaters were obliged by contract to live on the premises and to 'receive and entertain traveller guests' in the customary manner.   In 1820 the Haunch was being supplied with beer by the Saracen's Head, a pub which has now disappeared.

> On Sunday the 27th ult. died, to the great grief of her husband and family, aged 60 years, Mrs. Jane Cheater, wife of Mr. Thomas Cheater, of the Haunch of Venison public-house, in Minster-street.

Jane Cheater died in 1823. Thomas followed her in July 1831, and was buried in St Thomas's Churchyard.

Maria Cheater (Mrs Maria Potto)

Maria, the youngest surviving daughter, carried on the business, and a surviving receipt for fire insurance (£8 per year), the year of her father's death, has his name crossed out, and hers written in.

Maria married Firmin Potto at St Thomas's Church in April 1832. The witnesses were William Marrows Potto (Firmin's father) and Mary Arney, who was probably a relative of John Arney, who was a boot and shoemaker in Minster Street. Arney got into financial difficulties in 1834, and his shop was bought by Firmin Potto in May

> On the 28th ult., at Mr. Firmin Potto's, Minster-street, Miss M. Arney, very much respected by all who knew her.

that year (it is currently a travel agents, 2022). Mary Arney would die two years after Maria, at the Haunch of Venison, where she lived and was then 'assistant' to Firmin Potto. It appears that Maria Cheater and Firmin Potto both knew the Arneys.

As an ambitious young man, Firmin Potto carried on his shoe shop, but used the Haunch of Venison as the start of a successful Wine and Spirit Import and wholesale business. He was rising to the top of

Salisbury society, and was frequently in the newspapers. His brother
William was equally visible in Salisbury, with William specialising in
lavish dinners at his larger establishments, and one imagines that
Maria and Firmin must have had a lively social life. They did not have
any children, however.

Maria gave one pound and one shilling to Salisbury Infirmary
in 1834. The Infirmary relied on subscriptions from the public (Alas!
The gas street lighting did too, and the same newspaper lamented
that people were benefitting from the 'beautiful light', without
contributing funds).

> Lot 2. All that Freehold MESSAGE or DWELL-
> ING-HOUSE now in the occupation of Mr. Potto
> shoemaker, most desirably situated for trade, between
> the Cheese-market and Poultry Cross, in Minster-
> street, Salisbury.

When the freehold of the Haunch of Venison came up for sale
again in 1838, it was now said to be in the occupation of 'Mr Potto'
(and not Mrs Potto). The newspaper advertisement stressed its ties to
Salisbury Market, by pointing out its situation between the Cheese-
Market and the Poultry Cross.

Maria's brother, Charles, was a 'cellarman' all his life, and
lived in Castle Street. He might well have been the cellarman for
the Haunch of Venison (where he had grown up), for his sister and
brother-in-law. Firmin Potto also had cellars in George Yard (now the
Old George Mall), for his Wine and Spirit Import business. Firmin's
teenage niece, Jane Cheater, was his general servant.

Maria's brother, John, was a cheesemonger living in Gigant
Street, and successful enough in business to mention his sister Maria,
wife of Firmin Potto, in his will of 1841, although she pre-deceased
him by a few years. Since John also left shares in his estate to his wife,
children, and brother Charles, he must have been a successful trader.
Ten years later he had moved to New Street.

John Cheater was with Maria when she died aged only 50,
upstairs at the Haunch of Venison, in 1851. She had been married to
Firmin Potto for almost 20 years. Her death was caused by Chronic
Nephritis, which led to ascites, and was probably caused by either an
auto-immune disease, or an infection.

Chotie and Dicker © @chotiedarling.co.uk

C is for Chotie

It was not only the manageress of the Haunch of Venison (Dolly Bradbeer) who had a wartime romance during World War II. The old inn was also the backdrop to the love story of two childhood sweethearts. My thanks go to Chotie's daughter for allowing me to quote and use pictures from her web site

When you sit in a snug corner with a romantic partner, cosying up by the fire in the smoking room, spare a moment to think of Chotie, a teenager in the 1940s. 'Chotie' was the nickname of Barbara Chalkley from Poole, in Dorset, who met Richard Kelsey Williams – known as Dicker – at a local youth club, when she was only 14 and he was 16. He joined up (reporting to the Fisherton Working Man's Club, at the bottom of Wilton Road, Salisbury), when war broke out just two years later.

As the blog 'Chotie Darling' says, Dicker wrote to Barbara every single day of the war. Many of the letters were written from local army bases, at Quidhampton, Bemerton, and Dinton, providing a unique contemporary picture of Salisbury during the war years. He initially trained as a PT instructor, was appointed a corporal in 1940, and wrote his surprise at not realising that an acquaintance was *quite* so old – 'He's nearly twenty!'.

When Chotie and Dicker *were* able to meet up, it was in Salisbury. The Haunch of Venison soon became their favourite, and they referred to the city as 'Haunch Town', in their private 'lover's shorthand'.

It was Firmin Bradbeer and his daughter Dolly, who had the pub then. Dolly herself was in a romance with Captain Jack Edwardes, an RAF officer and ENSA performer. Dicker was encouraged to use the Haunch since it was frequented by officers, and he was no longer able to fraternise with lower ranks, who used pubs like The Rising Sun. The Haunch was a respectable Inn, and the couple particularly liked old places (they chose the Spreadeagle in Midhurst for a honeymoon).

'I could get next Sunday (30th) off? When I could perhaps meet you in the neighbourhood of the 'Haunch of Venison?"

May 14th, 1944. By this time, Dicker had been promoted and was serving in the 61st Recce Reg RAC: 'I imagine that we could fix up somewhere to stay in the Haunch town'

They stayed for one night at the 'Haunch of Venison' (they rented rooms), on Friday 19th of May. D-Day was looming. Chotie had to go AWOL (she had joined up, as soon as she was old enough). They had 'separate rooms, but he wanted us to be together before he went to France. It was very romantic, our young hearts breaking'. She describes the rooms being opposite each other, and so they slept in the rooms at the top of the building. Chotie wouldn't see Dicker again until the following year, when the couple married, with just a few days leave.

On 26 March 1945, having heard that Dicker's brother was stationed close to him, Chotie wrote 'It's marvellous that you are so near each other. I hope you manage to meet. (…) I spend quite a lot of time just dreaming of things to come (…) I think that I had better see what I can do with a Missen, probably have to.'

Dicker Williams was killed in Germany on 30th March, 1945. It was in a random accident where, having spent a relaxed day socialising with his brother, his car ran over a bomb crater and he was thrown from the car and killed instantly. His brother walked back to camp to give the bad news. Dicker had survived active service in Normandy, Belgium, The Netherlands, and the Ardennes, and was amongst the first troops to liberate the Concentration Camps in Germany. He had been married to Chotie for just three weeks.

C is for Churchill

Two famous historical people who are associated with the Haunch of Venison are Sir Winston Churchill and President Eisenhower of the USA.

Churchill and Eisenhower drawing © Haunch of Venison

Winston Churchill knew Salisbury well, having made several visits in his youth. An interesting little-known fact (according to Wiltshire & Swindon History Centre), is that he was one of the first people to learn to fly before World War I. There is even a picture in the Science Museum, taken in 1914, of Churchill getting ready to fly with the RFC (forerunner of the RAF) at Upavon, which is 33 minutes by car from Salisbury.

Firmin Bradbeer, then landlord of the Haunch of Venison, spent World War I in the RFC. The pub was frequented by many RFC pilots, in 1914, as can be seen by the Haunch's Visitor's Book, now in Salisbury Museum.

Churchill often came to Salisbury Plain during World War II. He is pictured at Fovant camp. He visited Larkhill in 1940, and

The Double Cube Room at Wilton House

Netheravon in 1942. Leading up to D-Day, in 1944, Churchill was staying at the Red Lion Hotel in Salisbury, and planning the liberation of Europe with General Eisenhower in the Double Cube Room at Wilton House. Tradition has it that, whilst showing General Eisenhower Salisbury during the preparations for D Day, they visited the Haunch of Venison, where they were able to find a quiet corner to continue the important conversations in private. It might be that although the Haunch of Venison's quaintness and antiquity would be something in itself to show General Eisenhower, the pub's links to the RAF, and 'officer' clientele would be another attraction.

The visitor's book was no longer in use by World War II, and 'off duty' discreet visits to pubs, would not be reported in the newspapers, however the staff and locals would have been well aware of their important guests, and have remembered them forever, passing down an oral tradition that I certainly believe.

C is for Coins

Edwardian woodcarving of a haunch of venison with coins

'It was the night of decimalisation' (15th February, 1971) recounts long-time customer, Les Mitchell. 'We were all sitting on 'Death Row', when suddenly Roy Spring got up to show us the new money, and what the equivalent was in the old money, and he wedged the coins up above the fire place. Some tourists came in and saw the coins and they, straight away, put more up there − they automatically thought that it was like a Wishing Well, you see. That's how it started'.

David Taylor (who, later, lived upstairs) said 'back then, if you were short of money for your next drink, then the unwritten rule was that you could borrow from it − but you always had to put it back. It was like an overdraft to spend only on beer!'.

Anastasia Samoilova thinks that the tradition mentioned by David Taylor goes back to before 1971: 'I have read that tradition in a 1960s guide book, about the Haunch' (I have yet to trace the book, but I'm sure that it exists).

Nowadays, the coins regularly go into the Charity Box, and not into the glasses of the locals!

C is for Cooper

For a few years, from, 1681, Thomas Cooper and his wife lived in part of the merchant's house, which had been divided into two at this date. They bought it from Thomas's uncle, Henry Mason, who continued living in the other half. Thomas's home included the hall, which is now the dining room of the Haunch of Venison. According to John Chandler, this was probably partitioned to make a bedroom (as no bedroom was included in the rooms which hc'd purchascd). Thomas was a shoemaker, and his daughters would later share ownership of this part of the house.

Samuel Cooper was the cousin of Henry Mason who bought the other half of the house from him in 1688.

Henry Cooper (no relation, as far as is known) never lived in the Haunch of Venison, but owned the building for many years, during the occupation of Firmin Potto. Henry appears to have inherited the Haunch from his father, William Cooper, who bought it from James Butcher (who had bought it from the Fawconer family). He was a wealthy solicitor in Castle Street, living in the building which would later become known as the restaurant used by the Russian father and daughter in the Salisbury novichok poisonings. Henry would seem to be an uncle of the blind Post Master General and politician, Henry Fawcett. He was a customer of Firmin Potto, for wines and spirits, which he deducted from the rent which he collected for the Haunch of Venison. He died only a short time before Mr Potto, who had bought the freehold of the Haunch from his Estate, at auction in 1874.

C is for Crew

It can be difficult to find concrete information about the landlords of the Haunch of Venison, before the census, and without knowing where to search. The information about landlord Thomas Crew is surely there to find, for the sleuths among you! A Thomas Crew is given as landlord in 1791. Some clues as to who he was, follow (although they may be red herrings!).

A baby, Thomas Crew, was christened in St Thomas's Church (behind the Haunch of Venison) in 1792. His parents are given as Thomas Crew, and Caroline Matilda Crew. Caroline might be the Caroline Papps, from St Edmund's district of Salisbury, who became Caroline Crew upon marriage.

A Caroline Matilda Crew died in Bath in 1812. Whilst 'Caroline Matilda' is a common name of the period, being named after a daughter of a then Prince of Wales, and sister of the future George III, it is possible that she is the same woman who was the mother of baby Thomas, because a Thomas Crew appears in Bath on the earliest census return in 1841, and he was a 'letter carrier' born in Salisbury in 1792. If anybody can find a Bath innkeeper named Thomas Crew, we might have a start!

D is for Death Row

The longest customers of the Haunch of Venison still call the long bench facing the entrance 'Death Row'. 'Or, 'God's Waiting Room' says David Taylor, who lived upstairs in the 1970s. Les Mitchell remembers, 'the regulars used to sit on that bench and around those tables' (*the regulars, these days, still have a tendency to do so*). Les continues, 'and the senior regulars – those who had been coming here the longest time – were allowed to sit closest to the fire. That was the way we did things. And one by one they died off, as they moved up the bench'.

The notorious 'Death Row' bench

D is for Dining Club

One of the things that the Haunch of Venison was famous for in the 1980s was its illustrious Dining Club. The idea was that of Salisbury local celebrity, Roy Spring, who was Clerk of Works at Salisbury Cathedral, and dreamt it up with some of his friends: Salisbury's head postmaster, Jim Jessop, Les Mitchell, Ken Lailey, Alec Walk, Bob Robert, Tony Redding, and Des Mist. It was to be a 'gentleman's club'.

The concept was to recreate 18th-century menus, three times a year, and sit down to a formal, candlelight dinner, in the dark panelled Smoking Room, in evening dress. Roy loved the 18th-century book, *Diary of a Country Parson*, and wanted to recreate some of the period menus. He told the *Salisbury Times* in 1980, about the inaugural February meeting: 'It does not mean that we will be meeting to gorge a full 18th-century meal, because we could not afford it, but there will be hearty indulgence in such mouth-watering dishes as boiled leg of mutton, caper sauce, and roast capon, on the first occasion, with a dish of fried sprats to start off, and Stilton and port on the table afterwards'.

Landlord Bill Jakeman, who was in charge of the kitchen said, 'Recipes of the 18th century are few and far between. In that period, they indulged in cauliflower, spinach, and sorrel a lot, as a garnish (...) English lamb, cooked in a straightforward, simple way'. Roy went on 'the October dinner will be near to Michaelmas, and the obvious choice for that meal must be goose. At Christmas, as in the 18th century, there will be none of the frozen turkey, that would be an unforgivable sin, but a delicious round of beef, roasted to the spit.'

Roy Spring on the spire of Salisbury Cathedral © Ben Spring

The food was accompanied by the appropriate choices from the cellar, 'The dinner will begin with malmsey and madeira. During the dinner, ale will be served with a bowl of mixed spice. mulling irons will take off the chill, and adding zest to it. With the Stilton there will be vintage port.'

Roy Spring's Churchwardens pipes © Nick Spring

As smoking was then allowed in pubs, the Smoking Room (House of Lords) lived up to its name, when members of the Haunch Dining Club smoked long churchwarden pipes between courses. Nick Spring (Roy's son), still has two of his pipes, which then sat in a case upon the wall, near the fireplace, in the same room. "Churchwardens' are very fragile', Les Mitchell told me. 'They'd often break. Mine didn't because mine was unused. I'd be sent to buy the tobacco – Roy had the tobacconist make up a special 18th-century mix' first of all, we got it from Pothecary's in Fisherton Street, and then there was a pipe shop which opened up in the Cross Keys Mall. He used to make his own pipes there, and he would get the tobacco for us. Then he packed up, and I used to have go all the way to Bath for it – and I was the only one who didn't smoke! The pipes were very dangerous – they gave people lip cancer'. The pipes had red tips to protect the lips. Les has kept the pipe cabinet.

Les remembers, 'the dinners were very expensive, and so we would pay into a fund each week – so at least we knew that we went into dinner with something in the kitty. It helped! It was insufficient for the first dinner. We often bought our own meat, and the Haunch would cook it. If there were any left over, we'd take it down to the bar. Towards the end, it was more about the Stilton and Port!! We did try to revive the Dining Club, later, after Bill was gone. But it was never the same.'

D is for Drake
An early lease between the then owner of the Haunch of Venison (Fawconer) and Thomas Cheater, refers to the Haunch as having 'lately been in the occupation of Thomas Drake', so that we can surmise that there was a landlord called Thomas Drake at the end of the 18th century, in the reign of George III.

E is for Edwardes (Jack)
It is a little-known fact that for a few brief years in the 1940s, the flamboyant comic actor, Jack Edwardes, was considered the Landlord of the 'Haunch of Venison' because he was married to the manageress and landlady, Dolly Bradbeer/Edwardes. Look at the height of the ceilings in the bar, and the tiny stairs leading to the Lords, and then imagine a huge heavily built, pipe-smoking, man, swinging around in the tiny space. Next imagine him in 1940s woman's clothing and make-up, serving pints of beer from behind the pewter bar (as I feel sure that he would have done occasionally, for the pleasure of the regulars), because Jack Edwardes was an actor-comedian who made a speciality of female impersonation.

Jack was 6 ft. 4 ins. (he was a member of the London Topliners club for tall people), and a pilot by trade. He was born in 1913, in Kent, and was nine years younger than Dolly. According to one interview that he gave, he had started to train as an architect on leaving Chatham Grammar School, but gave it up because his maths was poor, and instead joined the RAF. He would do a total of thirteen years in the RAF, altogether.

He originally joined the RAF in No. 10 Bomber Squadron, on a short service commission, between the wars. He then worked as a commercial and test pilot for Brooklands Aviation Company, who were developing the Hawker Hurricane, and the Vickers Wellington. Whilst there, he married his first wife, Joy Tuttle, in 1936, and by 1937, Jack was in the RAF reserves (class F), stationed abroad in Iraq, returning to England in 1939, via Australia. Still in the volunteer reserves as a 'Pilot Sergeant', he was among the men who took over the Squires Gate Airfield, Blackpool, in November 1939, as part of the No. 9 Civilian Air Naval School (C.A.N.S), flying two-seater Tiger Moth, Hawker Hind, and Hawker Audax aircraft. He became part of Coastal Command, checking out ships using the Irish sea, from the air. Coastal Command were responsible for protecting allied shipping and supply lines from U-boats and air attacks, and they saw frequent 'action'. It was during this period that Jack met 5 ft. 1 ins. tall Charlie Springall, who was a rear gunner and still a teenager. Charlie Springall would later become a household name, as 'Charlie Drake'.

Jack Edwardes and Charlie formed a naturally comic looking pair, and both were talented performers (Charlie had been a child actor). Towards the end of the war, they performed together for ENSA (the Entertainments National Service Association – also known as 'Every Night Something Awful'). Jack also performed comic sketches for Ralph Reader's Gang Show, and even appeared in a show called 'Airmen in Skirts'. He wrote and produced a comedy sketch show called 'Out of The Blue', which briefly opened in London's West End.

It is very difficult to know how Captain Jack Edwardes met Dolly Bradbeer, but Marjorie Bradbeer mentioned in a letter her sister's RAF friends, and the pub was known as one which was used by officers, and the landlord (Firmin Bradbeer) was himself ex-RAF. One can imagine then, that Jack was taken to the pub by mutual friends, probably before World War II started. By the time that he got together with Dolly, he already had an infant son with his wife, Joy.

It appears to have been a whirlwind wartime romance. By 1943 Jack was divorced, and by 1944 married to Dolly. She was forty – and in this period, would have been considered on the shelf – and he was thirty-one. They married at Salisbury Registry Office, and for Firmin, sometime churchwarden of St Thomas's Church, it must have been a disappointment that they could not have a church wedding. However, Firmin Bradbeer appears to have bonded with his new son-in-law, and certainly the pair had a great deal of interests in common. Indeed, Dolly seems almost to have married her father, as a list of the duties which Jack carried out for a show given at Ventnor, Isle of Wight, in 1946 display a range of talents just as versatile and exhausting as Firmin's: 'he combined the duties of manager, producer, compere, comedian, chorus and community singing leader, scenic designer, dance organizer, stage hand, and electrician', said the local papers.

Mr. Jack Edwardes as carnival "Queen" of Salisbury's Battle of Britain Week, pictured above before the "royal court" moved off for the procession on Wednesday. Children in fancy dress costumes (right), enjoy Punch and Judy at Victoria Park later in the afternoon.

Jack Edwardes as the Carnival Queen © *Salisbury Newspapers*

Whilst in Salisbury, Jack Edwardes continued his theatrical career, writing, producing, and acting in two revue shows at the Palace Theatre in Endless Street, 'Into the Brew', and 'What's Brewing'. and his theatrical costumes (including women's clothing) are listed for insurance purposes, in the Haunch of Venison archives at Salisbury Museum. He also announced that he was standing for election to the local council, on behalf of the Conservative party.

Jack was on the National Council for the RAF Association, as well as the Salisbury Executive Council, and organised the Battle of Britain celebrations in the city. Dolly led the Ladies Branch of the Association, and wore a diamond brooch with the RAF insignia. Raising money for the RAF Benevolent Fund, the *Salisbury Journal* carried a touching piece about a small boy in Harnham selling his own toys and then running down to give the money to Captain Jack Edwardes, landlord of the Haunch of Venison. The object of the Benevolent Fund was to help ex-RAF men find peacetime jobs, and to provide an income for those who had become disabled after accidents, or being shot down.

The celebrations began in 1946, when an annual Battle of Britain Week was declared, always to be celebrated on September the 13th. Salisbury witnessed over 300 aircraft of the RAF and Naval Air Arm (including Coastal Command) fly over in massed formation, during that afternoon: part of the area in which the Battle of Britain had been fought in 1940.

In 1947, 77 mosquito planes set off from Yeovil, flying over Bath and Bristol, finishing in Salisbury. Jack even rode around Salisbury dressed as Salisbury's Carnival Queen. There is a picture of him sitting on Salisbury Guildhall steps (in a sombre suit), with the city dignitaries. Dolly is sitting on the other side of the mayor, dressed in black, mourning her father (Firmin Bradbeer, ex-landlord of the Haunch of Venison) who had died a few days beforehand. Jack also wrote and produced the 'Searchlight Tattoo' show for the occasion.

In 1947, Jack Edwardes was still living at the Haunch of Venison, and one presumes acting as 'mine host', but by this date the couple were separated. The reason for the marriage breakdown is given as his 'Misconduct' on the divorce papers. 'Misconduct' means 'adultery' and this might have been with his ex-wife, Joy, whom he remarried shortly after his divorce came through a few years later – going on to have another son. However, since the separation appears to have been fairly amicable, perhaps Jack merely volunteered to chivalrously

Jack Edwardes on the Guildhall steps © *Salisbury Newspapers*

take the blame – this was a quite common arrangement in a time when 'no fault' divorces didn't exist, and gentlemen would not accuse a lady of the fault. Whatever the true situation, it was Dolly who had moved out of the pub (to 1 Prospect Place) even though she held the licence for the Haunch, and had managed the business for years. It was Jack Edwardes who stayed on at the Haunch of Venison, and is named on Mr Bradbeer's death certificate, as being present at the death.

By May 1948, Jack Edwardes had left Salisbury, and the Haunch of Venison was handed back to Simonds Brewery, who installed a new landlord (Clifford Johnson) in that month. But Jack was not to forget his experiences as a pub Landlord, as we shall see.

Jack Edwardes continued to work tirelessly for the RAFA, organising sixteen big shows at the Royal Albert Hall and other major centres such as The Royal Festival Hall, and the Usher Hall Edinburgh. He made a 3x replica of The Battle of Britain window in Westminster Abbey, himself, for the show. He was the Entertainments and Publicity Officer at the RAFA headquarters, and proved very inventive, organising a race between RAF men trying to go 100 yards on Penny-Farthings – faster than he and a member of his RAFA staff could do a lap of Herne Hill cycle track, on a tandem; He got the event covered by the BBC. Soon he was making a name for himself on the radio.

In 1950, he remarried his first wife, Joy, and soon had another son.

However, in 1952, everything changed for Jack...he entered a competition run by 'Quaglinos' nightclub to find new 'Variety' talent for first class Cabaret, beating huge competition (the female winner, was singer Pearl Newman). Jack was still doing a female impersonator comedy act. Part of the prize was a contract with a Theatrical Agent, and he received some publicity in the *Stage*. It is supposedly in the waiting room of his agent that Jack re-met his war time fellow performer Charlie Springall, who shared the same agent, and was now calling himself Charlie Drake. According to Turnipnet.com, the pair were both sent for auditions at the famous Windmill Theatre, and failing them, decided to throw their lot in together as a double act; their first job was at Butlins Holiday Camp in 1953.

It was Charlie Drake who invented the hapless duo 'Mick and Montmorency', writing the scripts. The gags were 'Laurel and Hardy' style slapstick, and based around the naturally comic appearances of 5 ft. 1 ins. skinny Charlie, and heavily built 6 ft. 4 ins. Jack. Spotted by a BBC Producer, they were invited to appear on Children's TV as part of the Children's comedy show 'Jigsaw', and then were poached by the 'other' channel, Associated Rediffusion, for their own show known both as 'Mick and Montmorency' and 'Jobstoppers', which was a huge success, and even had its own associated comic book magazine. Together they made 91 episodes. Details about Mick and Montmorency can be found on turnipnet.com. Jack and Charlie continued to do pantomime, as celebrity television stars, and travelled all over the Country. The series lasted from 1955-1958.

The partnership ended in May 1958 because Charlie Drake wanted to go solo (he would go on to become one of Britain's most famous comedians in his heyday), and although Jack tried the same comic little/large formula with other partners like Felix Bowness, it simply didn't work.

Jack Edwardes stayed on national television until 1963, however, in a live broadcast show (15 minutes a week), which was a 'soap' based around the eponymous pub 'Jim's Inn' where the landlord and landlady discussed 'products' with their customers, in a natural way. Jack played 'Jack', a local farmer, who had the catch phrase 'two Ben Truman's in a pint pot, please.' When this type of advertising was banned in 1963, Jack claimed that it was the brewery which approached him and asked him to take over the historic 16th century pub, the Kings Arms, in Frating (Essex). Jack had already moved back to the area, in which he had grown up. Of course, he might simply have wanted to settle down bringing up his new family, and running a pub was something he knew how to do very well.

Jack had met Pat Keeble, a mother of three children, in 1954, and since he was a television celebrity, her outrageous divorce made the front page of the scandalous newspaper the *Daily Herald* on 30 July, 1958. Jack Edwardes's divorce from Joy, with whom he had two children, came through the same year. He came over in Court as a 'ladies' man', and a brief appearance on Charlie Drake's first turn on 'This is your Life' TV show, shows him to have a sweet charm. However, despite the judge's understandable scepticism over the advisability of marrying Jack Edwardes (and he perhaps did not know about the brief marriage to Dolly Bradbeer), Pat went on to marry Jack the next year, and by the time that they took over the Kings Arms they had two small boys together.

The pub was a huge success, with a barn converted into a restaurant which was praised by prestigious food guide Egon Ronay,

Wife was 'infatuated' by TV actor

A WIFE became "completely infatuated" with actor Jack Edwardes, the tall half of the "Mick and Montmorency" team on children's TV, said a Divorce Court judge yesterday.

"She wrote to him : 'You have known that I would come to you under any conditions that you would care to make, live with you or be near you, to be there when you felt you wanted me ... marry you, even work for you.'

"But the wife Mrs Patricia

Keeble, would be wise to give the deepest consideration to marrying Edwardes, said Mr. Commissioner Rewcastle.

For when Mrs. Keeble's husband found out about their association, Edwardes wrote— "to get out of trouble—" I have met again a girl I met at Butlin's. I thought I loved you, now I realise I do not."

The judge granted a decree nisi to Mr. Harold Keeble, of Onslow-gardens, Kensington, be-

cause of his wife's adultery with Edwardes.

But he also granted a decree to Mrs. Keeble on the ground of her husband's cruelty.

He said that Mr. Keeble put her out of the house in the early hours of a December morning. She was wearing only a nightdress, a coat, and slippers.

Later he went after her in his car and drove her to the river towpath. He dragged her out of the car, then swung her in his arms, counting "1-2-3."

He did not throw her in the river but dragged her back to the car by her hair and coat.

and multi-talented Jack did some of the cooking himself. Attractive Pat was described as 'the perfect hostess' and the pub was frequented by showbusiness friends of Jack, such as Bruce Forsyth and Anthea Redfern, and Jimmy Tarbuck. One article went as far as to say that it was amazing how well Jack had done, considering his lack of experience of the pub trade. The marriage appears to have been a happy one, and there is a picture of the pair, beaming out from behind the bar at the King's Head in 1970 – Jack is described as being 17 stone.

After a brief spell at another local restaurant in 1977-78, the couple eventually retired to the Yeovil area, where Jack died in 2001, aged 88. All his obituaries state that he was married only twice (although it was actually four times), and Salisbury and the Haunch of Venison have been written out of his 'story' – just as the Haunch of Venison quickly forgot Jack Edwardes. Nevertheless, Jack was at one time one of the most popular personalities in Salisbury, and the person who stayed with Firmin Bradbeer till his deathbed, and was considered the landlord of the Haunch of Venison.

E is for Eels

Whilst the 'eel sign' above the bar was put there by landlord, Tony Leroy, nevertheless, most pubs serving food in Salisbury, would have served eels at one time.

E is for Epicurean

In 1963, Samuel Chamberlain produced a book for the Gourmet Distributing Corporation called *British Bouquet. An Epicurean Tour of Britain.* It later inspired a TV programme called 'Terry and Mason's Great Food Trip' in 2015.

It's very startling to open an original copy of the book, because opposite the title page is the picture of a building startlingly similar to the Haunch

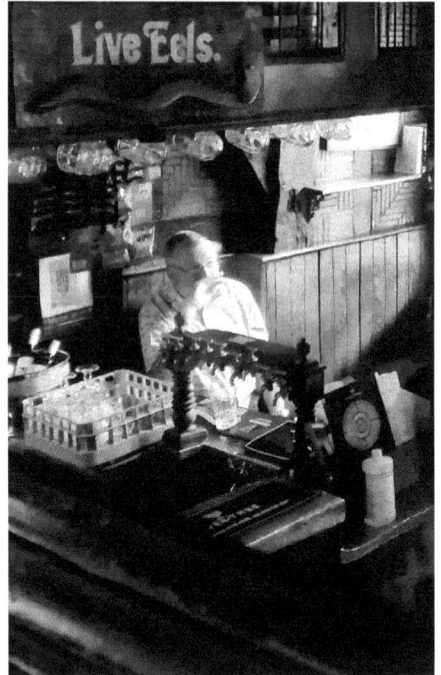

The 'Eel' sign above the main bar

– but which is in Canterbury High Street (The façade has been altered since 1963, and is now a shop front).

The church standing behind the Haunch of Venison is St Thomas of Canterbury, and the Canterbury building is in front of Canterbury Cathedral. However, since both the Canterbury building and the Haunch have façades altered in the 18th century, the resemblance is probably a coincidence. Nevertheless, it is worth considering the fact that the Haunch of Venison was originally built as a church house, when comparing the two buildings.

Canterbury High Street & 19th-century engraving of the Haunch of Venison

Chamberlain visited when the 'moustached manager', Mr Bennett, was showing his solicitude to the customers of the Haunch. Chamberlain also recommended the White Hart Hotel, the Old George (now Boston Tea Party) and the County Hotel (now Wetherspoons), but he said 'if you are in Salisbury for the day only, the Haunch of Venison seems destined to fill your time with a full measure of contentment.'

What did he suggest visitors eat and drink? 'A dry sherry or a beaker of ale before climbing the winding stairs to the timbered dining rooms above. Here you may order a good English meal a la carte, with Whitstable oysters, Dover sole, Aylesbury duck, or a dozen other delicacies, knowing that they will be well prepared and well served'.

E is for Execution

It is a difficult thing for us to imagine today, but up until 1855 Salisbury saw the public executions of many people. Up until 1822 many took place outside the old gaol, which stood where the Clock Tower stands today (with earlier ones taking place on the Market square, and others taking place on the corner of Wilton Road and Devizes Road). The Haunch of Venison must have surely been packed out on such occasions with rowdy revellers, sombre sightseers, and tearful friends of the condemned.

When there was an execution, it was a busy day indeed for the pubs of Salisbury, with people walking into the city from the surrounding area to gawp in awe, but also to listen to broadsheet hawkers singing tales of warning (particularly in the case of murder), and to buy souvenirs and refreshments. They thronged to the inns nearby to the execution site, and the Haunch was just around the corner.

One particular two weeks in 1801, when Thomas Cheater had just arrived to be landlord of the Haunch, must have been particularly busy, because eight men were hanged after the March Assizes, held at the Guildhall, over three different days. Although there were around 200 crimes punishable by death at that time, usually many were commuted because judges and juries were often very sensitive to the severity and finality of the punishment for relatively trivial crimes – not so this time! Perhaps they were swayed by the argument that heavy punishment was a deterrent, because they had 70 prisoners to judge ('a third more than ever before').

Minster Street must have been filled again with people flocking down towards Fisherton Gaol, and the sound of fanfares and horses, as the procession of dignitaries arrived to witness the grisly spectacle.

Some of the earlier executed men were buried anonymously in St Thomas's graveyard, just behind the Haunch of Venison. The mummified hand found in the fireplace of the Haunch's smoking room was most probably a 'hand of glory', and apotropaic, and the source used for this sort of talisman was generally from an executed man (these hands were said to have special properties, and people would rush to the gallows to rub the hand of a hanged man over skin complaints). I suggest that the relative proximity of the Haunch of Venison to both the gallows and the graveyard was once important, and it partly explains how the hand got there.

F is for Fawconer

The Haunch of Venison was in the hands of the Fawconer family from 1740, to 1803. The Fawconer family were very well known in Salisbury and Dorset. Edward Fawconer had been a rector in the village of Britford, just outside Salisbury, born in 1617, and his son, also Edward, was born in 1636. The younger Edward was a 'Lace Man' and described as 'an Alderman of Sarum' in 1680; he is presumably the Edward 'Faulkner' who was Mayor of Salisbury in 1686.

Of the Mayor's children, the second son was William Fawconer who became 'Sword Bearer' to King William III (He died in London with no children surviving). The fact that a Fawconer had such a position with royalty is not so surprising when we learn that a relative, Margaret Fawconer of Salisbury, had married John St Lo of Little Fontmell, Dorset. On John St Lo's Father's side of his family, he was related to the Hyde family (1st Earl of Clarendon, and father of James II's first wife). That meant that Queen Mary (King William III's wife) and Queen Anne were distant relatives by marriage.

Edward's daughter, Thomasine, married a London mercer. Johnathon Fawconer, buried in St Edmund's Church, was a merchant 'Lace Man', who actually died in London.

The Mayor's other son was Samuel Fawconer, born in 1694, who 'kept the Lamb and Flag, High Street, Sarum' (now Mitre House, on the corner of the High Street and New Street). He married Anne Fulford in London. He was a hosier by trade (says Maskelyne, in *Wiltshire Notes and Queries* I, although letters at the Wiltshire & Swindon History Centre give him as a shoemaker). 'Although he had some legitimate children, he was also said to have some illegitimate ones,' Maskelyne continues. He was evidently wealthy – and was mentioned in his father and brothers' wills – because he bought the Haunch of Venison Inn firstly, and then, in 1741, the merchant's house next door (the merchant's house was then divided into two halves, and he bought both, but did not make them one). This is important for the history of the Haunch, because the two buildings then had one ownership. It is also the first time that the Haunch of Venison is described as an Inn, having that name, although it probably was earlier. John Chandler suggested that Samuel probably moved into part of the merchant's house; if so, he evidently enjoyed the large fireplace in the upstairs dining room of a winter's night.

Like so much concerning the Haunch of Venison, then, we should not get the idea that Samuel Fawconer was a 'simple' artisan/ tradesman and inn keeper. Maskelyne, who wrote about Wiltshire history, considered the Fawconers to be 'Gentry'. There would later be a legal dispute over Samuel Fawconer's purchase of the Haunch of Venison from Sir Alexander Powell in 1740.

In 1816 (after the Fawconers had sold the Haunch to James Butcher in 1804), letters between solicitors (held in Chippenham) reveal that descendants of the Powell family had earlier begun a legal dispute claiming that Sir Alexander 'had conveyed the Haunch of Venison to Hugh *Lebonet* (?) for the use of Samuel Fawconer, *shoemaker,* for life, and then to the use of his wife Frances, for her life'. After their 'deceases', it was to go to the heirs of Powell. It was claimed that Sir Alexander had left the Haunch to his wife in his will. One can consult Sir Alex's will on Ancestry, and it doesn't itemize his property, probably because he had so much.

The first Samuel Fawconer, however, left to his wife, Frances, in *his* will, the building 'commonly known or called by the Sign of the Haunch of Venison which I bought from Sir Alexander Pool'. (Powell). He wrote in his will of 1755, 'Samuel Fawconer shoemaker, for himself, his heirs conveyed and granted that Samuel Fawconer and his heirs and all other persons . . . after him be seized of the Haunch of Venison for ever thereafter'. The Fawconers solicitor would later write: 'I am not certain but it clearly appears by that will of Mr Samuel Fawconer that he conceived that he had the right to dispose of it in the way that he has . . . however the limitation in the settlement may oppose it.'

Frances Fawconer left the Haunch to their eldest son, Samuel. Samuel and Frances Fawconer's sons Samuel and Edward both went to Merton College, Oxford University, and both became wealthy clergymen in Dorset. The elder son, Samuel, married a baronet's daughter, and had a coat of arms. He left the Haunch to his second wife, Martha Knight, who inherited in 1783 (and leased it to William Butcher). There were no heirs and so this direct line died out, and it was Samuel's brother, Edward who inherited the Haunch.

Edward had firstly wanted to leave the Haunch to his daughter, Frances, but she died unmarried, so on 24 January, 1801, Edward made a will leaving the building on 'Oatmeal Row aforesaid being a Publick House now commonly called and known by the name of the Haunch of Venison, to my son Edward Fawconer, now a Lieutenant in the 17th regiment of foot'. It was Edward junior, by then a Captain, married to Martha, who sold the Haunch of Venison to a brewer by the name of James Butcher. The Reverend Edward Fawconer had inherited the 'Haunch of Venison' and the Merchants House. James W. H. Fawconer (a surgeon), Edward-the-soldier's elder brother, inherited the house.

It was James Fawconer who was in dispute over the ownership of the Haunch of Venison concerning the intentions of Sir Alexander Powell, and whether the building could be disposed of. Thomas Cheater was in occupation of the Haunch of Venison in 1816 (and had been for many years), and his agreement was with the lessees of James Butcher, who then owned it. James Fawconer instructed his solicitor to evict Mr Cheater, because he wanted to take possession. The solicitor wrote: 'I am perfectly ready to desist in this ejectment if Mr Fawconer is not entitled. My client is J.W.H. Fawconer.' John Chandler wrote in Endless Street, 'Falling on hard times in 1815, J.W.H. Fawconer mortgaged his share of the inheritance'. Money problems might have been at the root of the legal disputes (or vice versa). He sold the house around 1821.

F is for Fire

It is a miracle that the Haunch of Venison is still standing, given its age and the constant threat of fire that it was under in the past. Difficult to realise today, but fire was a cause of major destruction to towns and villages, and would spread quickly through timber-framed buildings, huddled together, causing the internal structures to collapse (Blandford Forum, Amesbury, Sixpenny Handley, Marlborough, all suffered from major fires).

Firmin Potto, a 19th century landlord, was evidently petrified of the Haunch of Venison catching fire, and instructed Louisa Potto, in his will, to 'keep up the fire insurance'. Wiltshire & Swindon History Centre has a collection of paperwork showing that Firmin Potto, and both his wives, had certainly 'kept up the fire insurance'.

We know that the Haunch of Venison has caught fire many times, although mostly the fires are not documented. One occasion was in January 1912, when the corner building next door to the Haunch caught fire – then, Powney's shop. Firmin Bradbeer and his family were apparently not there at the time, and it was 'Miss Wilkes' and Eva Simmonds the barmaid who were awoken by the smell of fire. Eva ran outside to see smoke billowing from Powney's. The fire did char the roof of the Haunch of Venison, but most of the damage was done by water used to extinguish the blaze, which ruined the bedrooms. Mr Bradbeer was happy that the fire had not touched his new Grill Room.

The Cloisters Bar during a fire in 1952, note the fireman in the doorway
© Salisbury Newspapers

Chimney fires used to be a regular occurrence under landlord Tony Leroy, and regular Les Mitchell remembers the fire engines blocking Minster Street, 'the firemen got used to it. They used to stay for a 'half', after they had put the fire out!'

'We liked the firemen!' says former waitress, Val Gainsford 'I don't know how many times they held up Minster Street. Once the flames were shooting up the stairs (*from the lower bar to the passage*)'.

Tony Leroy told the *Salisbury Journal* in 1988 that although the chimneys were regularly swept, there was a fire on average twice a year, and he hoped that a sleeve could be inserted by the brewery, to prevent further fires. According to Les Mitchell, who is a retired building surveyor, the problem used to be the junction where the chimney of the downstairs bar met the chimney of the Smoking Room, which would collect soot and catch fire. The installation of a wood burner has stopped the problem.

Other fires were surely caused in the distant past by a wooden beam which crossed the chimney and was charred, showing that it had caught fire This might have been to suspend the spit and smoke jack which used to be in the downstairs chimney.

The fireplace in the smoking room was partly blocked in with wooden barrel staves, which were partially charred through, according to Firmin Bradbeer, in his booklet written after renovations. The bressummer beam in front of the open fireplace, has been partly restored, and there are signs of fire damage to ceiling beams in the Lords.

In 2009, the kitchen of the Haunch caught fire just before the lunchtime service. The staff managed to put it out before the fire brigade arrived, but 'a 36-year-old woman was treated for smoke inhalation', according to the *Journal.*

Added to the hazards from the open fireplaces, both downstairs, but also upstairs and in the private rooms, and the kitchen, we can add the fact that many people have smoked in the building in the past. Not only the customers, but the landlords and staff, as well as those renting rooms, either privately, or as hotel customers. One can imagine the servants zealously emptying the ash trays each night into the waste paper baskets, and sleepy customers lighting up cigarettes in their bedroom after a huge dinner and too much port.

Of course, there were the candles carried up to bed, and flammable fabrics. Later came the gas lighting and paraffin lamps, and then the early electricity, which often involved bare copper wires – Firmin Bradbeer had the whole of the front of the Haunch lit up in fairy lights in 1906 (for a Carnival).

Today, the rooms above the Haunch are unable to be let due to the lack of a fire escape. Ex-manageress, Justyna Nugent, recalls a rope in a metal ring, which let out slowly and could be used to abseil from the second floor of the building. Val Gainsford adds 'The rope was in the bathroom. It had a strap harness. I showed it to a fireman and he said 'don't ever use that – you'd die. You'd be better off facing the fire!' I said 'We'd like a fireman's lift!'

Nowadays, fire regulations for public buildings have seen that the building is very safe, but it is a miracle that the Haunch of Venison has survived into the modern age.

F is for Fireback

Sitting at the back of the fireplace in the merchant's house dining room is an 'Armada' fireback (metal firebacks project the heat out into the room). The design is very popular, and is so called because of the date, 1588, which coincides with England's victory over the Spanish Armada in the reign of Elizabeth I. Armada firebacks have a varying number of anchors, together with upright vines with grapes, roses, ropes and Fleurs de Lys. The differences between Armada firebacks are due to the fact that they were cast from a number of assembled panels, which could be changed to different combinations. The initials IFC are generally accepted to be those of the person for whom the original fireback was made – with a date of 1582, according to the V&A museum, so the first casting was not to commemorate the

The 'Armada' fireback in the large dining room © *Baptiste Vitorino*

The large fireplace without the fireback
© *Salisbury Museum*

Armada, and the date was changed for subsequent castings. A fireback nearly identical to that of the Haunch, with the date 1588, can be found at Chawton House in Hampshire, said to be the recasting of a fireback given to John Knight by Elizabeth I to thank him for a donation of £50 to fight the Armada (it has IK instead of IFC).

Armada firebacks were usually made in Sussex, where there was plenty of iron ore to be smelted in blast furnaces. The decorative panels were carved in wood, and pressed into sand mixed with a little clay to harden it, to form moulds into which the wrought iron, remelted, could be poured.

Many re-castings of the Armada fireback have been made over the centuries, and many date only from the 19th century. Because they don't have any information on the backs, due to the casting method, individual ones are very difficult to date, and they are often mislabelled by antique dealers and museums alike, and so I will not attempt to date the fireback in the Haunch of Venison.

How long this one has been at the Haunch is not known, but it is not present in this picture of the fireplace

F is for 'Firm Inn'

The 'song' 'The Firm Inn' (Ours is a nice 'ouse ours is.) was written by the landlord Firmin Bradbeer, and gives a unique snapshot of the Haunch of Venison, and its customers and staff, around 1920. The song has come down to us, kept by Dolly Bradbeer, who was 16 that year, and through members of staff who were given a copy – it obviously brought alive their memories:

The title 'The Firm Inn' is obviously a word play on Firmin. The subtitle 'Ours is a nice 'ouse ours is' refers to a hit 1920 song, sung by Harry Fay, a comic music hall star, who made many records under different pseudonyms. The lyrics of that song give a good idea of how Firmin Bradbeer felt about the Haunch of Venison, beside the romantic Tudor version of his booklet:

Of all the 'ouses in the world,   there isn't one like ours is.
We never pay the rent and yet   the landlord never grouses.
We got no windows in the 'ouse   it 'elps to let the air in,
it also lets the foul air out   when Father keeps on swearing...
Ours is a nice 'ouse ours is,   ours is a very nice 'ouse.
  The roof's on the top of this pretty little shack,
  the front's at the front, and the back's at the back.
Ours is a nice 'ouse ours is,   it's got no rats nor mouses,
it's cheap, cheap, cheap   sweet, sweet, sweet,
ours is a nice 'ouse, ours is'

The song goes on to describe a ramshackle abode, of which the bad tempered and impecunious 'father' is very fond. It also has the line, 'some fathers like to hold up banks – ours holds up public houses'. Firmin Bradbeer was the treasurer of the Licensed Victuallers Association.

We know from insurance papers for the Haunch, that Mr Bradbeer had a collection of gramophone records, and perhaps 'Ours is a nice 'ouse' once played through a trumpet loudspeaker on a wind-up gramophone, and echoed through the building. You can listen to the song on Youtube 2022).

However, the Firm Inn was not written to be sung to the tune of Harry Fay's song, but to an Irish ballad called 'Little May' (also known as Molly-O) mentioned in the first verse:

All the Haunch is full of music   Little May.
All the customers are singing   Little May.
All the tankards full of bitter;
Never froth but always bitter;   Little May.'

One can imagine the customers, late one night in the Haunch of Venison, raising their tankards – the regulars kept their pewter ones behind the bar – standing shoulder to shoulder at the counter, or lined up along 'Death Row', in a sing-song of Little May.

Every 'R.A.F'. boy speaketh Francais   Little Mick,
Every 'night night' always 'bon soir',   Little Mick.
And her tankards all are shining,
All her taps and counters shining,   Little Mick'.

The pub was frequented by the RAF (Firmin Bradbeer himself had served in the RAF), and the Visitors book is signed by RFC pilots in 1914. These very young men (for the most part – fighter pilot of flimsy bi-planes having a short life expectancy), evidently wanted to show that they had been flying over France during the recent Great War. Or they wanted to give people the impression that they had. Was Little Mick an Irish pilot who led the customers in a lilting rendition of Little May, one night? Or was the song sung in a nostalgic homage to Mick Mannock, a World War I fighter ace, who had won 61 aerial victories before he was shot down in 1918. He was one of the most decorated men of the war. Very slight, he was of Irish stock, and was very musical. It is very probable that most of the RAF boys of the Haunch had known him, or crossed his path, as he had been based near Portsmouth. The two female barmaids and waitresses were Gwen Burden and Elsie Gray, and perhaps Firmin uses 'her', rather than a name, so as to let them share the praise. They were both in their 20s.

And the cellar has for keeper	Our Ole Bill,
And each cloudy bitter worries	Our Ole Bill,
Never late is he each morning;	
'Damn those girls', he says each morning;	Our Ole Bill.

The cellarman was Bill Golding, but since he was something of a Salisbury Celebrity (or rather, figure of fun), he has his own entry.

In the Dining Room the perfect	Only Tim,
In the morning and the evening,	Only Tim.
One and only is our waiter,	
'Plus Four' is our only waiter,	Only Tim.

Sadly, we don't yet know the name of the perfect, 'Tim', or even if Tim was his real name, rather than a nickname. 'Plus fours' were the latest trouser fashion in 1920, and would be popular over that decade, fitting in with a more relaxed lifestyle. They had developed from sportswear, and were worn four inches below the knee. This gives an impression that Tim is a young man, and very fashion conscious, which is perhaps why Firmin Bradbeer has chosen to tease him about

the 'Plus fours'. The barmaids, Gwen and Elsie were also young –
Gwen was only 21, and Elsie 28; then, as now, the Haunch of Venison
had young staff, even if some of the customers remembered earlier
times. It is worth remembering that just as Firmin Bradbeer wanted
to preserve the history of the Haunch, and its Smoking Room, the
bar that he had installed was modern in its day – as was his 'London
Style' Silver grill – and he had one of the first telephones in Salisbury.
Firmin was a man who had spent time on airfields with young pilots,
he drove a car, and he knew the latest films and records. The Haunch
of Venison employed young staff in the 'roaring twenties', and it was
a totally different atmosphere to the Haunch when Firmin's brother
Frank Bradbeer worked there along with Louisa Potto and her elderly
relatives.

In the kitchen, in the scullery,	Mutt and Chop.
'In the Soup' and in the grilling,	Mutt and Chop.
Always civil, clean, and willing,	
Though 'damned hot' they're always willing;	Mutt and Chop.

Mutt and Chop were evidently the kitchen staff. 'In the Soup'
was a silent film of 1920, with Christian Rub. It was an American film,
so one imagines that the expression 'In the Soup' was American, made
fashionable with the film. 'Hot' meant 'fiery', and the expression 'Hot
Damn!' was a 1920s American slang term. Firmin might have meant
that these ladies were quite scary when under pressure in the kitchen,
but still ready to put themselves out.

In next door is heard the humming	Busy Bee.
Night and morn she's always busy,	Busy Bee.
Rubbing, scrubbing, shining, smiling,	Busy Bee.
Working always, ever smiling;	Busy bee

'Busy Bee' was Beatrice Golding, the daughter of 'Our Ole' Bill
Golding, the cellarman. She was 34 in 1921 (13 years younger than
Firmin). 'Next door' was the private rooms of the Bradbeer family, in
the Merchants House; they had their own servant. Should we detect
a particular tenderness for 'Busy Bee', who is always smiling? Sadly,
Beatrice would lose her two younger brothers to tuberculosis shortly
after these lyrics were written. Beatrice never married, perhaps

because of World War I wiping out most of the eligible young men. She died in 1960, in St Mark's Road, Salisbury.

F is for Firmin
Two of the landlords of the Haunch of Venison, uncle (Firmin Potto) and nephew by marriage (Firmin Bradbeer), have held the unusual name of 'Firmin'. Mr Bradbeer's son, who grew up at the Haunch of Venison, was also christened Firmin.

The name came about because Firmin Potto was born in Nayland in Suffolk, whose most famous resident was John Firmin – otherwise known as 'John Firmin of Watertown'. He was one of the Pilgrim Fathers who left England in the early 17th century, at the same time as the Mayflower, settling in Massachusetts. He appears to have sailed to America with Winthrop, returned briefly to Nayland, before going back to America. Firmin had many children, by two wives, some of whom stayed in England, around the Suffolk and Essex area. Firmin Potto appears to have a great grand-mother with the surname 'Firmin', and the name was then perpetuated as a first name in his family.

There were other people christened 'Firmin' in the UK – but they all seem to be related in some way to the Potto family.

G is for Ghosts.
Whether you believe in the existence of ghosts, or you don't, the Haunch of Venison has the reputation of being one of the most haunted spots in Salisbury. In 2019, EI Publican Partnerships (better known as Enterprise Inns) voted it their most haunted pub, after assessing '4,000 venues' across the UK.

Although I would not class myself amongst the 'believers', even so, I have spoken to credible witnesses whose testimony I believe, and I have personally witnessed some phenomena in the Haunch which I am unable to dismiss easily; certainly not without troubling question marks.

Here is a list of Ghost stories from the Haunch:

Downstairs Main Bar:
Smashing Glasses
The most striking phenomena in this bar are the smashing glasses
    Frogg Moody recounted in his book *Haunted Salisbury* watching

his pint of cider slide off the beer mat one evening and crash to the floor. Being, as I am, 'Mrs' Moody, I would not doubt Frogg's word! However, it is natural to be sceptical. Then, one day, I witnessed a similar occurrence in the following circumstances: Timezone Tours were giving a tour and I ran to use the loo in the Haunch of Venison, before setting off on our Walk. The barman was sweeping up broken

The bar during the time of Firmin Bradbeer and scene of many strange happenings © Salisbury Museum

glass from the floor, near the stairs to the loos; he told me that a beer glass had been accidently smashed. Returning to the Haunch, a couple of hours later, I was accompanied by local Historian Matt Pike, Frogg Moody, and my brother, Alex King. We had a copy of a broadsheet newspaper, and laid it on the first table near the Silver Street side. The newspaper covered the table and so our glasses were sat upon it. We were not there long, however, when a full pint glass, somehow, ended up smashed on the floor. No-one had knocked it, as far as any of us were aware, and it was sat, very heavily, on dry paper which remained dry after the accident. We bought another pint.

If you have to pay twice for the same pint, as well as submit to the discomfort of puddles of beer and broken glass around your feet, then – I suggest – you are doubly careful with the new pint. We sat the full glass on the table, well away from danger. It happened in less than a second, and so I have often questioned whether I really did see that glass – not slide – but JUMP off the table!

It was my first impression then, and I can't tell you anything different now. I'm sure that the full glass jumped. I do remember that when I spoke to the barman again, he remarked that it wasn't (as I'd thought), the third such incident that had happened that evening, but the fourth.

Yes, the tables are worn wood on uneven floors. However, if they were the cause, then surely glasses would smash all the time? Instead, such incidents are apparently all on the same evening, as if somebody wants to make their presence known.

Exploding candle holder

Anastasia, the landlady (2022) tells me that on such nights, she has seen a glass candle holder simply explode, although the fire was lit, and there were no extremes of temperature. Furthermore, the shattered glass fragments lay all together on the table, as if the holder had disintegrated, rather than touch anybody, or put glass in their drinks. I am unable to reach a conclusion.

Dog

A stranger, met on an off-chance in another pub altogether, claimed to be psychic. When the conversation turned to the Haunch, he claimed that he sensed the ghost of a small dog in the downstairs bar. In fact, he was apologetic to tell such an odd and unexciting story.

Inside info, or was it a lucky guess? Or, does the ghost of 'Jack' still yap-yap-yap around the feet of drinkers in the House of Commons?

The Jolly Cook

Trained psychic, Samantha Hulass, on a visit to the Haunch, with myself, sensed a plump and jolly female cook, whom we felt from her description was possibly Elizabethan, cooking in a cauldron over the fire. Samantha didn't know that the smokejack found in the chimney proves that it was certainly used for cooking, in the past.

Trained 'Medium' Samantha Hulass at the Haunch with her dog Pippin ©Alex King

The Lords:

The small upper bar, nicknamed The House of Lords, but also known as The Smoking Room, appears to be a particular focus for something – or some things – strange and unsettling.

An Evil Spirit

Marjorie Bradbeer, who grew up at the Haunch in the first part of the last century, mentioned in her letter. 'I felt again that evil spirit . . .' when she returned there, around the year 2000. It was Marjorie's

The 'House of Lords' bar where the past still seems to linger.... © *Salisbury Museum*

father who had discovered the mummified hand, hidden near the bricked-up oven, next to the fireplace in this room. Marjorie appears to have been a woman more pragmatic than romantic, destroying family photographs before her death, and one might speculate that it was 'the hand' which gave her the bad feeling.

The Ginger Lad

Samantha Hulass (trained psychic) saw an adolescent with red hair and acne near the fireplace, but felt that he had taken a wrong turn, rather than being evil. She did not know if he was the owner of the hand. He was a troubled youth.

The Shooting Cold

David Taylor, who lived upstairs at the Haunch in the 1970s, recalled the days when the Smoking Room was packed solid with customers even standing to smoke, between tables. The fire was going and the body heat was palpable, 'One day a sort of freezing cold – something – shot across the room from the fireplace, and out of the door.

Everybody felt it, stopped talking and looked at each other. Then they were saying 'What the HELL was THAT?'

Sitting lady
Former landlady, Justyna Miller, told me of the time when she and her partner were drinking in the restaurant upstairs with two American tourists, after the pub had been locked up. The staff had all gone home. The conversation had turned to ghosts, as it often does in the Haunch of Venison – perhaps it is something in the atmosphere. 'The man was really interested, and kept asking lots of questions', said Justyna 'but his wife just looked bored, and scoffed. She obviously thought that it was all nonsense. Then she went downstairs by herself to use the Ladies... She came running back up the stairs, petrified, saying to her husband 'I want to get out of this place NOW!' She wanted to leave by the Cloisters Bar' Justyna went on. 'Apparently, when she came out of the toilet, she glanced through the door of the Smoking Room, and saw an old lady in old fashioned clothes sitting close to the fire, looking back at her. She was very solid, but the air turned 'very odd' and 'not right' 'but not cold', is how it was described to me. The man wanted to see if the old lady was still there, but everything was just normal'.

The Stairs:
The Lavender Lady
The staircase and area near the ladies' lavatory, as well as the small dining room above it, is associated with a 'grey lady', seen many times, ascending and descending the stairs in her long dress. The particularity of this ghost is that she is heralded by a strong smell of lavender. Sometimes, only the smell is scented and the lady does not appear. 'Terry' who used to smell it, whilst waiting for his girlfriend who was a waitress there in the 1980s, told me that the hair on the back of his neck would rise, and he'd feel very strange just before he became aware of the perfume. David Taylor, described the odour as being contained in an invisible cube, which you could put your nose in and out of. What strikes me most about this ghost, are the number of people, including ex-waitress Val Gainsford, who have described the lavender smell to me and who, as far as I know, don't know each other.

The 'grey lady' was seen by Charlie Aldridge, who was interviewed for Frogg Moody's book *Supernatural Salisbury*. Charlie works for Pritchett the butcher, who have long been a supplier for the Haunch of Venison. One day Charlie arrived to deliver meat to the kitchen, which is at the top of stairs, on the first floor. The place was quiet. There was no one about. Charlie took his delivery up to the kitchen, which was empty, and banged down his load on the metal table. Opening the kitchen door, he made to go back down the stairs, when he saw the form of a lady on the staircase, standing just in the bend. He described to Frogg her distinct outline, and long dress – but although he could not see through her, everything about her face or the details on her clothing were misty and unclear. She had no colour. Charlie says that he turned around and fled

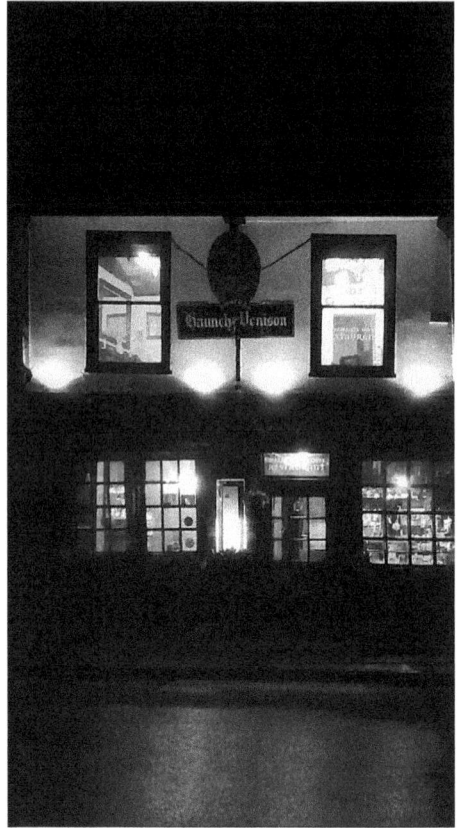

The Haunch of Venison – alone with its ghosts.... © Alex King

back into the kitchen, eventually composing himself to look at the stairs again. But by then, she had disappeared.

This grey lady has also been seen in the office upstairs by a waitress in the 1980s. She had never seen nor felt a thing in six years of working at the Haunch, and never gave would-be ghosts a thought, when one day, in broad daylight, the grey lady suddenly appeared and walked across the room before disappearing, leaving only a waft of lavender. It happened so quickly that the waitress had no time to be scared, but just looked on in amazement, unable to take in what she was seeing.

The Main Restaurant

The Main Restaurant was once the Great Hall of the adjacent building, built by a wealthy merchant.

Two Gentlemen

According to *Haunted Salisbury* (Frogg Moody), two gentlemen in Edwardian dress sit together at a table in the bay window. Mr Bradbeer and his beloved friend W. H. Jackson, whose death coincided with the Publican's slow decline in fortunes? (and close to whom, he asked to be buried).

Burning Lady

When speaking to the room at a Halloween event, hosted by Timezone Tours, a gentleman amongst the public suddenly turned white and asked to speak to me privately. He confided that, whilst I was talking, he had had a vision of a woman with her dress in flames, standing to the right of the fireplace, as you face it.

Women's long dresses were, in fact, a constant hazard when worn near naked flames (and whilst negotiating steps). Did some poor lady burn to death in what was then a private lodging?

The Opening Window

Whilst speaking to the 'Ghost Club of Great Britain' at a dinner held in the 'Haunch of Venison', about the ghosts of the Haunch of Venison (again, for Timezone Tours), the bay window, which had been shut and latched, suddenly burst wide open with a shocking force. No doubt, the sceptical amongst the diners thought that Timezone had engineered the opening window as a stunt. Far from it – we were more surprised than anyone, and like the smashing glasses downstairs, possible rational explanations were not very convincing. Coincidentally, the timing was perfect.

The haunted table

Ex landlady, Justyna Miller, told me in an interview about the strange things that had happened at a dining table which once stood in front of the fireplace, in the summer, but which had to be removed. According to Justyna, this particular table appeared to be the focus of something in the room. On two separate occasions diners, who were foreign tourists who could not have known each other, were perplexed when cutlery stood itself on end, and then toppled off the table. How could they have concocted the same story? The strangest incident came, though, when the dining room tables had been laid up for the

The haunted table which had to be removed © *Salisbury Museum*

next day, and Justyna had gone to bed upstairs. 'The tables were all set with white napkins, but when I got up for breakfast the next morning, this one table was set with red napkins.' Justyna continued, 'you know it was crazy. There was no one else in the building, and why would I have set one table differently to the others? It couldn't have been a mistake – I'd have noticed! I had never felt scared in the building but, after that, I asked my boyfriend to move in! I stopped putting a table there'.

The ghostly foot
Val Gainsford, who was a waitress at the Haunch for 12 years in the 1980s and early 1990s had this to say: 'I walked up the stairs one day, and as I turned the corner, I saw the back of a boot as someone walked up the three little steps and into the upper restaurant room. It was perfectly solid – like you are. Whoever it was had just gone into the room and I just caught sight of their foot. I don't know if they were a man or a woman, but it was a flat heeled heavy boot or shoe – I remember the heel clearly. It looked like something from the olden days. I thought that it was a real person. But there was nobody in the dining room. I remember it clearly. There is something there – definitely'.

The Secret Bar
The secret Cloisters Bar is the place where previous staff have most

The 'Secret Bar' – one of the most haunted rooms in the Haunch of Venison
© Salisbury Museum

often felt a 'presence'. I once visited it with a friend who is a successful and down to earth business man, whom I would not describe as 'imaginative'. He felt the atmosphere to be so heavy and magnetic that he could not stay in the room. He confessed that nothing on earth could persuade him to be alone there, because he felt that something unseen was watching us the whole time.

Upstairs
Noises
Valerie Gainsford told me that girls who stayed upstairs in the bedrooms, after working late, invariably spoke of strange noises and chills in the night.

Face at window
Thanks very much to Frogg Moody (*Haunted Salisbury*), for telling me about the woman's face often spotted at a rear window, overlooking St Thomas's Churchyard. Could this be the same lady as the phantom spotted inside the room (see above), and who might she be? Rather

fancifully, I wondered if it might be Mrs Louisa Potto (née Bradbeer), landlady for many years, looking down to the graveyard where her husband is buried.

Man in Braces

Former landlady, Justyna Nugent, who lived upstairs, told of waking one night to find a man in brown trousers and braces leaning over her bed, with his arms folded in front of him. The period clothing corresponds to Firmin Bradbeer, who lived above the pub in the first half of the 20th century, dying upstairs in 1947. Justyna's boyfriend (now husband), later awoke another time to see the same man.

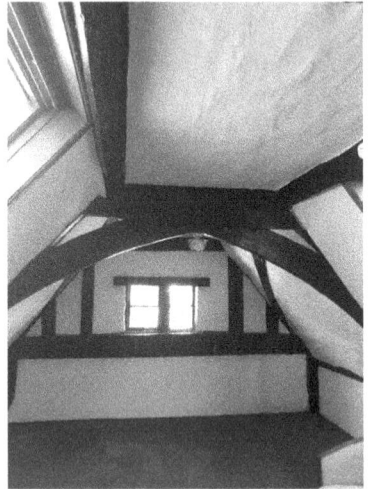

The 'Attic Room' – many manifestations have been witnessed here. © Ruby Vitorino Moody

Turned Slippers

When Justyna had a friend stay in another bedroom, at the top of the building, (see photograph), she would always find her slippers turned over, when she returned to the room – even though she locked the door, and started asking staff to witness the position of the slippers before she went out.

Outside:

Crying Woman

In the Alley behind the Haunch, a woman, said to be searching for her son, walks crying and wringing her hands. The woman had, so the tale goes, sent her child to buy a jug of beer to take out from the Haunch. The boy never returned.

Man in a suit

A ghostly man, in a 20th-century pinstripe suit, has been seen standing under the Poultry Cross, gazing up at the Haunch. Once again, I would be tempted (*if* I believed in Ghosts) to speculate that the ghost was that of Firmin Bradbeer.

Longfellow:

That Firmin Bradbeer, himself, was superstitious and believed that the Haunch was haunted, I have no doubt. Tellingly, he chose the following poem by Henry Longfellow 'Haunted Houses' to preface his own pamphlet on the history of the building, and so I will reproduce the same extract that he himself used here:

> All houses wherein men have lived and died
> Are haunted houses. Through the open doors
> The harmless phantoms on their errands glide,
> With feet that make no sound upon the floors.
>
> We meet them at the door-way, on the stair,
> Along the passages they come and go,
> Impalpable impressions on the air,
> A sense of something moving to and fro.
>
> There are more guests at table than the hosts
> Invited; the illuminated hall
> Is thronged with quiet, inoffensive ghosts,
> As silent as the pictures on the wall.
>
> The stranger at my fireside cannot see
> The forms I see, nor hear the sounds I hear;
> He but perceives what is; while unto me
> All that has been is visible and clear.
>
> We have no title-deeds to house or lands;
> Owners and occupants of earlier dates
> From graves forgotten stretch their dusty hands,
> And hold in mortmain still their old estates.

G is for Giants

When walking up the stairs to the smoking room, or descending from the restaurant, spare a thought for the very tall people who once lived at the Haunch of Venison, and probably often struck their heads on the door frames. Whilst Firmin Bradbeer and his daughter, Dolly, were both described as tall, Dolly's brother Firmin Pomeroy Bradbeer was 6 ft. 4 ins. as a teenager, and grew to be 6 ft. 6 ins., according to his nephew by marriage, Mr Tim Hayter. Jack Edwardes was 6 ft. 4

ins., and heavily built. Jack was a member of the 'London Topliners' Club, for tall people.

G is for Golding

Bill Golding was Firmin Bradbeer's cellarman in the 1920s, who would receive the beer, cider, and stout in large barrels from the station, in a horse and cart. He would then bottle it, and deliver it to

Cellarman Bill Golding outside the Haunch of Venison
© Salisbury Museum

the Haunch, twice a day, by handcart. He also had wine delivered by the cask, which was not only bottled and corked at the cellar, but the bottles were rolled in dust to make them look vintage, according to Arthur Maidment in his book *I remember, I remember*. The cellars were in Culver Street (now under a car park), and since Arthur lived in Culver Street, he liked to help Bill, as a young boy.

Bill Golding was born in Ford, Salisbury, in 1865, the son of an agricultural worker. He worked as a 'farm servant' as a boy, but as soon as he was old enough, he joined the Salisbury City Police force, marrying Martha Gillam, and having three children – Beatrice (who would work at the Haunch of Venison, as a domestic servant, 'busy Bea'), Herbert, and Sidney.

Something not mentioned by Arthur Maidment (if he knew it) is that, tragically, Sidney Golding died in 1920, aged 15, and Herbert Golding died in 1921, aged 21, both of pulmonary tuberculosis. This puts Firmin Bradbeer's 1920 song 'The Firm Inn', with its 'ever smiling' Beatrice in a sad light, since presumably it was written just before the death of Sidney. It was perhaps why Bill Golding liked the young Arthur helping him, since he had lost his own boys. Salisbury had almost an epidemic of tuberculosis between the wars, and indeed it would carry off Firmin Bradbeer himself years later.

Arthur Maidment also remarks that Bill Golding was almost a laughing-stock in Salisbury, because, as a police sergeant he had gained notoriety for lousing up on Salisbury's most infamous murder case. In 1908, a 12-year-old one-legged child named Teddy Haskell had had his throat cut whilst sleeping in bed, in Meadow Road, Fisherton, Salisbury. The child's mother, Flora, maintained that an intruder had come running down the stairs and thrown a bloody knife at her, before escaping down the passage and out the front door, following a burglary in the boy's bedroom (Teddy had been saving for a cork leg). Flora was herself subsequently tried for the murder, although she was found not guilty. One problem with the trial had

Bill Golding during his time with Salisbury Constabulary
© *Frogg Moody*

been that crucial evidence to nail a suspect had been lost when Bill Golding had stood by and watched Teddy's grand-mother scrub the traces of blood from the hallway and door, including any fingerprints. His only comments at the trial were 'my orders were to not let anyone upstairs'! Bill had also put the murder weapon (wrapped in paper) in his back pocket, and this had been subsequently 'lost', although not by himself.

Bill Golding was very strong, and would be in his rolled-up shirt sleeves, whatever the weather. He died aged 69 in 1935 of tongue and neck cancer, at the family home in St Marks Road. He is portrayed, along with a young Arthur, on the mosaic behind Culver Street car park.

G is for Gun

Above the fireplace in the House of Commons bar hangs a gun (2022); Anastasia and Ilya found it in the attic. Anxious to preserve the history of the Haunch, and seeing its age, they put it back on the wall. Locals told them that, once, there hung three guns on the walls of the lower bar.

Curious, I went with Ilya to Greenfields, Salisbury's gun experts in Milford Street, to speak to Jonathon Russ and find out more about it, whilst the rest of the staff hung around to hear what he had to say. 'It's not often that something so old comes through the door,' they explained – clearly passionate about their trade, and wanting to learn from what Jonathan had to say.

The gun dates from around the 1780s, 'perhaps earlier', said Jonathon. It's a 12-bore flintlock musket (apparently), that fired lead balls. The lead balls would be made by the rifle owner by melting lead and shaping them using a mould such as this. If they ran out of lead to mould, they might even melt down kitchen pots and pans, according to John Poulter, an 18th- century highwayman. Jonathon Russ told us that the owner of the gun would have put the lead balls in first, and then the gunpowder. To ignite the gunpowder and fire the gun, a 'cock' (that is the hammer) strikes the flint.

On this rifle, the cock has gone. 'It's snapped off', said Jonathon. 'It's maybe military, 'he went on. 'It doesn't have a 'crown' logo, and there's no 'mark' on the lock. It's quite crudely made, with no maker's marks.'

The rifle has got marks to show it was tested. The wood on

Engraved writing found on the gun which hangs in the 'House of Commons' bar
© Haunch of Venison

it is 'Probably beech. Not walnut as you'd get today.' But the most interesting thing on it is engraved writing on the top of the barrel: It is engraved with a language which might be from the Indian continent. Below it are 'scores', which might be 'notches on the barrel'.

H is for 'Three Hearts'

Found in the Haunch of Venison by Firmin Bradbeer was an old flagon 'bearing the impression of three hearts'. Mr Bradbeer doesn't say (in his booklet) if this was the same stoneware flagon found in the fireplace of the Lords. He does say that it was around 300 years old, and we know that he had taken his finds to Salisbury Museum for appraisal.

He speculates that the Haunch of Venison may have been an inn known as 'the Three Hearts', before it was the Haunch. The pub name 'The Three Hearts' is as rare as the Haunch of Venison, but there is one in Winchester. It appears to have a religious significance, with not just one 'sacred heart' but a whole trinity.

H is for Hammond

The first documented owners, and residents, of the Haunch of Venison are the Hammond family, who had the building from the 16th century until the mid-17th century, through several generations. The name is written with different spellings before spelling became standardised, including 'Hamon', which was a French surname.

The first Henry Hammond listed at St Thomas's Church was in the year 1523/24, who paid money for 'settes in the church this year'. These were probably wooden pews. There is no indication that this Henry lived at the Haunch. The Haunch of Venison had been built as a church house only 75 years previously. Interestingly, this Henry Hammond is recorded as being a 'brewar' (brewer). He is almost certainly related to the John Hammond, who also worshipped at St Thomas's, in 1546, who had 'tent'es on grene crafte', which is to say that he had woollen fabric stretched on frames to dry, on the Greencroft.

His son, Henry Hammond, definitely lived at the Haunch of Venison, as he is listed in the Easter Books, as doing so. Easter books list a tax paid each Easter by local residents to the Church – in this case St Thomas's. He paid for his 'pewes' regularly. He died in August 1598. This Henry was known as 'Henry Hammond snr' (probably because he was living in the Haunch at the same time as his son, also Henry Hammond. and he is often referred to by the modern sounding moniker, 'Harry Hammond'. Harry Hammond was a churchwarden at St Thomas's, and was responsible for doing some of the accounts listed in Swayne's book of accounts.

Henry junior also had a son named Henry Hammond (born 1596), a daughter named Anne, and a son named Walter (born in 1605). He is also in the Easter books. Young Henry was christened at St Thomas's Church. He grew up to be a stationer (he sold paper and ink to the church). His wife was Elizabeth. He died in 1669, after the restoration of Charles II, and was buried at St Edmund's Church. The reason for this is that plague victims had been buried at St Thomas's (according to Swayne's book of church accounts) and it was judged too dangerous to open the ground for six years afterwards. 'All the bells and ground' for him, cost his family 8s. 8d. Henry made a will leaving the Haunch of Venison to his sister Anne, for her lifetime, and then to his brother's son, also called Walter. The nephew Walter had married Katherine and the pair were living in Marlborough in 1671, when their son, with the unfortunate name of Harburne, was born. It was probably his mother's maiden name.

Walter and Katherine duly inherited the Haunch of Venison but seem to have hesitated to live there. In 1685 Walter and Katherine lost the Haunch of Venison which became part of a court case. They were taken to court by John Powell, who accused them of keeping him from the building – and other buildings with it, of which he was the rightful owner, as there had been a promise between them to give it to him. The transcript of the case in Wiltshire & Swindon History Centre goes on to say that Powell paid the couple £60 to quit the building. It would seem that Walter and Katherine had made a legal contract to sell it but had then backed out. The Haunch had been the property of the Hammonds for over 100 years. The Haunch passed to John Powell.

H is for Hand
When the landlord Firmin Bradbeer unblocked the fireplace in the Smoking Room (House of Lords) during renovations begun in 1903, he described finding a mummified hand. The fireplace had been partly blocked in with wooden barrel staves, which had been charred through in places, and had probably been plastered over originally. Eighteen sacks worth of soot from the chimney had collected in the space, and whilst cleaning it out a (probably) Dutch stoneware flagon was found, along with two playing cards, and a desiccated human hand. Firmin estimated that they were then around 300 years old.

Mr Bradbeer wrote: 'Lastly was found a mummified hand, and curiously enough, there is a tradition to the effect that long years ago a man was bricked up in the chimney with a pitcher of water – possibly the old flagon. There is little reliance to be placed in this 'yarn' but it is certainly not improbable that there may be some connection between the cards and the hand. It may be that a sharper of those days paid the penalty of cheating by forfeiting his offending hand. Rough and ready justice was often meted out in the 'good old days and our forebears had a delicate way of making the 'punishment fit the crime." The proximity of the Haunch of Venison to Butchers Row has raised the spectre of a bloody meat cleaver being involved.

Firmin took the hand and the cards to Salisbury Museum, and there is now some discussion as to what became of the hand. The Museum maintains that the hand either disintegrated or was lost during the move from St Ann Street to its present location in the Cathedral Close. Mr Bill Oglethorpe, both the friend and Solicitor of Firmin Bradbeer's daughters, as well as the friend of the past curators of Salisbury Museum, told this author that the hand and the cards were merely shown to the museum – and then taken away again by Mr Bradbeer. Supporting Mr Oglethorpe is the fact that the playing cards were later given to Salisbury Museum by Mr Bradbeer's daughters, after his death. So, what became of the mummified hand?

The famous 'hand' which can be seen at the Haunch of Venison © Frogg Moody

Whilst the Haunch of Venison was owned by Simonds Brewery, and whilst it was closed for building maintenance (which included spraying the beams against woodworm), a young workman – Barry Wix – was sent into the Smoking Room to correct a loose floorboard. Lifting the board, the workman was sent into shock to see a blackened and wizened human hand, posed palm upwards, and clutching some dusty playing cards. Describing the scene many decades later to myself and Frogg Moody (and recorded by Spencer Mulholland), the now elderly Barry Wix recalled his horror at the gruesome find, and that the then landlord (Ian Bennett) had immediately wanted to call the Police to report finding human remains. Warned not to speak of what he had found, for fear of spoiling the image of warm conviviality that the Haunch was keen to promote, Barry said that he was sent home and found on his return that the floorboard had been nailed back flat.

Did the undoubtedly superstitious Firmin Bradbeer replace the hand as closely to the place where he found it as possible? If he believed that it was a 'hand of glory', then he might well have done, since it is a common human reaction to replace aged anti-witchcraft charms back in the places where they were found, or blame subsequent bad luck on having moved them. Did Mr Bradbeer, who had a lively sense of humour, place new playing cards in the hand, to support his theory of a cheating card sharp? Was the hidden presence of the hand, which was most likely taken from an executed convict, the reason that Marjorie Bradbeer felt 'an evil spirit' in the smoking room?

And what did Mr Bennett do with the hand once it was found? He might have thrown it in the bin, but it seems unlikely that he would have touched it. Once assured by the Police of its ancient origins, it is far more likely that he simply ordered the head maintenance man to quietly nail the plank back down, and leave that spirit to rest in peace.

The floor of the smoking room sits directly above the cellar and there is no place for the hand to be hidden. However, close to the fireplace is another matter. If you are sitting on the bench close to the oven – just think! – you never know what may be sitting silently below your feet.

The story of the hand at the Haunch of Venison doesn't end there: The hand presently on display was made by Haunch regular, and special effects man, Ken Lailey, who modelled it on his own hand (according to his friend, Les Mitchell). Ken had worked on Dr Who, and had made the head of Worzel Gummidge (the Jon Pertwee version). 'Ken wanted to make a lifelike rubber hand, covered in blood, that would twitch' says Les Mitchell, 'but Tony (Leroy) wouldn't let him'.

'The first version that he made was just plaster poured into a rubber glove, and it wasn't very good, and he made a better one, after the first one was stolen'.   The hand at the Haunch of Venison soon became internationally famous when it was stolen; not once but twice! The first time was in 2004. It was posted back to the Haunch in a jiffy bag, causing Justyna Nugent the fright of her life when she opened the bag. The hand was then put behind glass and padlocked. 'Mummified Hand Stolen from the Haunch of Venison!' announced the *Independent* in March 2010. 'it's kept locked in a cage so whoever took it must have come prepared to unscrew the locks' said handyman Dave Prodger, talking to the BBC. Once again it was returned.

It seems as if Ken's hand has taken on something of the psychic powers of the real hand, which it represents, and whoever moves it feels a growing horror that compels them to see the hand returned to its place in the fireplace of the Haunch of Venison.

The owner of the real severed hand might be guarding it. Trained medium, Samantha Hulass, senses a redhaired youth with acne around the fireplace in the smoking room, who is 'a bit of a rogue, but not really evil'. Is he the cheating card player? Was he executed at Fisherton gaol or on the marketplace? One thing is certain – there is something strange in the House of Lords, and it is linked to the hand.

H is for Handcart

The Haunch of Venison used to have a handcart which was originally used to transport casks and bottles between the cellars in Culver Street and the Haunch of Venison, as well as the other pubs for which the Haunch was wholesaler.

Arthur Maidment, in his book *I Remember, I Remember,* believed that the handcart was specially constructed for the Haunch because it had a dip in the middle to fit a cask, and flat tables at each end to take crates of bottles. Rather picturesquely, the *Salisbury Journal* speculates that the handcart was later used to wheel home drunks, and it is sad that this tradition has not survived.

The Haunch of Venison handcart ©
Salisbury Museum

H is for Hardy

According to Firmin Bradbeer's obituary in the *Salisbury Times*, 1947, his poem 'Men of Wessex', which appeared in the magazine of the Wiltshire Rifles, of which he was a co-editor, was commended by Thomas Hardy. The word 'Wessex', might be a homage to Hardy. It is unlikely that Hardy was a frequent reader of the magazine, and more likely that he was shown the poem, and that his commendation was addressed to Firmin at the Haunch of Venison.

Thomas Hardy knew Salisbury well, and drew inspiration from St Thomas's church, which appears in Jude the Obscure. Did he visit the Haunch of Venison? The answer has to be, very probably.

H is for 'Haunch of Venison' pub name

The name Haunch of Venison is certainly unusual, and I have only heard of four others, all gone, but one is commemorated by the name Haunch of Venison Yard, off Bond Street, now home to an art gallery. Another was in Maidstone, Kent, and yet another in Leicester, and one in Whaddon.

Website 'TheStreetNames', when discussing the 'Haunch of Venison Yard' points out that the name used to be found on pubs sited near royal hunting forests. It also says that the word 'venison' comes from the Latin 'venari', meaning 'to hunt'. Salisbury stood near to the royal hunting forests of Clarendon and Grovely.

Other pub historians, when talking about other cuts of meat used for pub names, state that the names 'Round of Beef', 'Baron of Beef', and 'Shoulder of Mutton' came from butchers who also sold ale (pubs often had a dual vocation). The 'Haunch of Venison' stands close to the end of Butchers Row, and near to where the Butchers Guild once stood (at what is now the taxi rank, on New Canal).

Nevertheless, although 'Haunch of Venison' sounds like a quintessentially Tudor meat, deer were then reserved for the very rich, who owned their own hunting grounds, or to people to whom they had offered the meat as a gift. Venison was 'Gentleman's food', and was eaten only by the aristocracy.

It would seem that when the building became an inn, its owners wanted to show its richness and nobility (sitting alongside the merchant's house, as it did), and establish its superiority over the inns in Butchers Row. The smoke jack in the chimney shows that meat was being roasted on the fire.

I am indebted to historian Edward Stow, who tells me that an inn called the 'Haunch of Venison Hotel' once stood in Market buildings, 12 High Street, Maidstone, Kent. As a point of interest, the pub was close to a pawn shop where, in September 1888, Catherine Eddowes, the 5th 'canonical' victim of Jack the Ripper, bought a herself a jacket, on the way back to the hop fields from London; she was murdered at the end of that month.

H is for Horse Box

The tiny bar that sits to the right of the entrance, as you face the pub, is known as 'The Horse Box'. It's probably called this only because of its size, but according to Les Mitchell, the oldest regulars assumed that it was 'The Whores Box'!

The tiny room was formed when the jetty (the overhang from the floor above) was walled in. The support for the jetty can still be seen in the wall of the Horse Box. It is generally accepted that the Horse Box made a small private room. These became known as 'snugs' in the late 19th and early 20th centuries, and were often (but not exclusively)

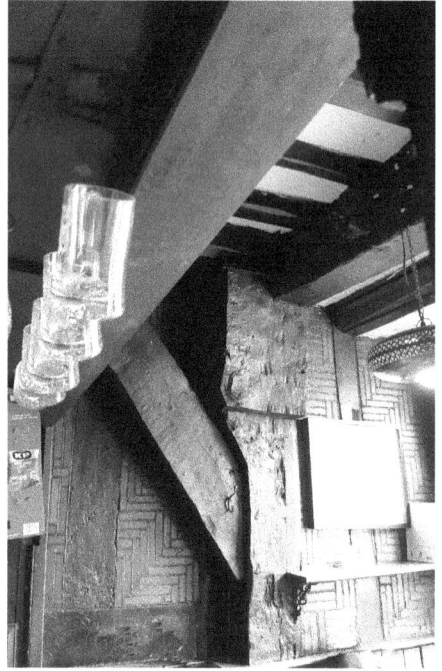

The 'Horse Box' bar. The support for the jetty can still be seen

where the ladies sat. If this was a 'snug', and it seems to naturally lend itself to that, then it must have had frosted glass, or curtains giving onto the street, and onto the passage, and was perhaps screened from the bar, because the whole point of a 'snug' was privacy.

The 'snug' was a concept that had begun in Ireland, and it allowed women, for whom drinking in public was socially unconventional (although not forbidden), to be discreet. It also allowed for private business to be discussed.

During the time Louisa Potto was landlady, women certainly did come into the public bar, since several incidents involving women drinking at the Haunch of Venison made the local newspapers. One involved a female pickpocket who took the purse of a female customer standing at the bar, after observing her paying. The other incident was when a female customer physically attacked another in the public bar (and the Judge made clear his disapproval of women drinking in pubs). The Haunch of Venison was a respectable establishment, and landlady Louisa Bradbeer was religious, as were her family. Women drinking in the public bar were not respectable, so these incidents are surprising.

The Horse Box was used as a Ladies Snug more during the time of Firmin Bradbeer, when one has the impression that it was a very masculine environment, and ladies were encouraged to have soft drinks upstairs. There were no ladies' lavatories downstairs, and women had to go upstairs to the bathroom.

Most 'snugs' were knocked down to enlarge the public bar when it became acceptable for respectable women to enjoy a drink alongside the men. However, the way that the Haunch is constructed has made this impossible. The Horse Box is therefore another part of history which has survived the years.

H is for hotel
In the 1950s the Haunch of Venison was an hotel, although it must have had only three or four rooms to rent. Still, it carried on the tradition that the Haunch was an inn and not merely a boozer.

H is for House of Commons and House of Lords
It was Firmin Bradbeer (landlord of the Haunch of Venison for most of the first half of the 20th century), who nicknamed the two

The 'House of Commons' and 'The House of Lords' © Salisbury Museum

bars of the Haunch of Venison proper, 'the House of Commons' (downstairs), and 'the House of Lords'. He used the terms to caption drawings of the two bars. Mr Bradbeer was the Prime Minister of Salisbury Parliament, which was a political debating society, and a conservative councillor for St Edmund's Ward. His daughter, Dolly, originally chose politics as a career, and one can imagine that local and national politics were hotly debated at the Haunch in this period. The terms 'House of Commons' and 'House of Lords' are still used by regulars talking about the bars.

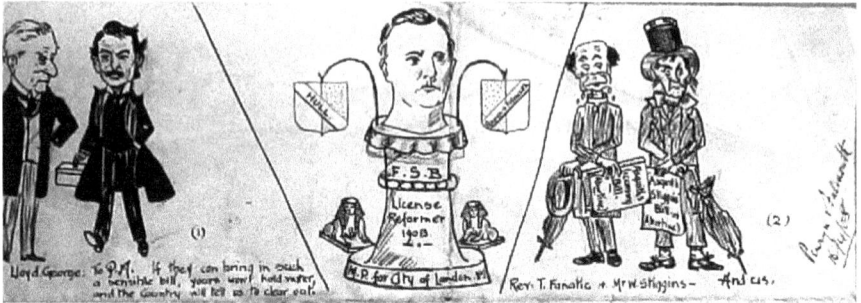

Firmin Bradbeer as Prime Minister in the Salisbury Parliament
© *Salisbury Museum*

I is for Idyllic England

It is remarkable how often, when reading old newspapers, the Haunch of Venison is mentioned as an example of something old, rare, and emblematic of an idyllic England that was passing even as the different authors wrote about it. Anchor Taverns wrote about the Haunch in its publicity:

> ONE is tempted to think that in THE HAUNCH OF VENISON all the elements that go to make the ideal Tavern of English tradition have taken actual shape. The corners and the angles, the low roof here and the twisty stairway there, the beams and the panels—no Dickensian description could do justice to this small jewel of architectural evolution.

It was something that Firmin Bradbeer understood well, when he wrote about his Inn, which he had known from childhood: 'Its history, could it be written, would speak of stirring days in England. Picturesque days. The glorious days of chivalry and romance.'

J.R. for the *Taunton Courier* in 1931, pre-war Britain, waxed nostalgic for pub names.

> Uncle Tom's Cabin at Wincanton, Bell and Crown at Zeals, The Chough at Salisbury, which was licensed in 1635. The Haunch of Venison, in the same town, The Hatchet Inn, Clump Inn, Sir John Barleycorn, The Oliver Cromwell, Hill Top Inn, Bee Hive, Cat and Fiddle, The Sailor's Return, and The Silent Woman, and many of these have well painted pictures on the signs.

Man O'Mendip sighed that the Haunch of Venison made him feel 'humble'. He was writing in 1947 for the *Western Daily Press*, just after the war had finished, and even as Firmin Bradbeer sat dying of tuberculosis upstairs at the inn, surrounded by his rare books and gramophone records:

> ❂ ❂ ❂
>
> OUR tribe were present at a thé dansant As the band tootled "Sonoma I hear your sweet bells ringing still," we departed in the appropriate dreamy mood to visit that poem in stone, Salisbury Cathedral, set in its vast green lawn from which the eye gently travels to the cross on top of the tapering spire— the tallest in England. Passing that old chop-house built in 1320—the Haunch of Venison, we felt humble

Ned Halley, writing about the 'Haunch of Venison' as his 'Watering Hole of the week' for *West Country Life*, when Tony and Vicky Leroy were Landlords wrote:

> THIS is a famous pub, but a marvellous one nonetheless. Alone among the ancient structures at Salisbury's gnarled old wooden heart, it is the ideal historic building.
>
> That is, the kind you can slope into from the rain-drenched street and get not just a warm welcome, but a snifter or two while you take in the architectural splendours.
>
> The Haunch of Venison was already here,

There's that word 'ideal' again!

J is for Jakeman

Ask any of the oldest regulars of the Haunch of Venison for their memories of the old pub, and a misty look comes over their eyes as they talk about 'the Halcyon Days', when Bill and Kate Jakeman ran the pub and the restaurant, and the place was heaving, shoulder to shoulder, with interesting and eccentric characters. 'It was a special time', says bookshop owner and musician David Taylor, who lived upstairs.

Bill was a chef by profession, and ran the kitchen, and Kate, his wife, was 'Front of House', and did the finance (she had worked in the Accounts department, and Front of House, at some big hotels). She was, by all accounts, a formidable lady, 'you wouldn't mess with her', says Bill – although looking at pictures of the outgoing and attractive Irish woman, it's hard to imagine that she was as 'scary' as her family, and Les Mitchell, fondly enjoy remembering her.

'One day the 'Kennedy sisters' turned up' says Bill, 'They (the Kennedys) were like American royalty. The Kennedys – there were two of them – were accompanied by three **huge** guys.' They all sat in the main dining room, which was filled with diners, 'and of course the Kennedy ladies sat with their friend, and the bodyguards went to sit at a table near the bay window, and they were all carrying guns' continued Bill, 'It was a hot day, and they took their jackets off. You could see the guns. I said that it was out of the question that they sat there with guns – there were other customers, you see.'

Les Mitchell recounts, 'Kate said, 'You can't come in here like that! Take those guns off and we'll put them in the safe!'. Bill remembers that she ordered the 'gorillas' to put their jackets back on, despite the heat. Either way, customers did what Kate told them! There were no guns showing.

This was all reminisced on a visit back to the pub in 2021. Bill told me how you had to be married to get a pub licence back in the early 1970s: 'You had to go to court – You had to. It (the licence) wasn't just handed over like a piece of cake'. The couple had to physically go to the court with the previous couple (Peter and Celia Ward) to take on the relay, 'it wasn't just applying online and getting a bit of paper in the post. And we had to have three interviews to get the Haunch. We had to go to Reading – to the Brewery. They were very particular as to who took it on'. The pub was then part of Anchor Taverns, a subsidiary of Courage.

'The biggest thing for us in 1970, when we moved in – to get our plans into action – was to clean the place up. There was smoking in those days, and it was absolutely dirty! We stripped the walls, the wood panels mainly, with vinegar and warm water. We did it bit by bit.'

'It was all carpeted. It wasn't all just plain wood'. Bill was talking about the floors, which were covered in a grand dark red Wilton carpet, upstairs and downstairs, and up the staircases. 'The carpets were already here' (*Gail Fawcett remembers them in the time of Ian Bennet*). Remarkably, they did not seem to be damaged by falling cigarette ash, as there was constant smoking, and people were stood up between the tables, drinking and having a good time. 'It was a lot of work to clean them'.

The attics had holes in the roof, 'the pigeons used to get in and roost'. Paul 'Nobby' Norbury, then an assistant chef, remembers as a teenager going up to shoot them, before the roof was repaired.

'Then we started looking at the food. I took over a menu which I didn't particularly want to do. I was instructed by the brewery.' The Haunch had a reputation for good food at reasonable prices, and the brewery didn't want change, they wanted somebody who could carry it on. 'They wouldn't let me do my own food; my own bar snacks.' For the first two years, the Jakemans were managers, and only afterwards were offered a tenancy.

Bill carried on, 'We opened the fireplaces, too, and started having real fires again (*see 'F' is for fire*) I got the chimney sweeps in, and the Fire Brigade to check them. I opened the big one in the upstairs restaurant, too. It used to look magnificent! (it still does) Cosy, homely, sort of thing, on a winter's night'.

'We used to roast chestnuts in the Commons', Les chipped in, remembering.

'And we put in boxes of flowers. Growing flowers. Fresh.' It's something that we're used to in 2022, but I remember the outside of city pubs being somewhat grimmer in the 1970s. Perhaps because they had traditionally been a more masculine environment.

Bill and Kate lived upstairs when they first moved in, for about two years, but then Kate fell pregnant with their son, Will (who is proud to say that he was conceived upstairs at the Haunch of Venison!).

'I don't think that I ever felt anything supernatural – but I'm not that way – but Kate used to say that she felt something eerie upstairs.'

Bill didn't think that living above the work was the right thing for a young family though, and was offered alternative accommodation by the brewery, who owned a house at 15 Salt Lane, neighbouring the Pheasant Inn (home of the old 'Shoemakers Hall', and another picturesque old building, worth visiting). Bill later bought a house in Salt Lane, at number 36/37, and a house for his parents, in Fisherton.

The food started changing, too. 'I started making progress', said Bill, getting out some old photographs to prove it. 'I had a cheese table there (*In the corner of the upstairs*

Kate Jakeman © Bill Jakeman

restaurant), and it started getting bigger, and bigger, and bigger. And fruit'. People paid for cheese and fruit, and then served themselves as they liked. 'We developed it, and then we used to put puddings on it, if and when we could, if they didn't melt'.

'We cooked Venison'. 'Nobby' worked in the kitchen (aged only 17), with Bill Jakeman and his 'second', David Bunch. 'We used to hang up a whole deer from a hook, and skin it – it used to lift my feet off the floor'.

'I used to get my venison over near Stockbridge', Bill was proud to say, 'they'd bring the whole carcass up the stairs to the second floor, and that is where the fridge was, and we used to dissect it, because I knew how to do that.' Bill had begun his working life as a butcher.' We used to bring the venison in through the front door, and somebody complained as to where I was getting it from (that happened three or four times), but I bought it from a big estate, and it was all above board. I got wild rabbits, hares, widgeon, teal, snipe – any type of game, I got it from Stockbridge. It was niche cooking really, and I used to have to be commercial in other ways. I got the beef – sirloins – in Salisbury, and they used to carry them across the Market Square.

I used to only keep the youngsters in the kitchen three or four years, train them up, and then I'd send them on their way to progress – once they'd learned everything they could with me.'

The tables were laid with highly polished silver cutlery, crisp white tablecloths, crystal glass wear, silver wine coasters and fresh flowers, and Kate would inspect them each day to make sure that they were 100% perfect. Bill enjoyed being a prankster and sometimes laid up some tables poorly to see her reaction – 'she would not hold back!' It ended with the staff waiting and watching for her to explode. 'She finished by clocking that it was Me, and burst into laughter, but she filled the air with expletives, to the absolute delight of all of the Team.'

The regulars at the pub still included pilots from the nearby airfields, and scientists from Porton Down ('they'd never tell you anything!' Bill complains!) There were also actors who were appearing at the nearby Salisbury Playhouse, and performers from Studio Theatre, which at that time was still in Milford Street (above the William IV pub. The Author, William Golding, was amongst them). Then of course, there were the Haunchonians (led by Ken Lailey), and the Dining Club (led by Roy Spring).

'The Theatre Crowd were lah-di-dah-di. They'd come in after seeing a performance.'

'And there were tourists,' Les added, 'especially American tourists. The place had a high reputation under Bill and Kate Jakeman, and tourists would come to see Stonehenge, the cathedral, and to dine at the Haunch of Venison. It had a reputation as being the number one restaurant outside London'.

Bill Jakeman returns to the Haunch in 2021
© Les 'The Lens' Mitchell

In fact, the Haunch of Venison was one of the few

British restaurants, then, to feature in the 'Michelin Guide'. 'The food was high-end Haute Cuisine. The service was the kind that you'd experience at the Savoy, or the Ritz'.

Bill was used to cooking for celebrities, because he had served a five-year apprenticeship with Michael Smith, 'one of the first TV chefs', at the Foxhill private Club in Headingly. 'It was frequented by the top brass of its day,' and he had gone on to work as sous chef and head chef at some top hotels.

'I remember Tennessee Williams coming to the Haunch of Venison – and where he sat (at a table in the lower restaurant, closest to the door)' Bill said, 'and Lady Phoebe Phipps (born Pleydell-Bouverie, daughter of the Earl of Radnor, and mother of American racing driver, sculptor and painter, Hubert Phipps) would often eat alone in the restaurant at lunchtimes'. She would drink a lot.

'We used to see so many celebrities that nobody bothered with them' Les said. 'They used to like that, because they could just relax; we saw so many. Some didn't like it, though; Marty Wilde started saying 'don't you know who I am?'.

'There was a singer who came – he wore make-up. Extreme make-up'. It was the 1970s. 'He had an entourage. 'There were 14 of them came at 2 o'clock, and I laid a long table for them. It was Marc Bolan and T-Rex. He was only a tiny feller. Yes, it was definitely Marc Bolan.'

'Bob Monkhouse would come in – when he performed.' (Bob Monkhouse, a popular comedian of the time, opened Salisbury Tesco, chipped in Frogg Moody).

'The place was always busy' Bill went on, 'I used to have Thursdays off because that was the quietest night'.

We were sitting in the Smoking Room. There had been some big changes since Bill had last seen it, forty years earlier, 'There used to be two settles, big, antique, red leather settles, one each side, and a long table, with a drop leaf. And there used to

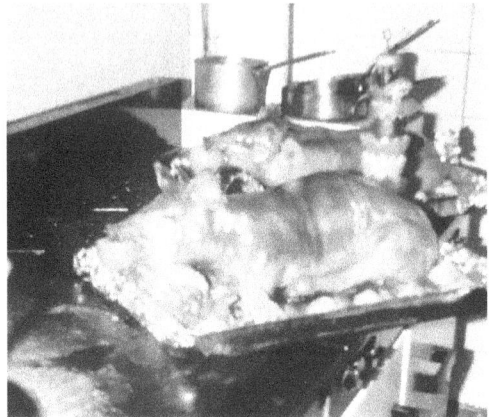

Roast suckling pigs © Bill Jakeman

stand a chair in the corner, beautifully carved, beautifully worked. It's gone now'.

Eventually, Bill and Kate Jakeman moved on. 'We felt that we'd done what we'd set out to do and it was time to do something else. We wanted to go back to Yorkshire. We wanted fresh scenery and new challenges'. It was 1981.

'It was a sad day when they left', says David Taylor. 'We had a lock-in after they had done the final shift, and Bill fetched some good bottles of wine from the cellar, and we sat by the fire.'

'It was never the same after they left', Les finished.

J is for John, Augustus

Augustus John signed the visitor's book of the Haunch of Venison (in S. Museum archive). It is marvellous how the over-large and flamboyant signature in green ink conveys Augustus's huge ego, and artistic nature.

From the RAFC signatures around his, one can see that the date was during World War One. Augustus John was not only one of Britain's most famous painters at the time, but he was also a notorious alcoholic and loved pubs. He was living in Fryern Court,

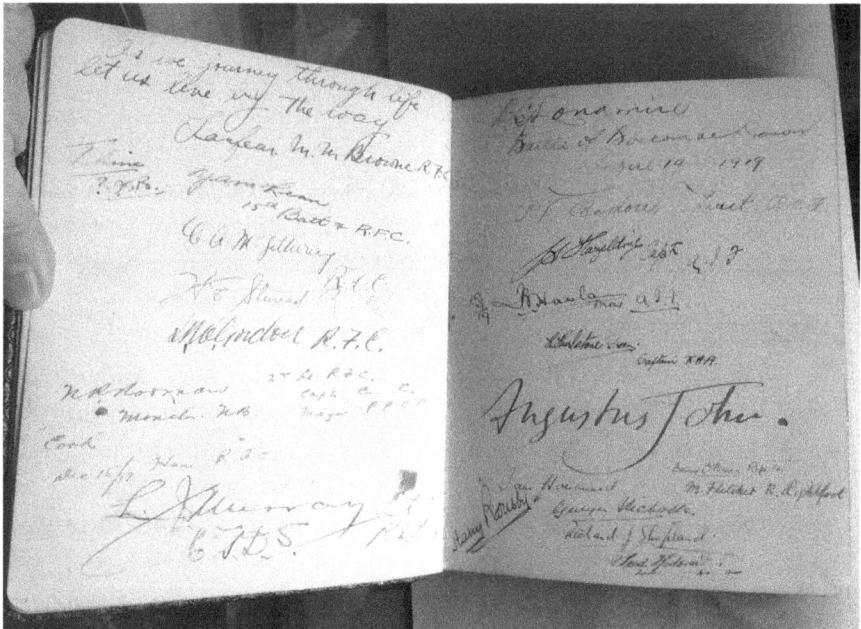

Picture of Augustus John's autograph ©Salisbury Museum

Fordingbridge in this period. He was a romantic, who loved antiques, and I would imagine that he did not pop into the Haunch just the once.

J is for Jole

Robert Jole (1580-1631) was born in Salisbury. He rented the merchant's house in 1612, when his son, Roger, was two years old, and he was then listed as a tanner. He is included because the hall which he would have lived in is now the upper restaurant room of the Haunch of Venison and he is a colourful character. Robert Jole is interesting for a variety of reasons: The first is that he was Mayor of Salisbury in 1623, at which time he was said to have a 'furious and fiery nature'. His colleagues were so afraid of being assaulted by him, that they that they would not go to see him alone. He was, by now, a brewer. He made the Salisbury records during his mayoral year by getting so drunk that he fell into a 'filthy mirey ditch', and then, after clambering out of it with difficulty, he found himself accidentally walking across the river. Which must have sobered him up.

As a brewer, Robert Jole soon clashed with John Ivie, who became Mayor three years later, and after whom Ivie Street is named. Ivie wanted to tackle the problem of drunkenness in the city. This must have been a very real problem, because when John Taylor, the 'Water Poet', boated through Salisbury in 1623 (mooring up at the spot which is currently Wetherspoons), he remarked on the dreadful drunkenness of Salisbury citizens! Ivie started a municipal brewery to break the stranglehold of men like Jole, and channel the profits back into helping the poor. He began issuing 'tokens' for poor relief, which could not be spent on drink, and when the plague struck during his time as mayor, he ordered Inns and alehouses to be closed. This brought him into opposition with Robert Jole.

When Jole moved into the merchant's house – and we can imagine him quaffing from jugs of ale in front of the roaring fire in the what is now the restaurant. He certainly worshipped in St Thomas's church, because he appears in Swayne's *Churchwardens Accounts* as having made a small donation to the church (a measly sum compared to others, I seem to remember.)

Since the Haunch of Venison was such a very short distance to go for such an enthusiastic imbiber, it would be fair to speculate that Robert Jole sat in the smoking room with his clay pipe and pewter tankard many a night when he lived next door – if the house was by then an Inn (and it probably was.)

K is for King Henry VI

The King of England at the time that the Haunch building was constructed as a church house was King Henry VI. He was an unhappy King, whose father had won the Battle of Agincourt (putting immense pressure on him), and he had become king of England at only nine months old. Although a gentle devout scholar (he would found Eton College), his widowed French mother was warlike. Henry was also crowned King of France.

At the time of the construction of the Haunch, Henry was beginning to suffer from mental illness, and England lost Normandy, partly due to Joan of Arc. Henry lost support, and divisions amongst the nobility led to the War of the Roses. Henry was a Lancastrian, and he was attacked by other members of his extended family – the Yorkists. Deposed, he was crowned king of England for a second time, but later again imprisoned. He was eventually murdered in the Tower

King Henry VI from Salisbury Cathedral West Front

of London in 1471 – clubbed from behind, whilst at prayer.

Henry's first bout of mental illness actually came while he was staying at Clarendon Palace, just outside Salisbury, in 1453. He left his mark on Salisbury Cathedral, by giving permission to build a new library, and donating thirty trees to build the first bookshelves.

The approximate date that the Haunch of Venison was built also had a rather horrible meaning for Henry VI, concerning Salisbury. His confessor and adviser, present at his wedding, was the then bishop of Salisbury, William Ayscough. In 1450 'Jack' Cade from Sussex led a popular rebellion in the south of England against the

King, marching on London. The rebellion led to the murder of the bishop of Salisbury, trapped in a Edington priory near Westbury as he fled to Sherborne. Jack Cade was eventually killed in a fight out, without being taken, and was never tried. His dead body was cut up into pieces to be displayed in Kent, and Sussex (where most of the rebels had come from) – and above the walls of Salisbury Cathedral Close.

K is for Kipling

Rudyard Kipling signed the Visitors Book of the Haunch of Venison. His parents lived in Tisbury, near Salisbury, where they were buried. Kipling would spend months at a time in Tisbury, when he was writing, to get away from family distractions at his home in Sussex. His fame was at its height before World War I, when he signed the book (his is the very first signature in it), because he had won the first Nobel Prize for Literature in 1907.

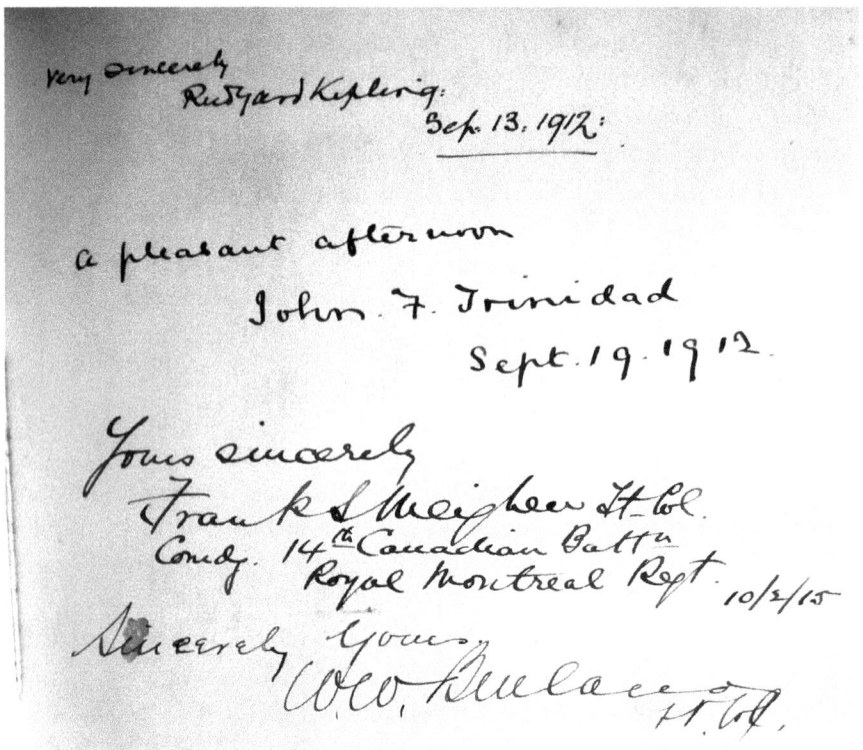

The signature of Rudyard Kipling in the Haunch visitor's book © Salisbury Museum

L is for Leroy

Antony and Vicky Leroy took over as Landlords of the Haunch of Venison in 1981, and so began a new era, that would last for 31 Years.

Tony had been in the music business as Managing Director of several music publishing companies at one time, and still had something of that glamour about him, with a passion for vintage Rolls Royces and Bentleys. One regular, who had been used to Bill and Kate, was taken aback when the flamboyant Tony walked in wearing a fur coat. 'He looked more like the boss of a casino, rather than a publican'.

One curious myth that has circulated in Salisbury, is that Tony was the English pop singer 'Leapy Lee', famous for the pop song 'Little Arrows', a hit in 1968. Leapy Lee was actually folk musician Lee Graham, and 'Little Arrows' was written by Albert Hammond and Mike Hazelwood. Tony is curious to know how the myth started, as he had never had any connection to Leapy Lee.

He was an experienced publican though, 'I think over a period of ten years I must have had eight or nine pubs'. When he took on the Haunch of Venison, he also had the Greyhound in Wilton, and the Grosvenor in Stockbridge. Val Gainsford who was a waitress at the Haunch reminisces 'We used to call it the Leroy empire. He had the Bull at Downton as well – and the Royal Oak at Wishford, as well as the Abbey at Romsey'. However, Tony and Vicky chose to move into the Haunch. 'The accommodation was historic . . . rambling . . . and had a warmth', explains Tony.

It was the brewery, Courage, who asked Tony Leroy to take on the pub when the Jakemans announced that they were leaving, and Tony still remembers walking in for the first time 'I was astonished by it . . . my wife and I felt privileged to be offered this property.'

Continues Tony, 'They (Courage) thought I could improve local drinking trade . . . they were right. How did I turn a very small bar into a great success (beer-wise)? When I took over the Haunch, it was trading at 105 brewer's barrels and 148 gallons of wines and spirits. In those days we closed from 2.30 pm until 6 pm. They used to queue outside at 6 pm, waiting for us to open. If you were not in by 6.30 pm, forget it.' This is confirmed by local historian Frogg Moody. 'The Haunch of Venison was not on my drinking circuit back then. But only because it was so packed that it was impossible to find a seat or get served in there . . . it was a very popular pub'.

Val Gainsford says 'If you opened the door Friday nights, you'd knock the glass out of some one's hand. But they didn't seem to mind, they (the customers) were lovely, lovely people. You felt safe and secure there. We were all friends. It's a whole way of life gone.'

'We had three behind the bar, and most evenings Kevin running around collecting glasses and emptying ashtrays and so on,' Tony says. David Taylor, a regular of the time, remembers Tony

Tony Leroy in the 'House of Lords'
© Tony Leroy

standing at the end of the bar smoking endless menthol cigarettes, and drinking G &Ts out of a goldfish bowl glass. 'It was an assault course to get to the bar Fridays', he says. 'There was a guy called Presley behind the bar, and a camp guy called Dennis who worked on the ships – he would work behind the bar between trips.'

Val remembers Dennis. 'He was always clean and spotless, neat and tidy, smelling of aftershave . . . he was excellent; on the ball; always early. He used to serve them in rotation, and if it was your turn to get served, well, you'd order a few drinks in advance, because goodness knows when your turn would come round again.'

The Cloisters Bar (the Haunch of Venison's 'secret bar') was opened for a year or so, to serve more people, but it was not very practical, as it is so small. 'You couldn't keep the beer cold', Les Mitchell told me, 'And it didn't warrant another member of staff there'. 'Tony wanted me to take over the Cloisters Bar, but it never really happened', says Val.

It is difficult today to imagine pubs which got so regularly packed, and with the cloud of cigarette smoke which hung over the room. The limewash between the ceiling beams of the smoking room was orange with nicotine. 'It had taken years to get there,' Dave Taylor told me, 'One day someone dipped their finger in their beer and wiped off the nicotine in a little pattern. Tony banned everybody who was in the room!'. Tony doesn't think that the smoking ban hit the Haunch an iota. Les Mitchell told me, 'People would line up on the pavement to smoke. On one occasion – I think that it was a royal wedding – they were sat on the pavement smoking, with their glasses next to them. Passers-by had to step over their feet. But no one complained' (!)

One reason that the pub was so popular was the quality of the beer. Dave Taylor goes on, 'Tony Leroy insisted that the brewery send him their best beers for the Haunch, 'Courage Best', and

Vicky Leroy © Tony Leroy

'Directors,' Tony adds, 'and after each and every barrel we cleaned the line without fail. Even the lager'.

Tony Leroy thinks that the popularity of the pub was down to the customers. 'They were so varied. Different occupations. Different ages. Different backgrounds – so diverse. It was uniquely amazing.... never a fight. I don't think that I was a typical, or much liked, publican (Tony is harsh on himself, as he became an iconic publican in Salisbury) . . . but I treated everyone exactly the same. I knew their names, their drinks, their likes, aversions, sports, hobbies. In short, I bothered to know them as people first, and a long way behind as 'punters', as my fellow publicans at that time described their customers. I loved it.'

David Taylor told me, 'The Haunch of Venison was a natural watering hole for strangers to Salisbury, and they probably outnumbered those who were born here. I remember 'Old George', who was Cornish, and had a finger missing. He'd been a builder and he'd tell very funny jokes. He'd sit in the Horsebox at lunchtime with John Pingleaux, who was from Jersey, and wore a smart jacket and cravat, and was like Terry Thomas. He was an alcoholic at the time and had a private income. He was in his 50s. He eventually got sober and went back to Jersey. He is well remembered'.

Les Mitchell says 'I was working behind the bar once, and it was Salisbury Fair, and Tony went out with John Pingleaux. Well, Tony says 'don't serve anyone who is drunk', but when they came back, they were both drunk and they wanted to carry on drinking. Well, I took Tony at his word and I refused to serve them! Tony was very annoyed, he roared, 'it's **my** pub!'.

'Lunchtime, and evening there was a definite community of young professionals. There was no live music, nor juke boxes, just a haze of smoke and the hubbub of intellectual conversation. There were a lot of college lecturers. It was an intellectuals' pub,' David Taylor goes on, 'I remember Nick McIver. He once got his guitar out and did a 45-minute version of 'No Woman No Cry', in the Horse Box. There were a lot of characters. There was a cell of feminists . . . strong women . . . strident. There were lots of actors from the Playhouse. And Les Mitchell, Roy Spring, Ken Lailey, people like that who had the Dining Club.'

Val remembers, 'There were the Haunch Hash Harriers Running Club – they would follow a 'fox and hounds' trail of cooking flour, and come back for a drink. There was Sir Edward Heath who would come in (an ex-Prime Minister). Roy Spring was a lovely, lovely, man – the Dining Club would be all dressed up in dinner jackets and bow ties. There was Jim Gee. There was young Chris from Thomas Cook's – he used to say 'any woman over the age of 18, and under the age of 80, is fair game!' There was Colonel John Stubbs – he was a nice man – and Major Colin Stanton – they both drank in the Haunch. They were superb model makers. They made a model of a converted 1956 Landover; they designed it. It used to stand in the Haunch. There were lots of visiting Americans, Canadians, Australians, and New Zealanders – they made a bee-line for the pub (this author remembers meeting Kiwi Jim, who would come to England regularly to visit the Haunch of Venison). But our bread and butter were the regulars. Those were the days – they'll never come again...'

'There would be lots of fun with the phone,' says Dave Taylor, (this was before people carried mobile phones, and most pubs let people use a public phone), 'The phone was in the doorway to the cellar, and anyone making a phone call would have to sit on the cellar steps. The phone would ring and someone would answer and call out something like 'it's stunning Bernadette in Bahrain to speak to John.'

'Once we had a Stripper-gram arrive. She came accompanied by a bodyguard, and they were both dressed as policemen.' Les Mitchell laughs. 'This policewoman started stripping off in the House of Lords. Tony wasn't half annoyed when he found out. But probably because he missed it! Tony would be away a lot, fishing in Ireland. Vicky ran the place then. She was beautiful and drove a pink Rolls Royce.'

'Vicky Leroy was a lovely lady' says Val, 'She was tall and slim with short dark hair – 'Ladylike'
is how I would describe her – yes 'Ladylike'. She did the nitty gritty, day-to-day running of the place, and she was a very hard worker. She was very well liked by the staff, because she could turn her hand to anything. If there was no chef, then she could cook as well as anyone, and do the silver service. I have worked with Vicky in the kitchen and me in the dining room.'

It was Vicky who employed Val. 'It was 1982, and Tony and Vicky had only been there about six months. I had only been married (to Tom Gainsford) a few months. My son, Nick, was the washer upper at the Haunch, and I took my mother there for lunch in the House of Lords, and Nick introduced me to Vicky. She was desperately short of staff, because they employed a lot of students who would leave to go back to Uni. I was older. She asked me if I wanted to work – I didn't really need the job, and I was just married and didn't want to work late, but I said that I'd help out for three weeks, so that she could find someone. But three weeks turned into three months and then she'd say 'please, please, please stay until Christmas.' Val ended up staying for 12 years.

'The lower dining room would have the snack side – pub food – ploughman's, cottage pie, game pie, sandwiches . . . The most popular dish was 'three sausages, bread and mustard.'

Val continues, 'The upper dining room was all silver service. There was virtually everything that you could wish for – soups, pates, snails, frogs' legs . . . for the mains there was roast venison, of course, Dover Sole, lobsters . . . I didn't know how to do silver service, but the chef, Tim Philbrick, took me in the kitchen and showed me how-to pick-up peas with a spoon and fork – he said 'if you can pick up the peas with one hand, then the rest will be fine'.

Val told me about a catering student who was carrying a large silver platter laden with roast venison into the grand dining room, 'She caught her foot on the top step as she walked in, and the platter flew off her arm and sailed across the room and straight into the roaring fire! I could hear the meat sizzling! I shouldn't have laughed, but you know it was so funny . . . she was mortified, but luckily, they had plenty more venison in the kitchen.'

She remembers the big walk-in fridge upstairs, 'there was a security key dangling in case you got locked in. It was creepy; there were whole deer hanging up in there. I didn't like it. The red wine was kept upstairs, too. The white was downstairs in the cellar under the bar – the steps were steep and narrow with no handrail.'

'They used to have parties to celebrate the arrival of the Beaujolais Nouveau. The office staff from UK Provident always came in, and they'd say 'stay and have a glass with us'. It was a big family. We worked so hard, but we had so many laughs. Tom would come to pick me up, and he'd end up folding dozens of napkins. We were meant to go home, but if customers kept on ordering, then we'd just stay – we'd never say 'no'. We often did extra hours without overtime, but people didn't mind. We just enjoyed the job.'

Val remembers that some of the young girls who worked at the pub were quite scared of Tony. 'You could tell if he was in a bad mood by the sound of his footsteps on the stairs, and the youngsters would hide, but I got on well with him, he was good fun. He was great friends with Dave Prodger, who was the general odd job man – if you can call it that. Tony once got into a temper because he couldn't find a teaspoon for his coffee, and he roared at Dave to tie a spoon to the mixing machine, so that it would always be there. Well, Dave bound it so tightly to the machine that you couldn't pick it up – because we enjoyed teasing Tony. Vicky would just roll her eyes and say "take no notice".'

Les Mitchell says, 'Tony had a short fuse. He'd sometimes ban everybody in the pub, even if they had nothing to do with the incident that had annoyed him. Then they'd all move to the George and Dragon. Then, after about three days he'd send McIver or some-one to tell them, 'You can get a free drink if you come back'. Everyone laughed!'

But Tony was often away. 'He loved fishing in Ireland, and I think that he had property there. He'd go away for weeks to Ireland. Sometimes Vicky went with him – and it was in Ireland that she wrote off her Rolls Royce.'

Val left shortly after Rupert Wilcocks arrived to take over as chef and run the restaurant. Justyna Nugent (who would later go on to become pub manageress), told me that Rupert ran the restaurant as 'No. 1 Minster Street' as a manager/partner. Says Val, 'I left because I didn't really need the job, and I wanted to spend more time with Tom

– it was nothing to do with Rupert. The restaurant did change though. I was surprised when they took up the red carpet and stopped the silver service. It was more modern food.'

The exposed floorboards were fashionable, and silver service was dying out all over the country, just as the 20th century was drawing to a close. The fashions were changing.

Rupert Willcocks made a success of the restaurant, but Tony and Vicky Leroy had already moved to France by then, leaving Arnauld Rochette to manage the pub – and then Justyna. Like the Jakemans before them, Salisbury never forgot the Leroys.

Tony and Vicky Leroy waving goodbye to the Haunch © Tony Leroy

L is for Lesbians

In 1988, under the premiership of Margaret Thatcher, a law was brought in ('section 28' Local Government Act) which forbad local authorities from promoting homosexuality (David Cameron later apologised for it).

The LGBT (although the term was not yet coined) community organised some widely reported demonstrations against the unpopular Act, which included marches in Manchester and London, and storming the the BBC. However, the headline which surely garnered the most publicity was when a group of lesbian activists decided to abseil into the House of Lords at London's Houses of Parliament, led by Sally Francis. The event was in protest at the support of the act, by peers.

Sally Francis and five of her friends bought some strong washing line from Clapham Market, and sat in the public gallery (four of them guests of a peer). When the act was passed, two of the women jumped over the balcony and abseiled to the floor of the Lords, using the washing line. They were not arrested, and had an initially hard job convincing journalists that it had happened – but they suceeded in grabbing headlines.

NOT A GAY DAY
IN THE LORDS

HAUNCH of Venison regulars, are at a loss to explain newspaper headlines which claimed "Lesbians abseil into House of Lords".

All was quiet in the Salisbury pub, the day following the alleged incident.

The wood panelled bar known as the 'Lords', situated between the tap room and the toilets, had apparently been the scene of a gay rights protest.

"I saw nothing," said one disappointed local, adding: "I want to know why the House of Lords was still open after closing time".

A spokesperson for the Haunch said: "We give the locals enough rope, without them bringing abseiling tackle into the bar."

Following suggestions that the protesters were led by a shaven headed demonstrator shouting, "shame on you", the spokesperson replied: There are always complaints when beer goes up. There are a lot of bald people in here."

Landlord at the Haunch, Tony Leroy, was unavailable for comment. Rumours that he was locked in a room above the pub, hastily writing a vegetarian menu, are unfounded.

Extra publicity was garnered when jokes were made in the papers about the Haunch of Venison pub in Salisbury – the pub's tiny smoking room is known locally as 'The House of Lords'. What the papers didn't mention was that the Haunch had a group of lesbians amongst their regulars. The joke reinforced the demonstration made by Sally Francis and her friends by keeping the story in the public mind.

M is for Marshall

Alex Marshall held the licence from 2012 to 2015. He was also licensee of the Pheasant Inn, and Tracey Thorne was the General Manager of the Haunch of Venison, taking over from Justyna Miller.

A 'winding up petition' was issued against the former tenant (Tony Leroy) in April 2012, and the Haunch went into receivership. The pub re-opened quickly, with Alex taking over, although the restaurant remained closed for a while.

According to the American blog 'Road Trip' ('a sales guy's guide to travel, food, and music in the mid-west and beyond), Alex is 'a gregarious guy with a faint resemblance to Tom Hanks'. Road Trip noted that Buzzfeed.com had recently voted the Haunch of Venison one of the '25 English pubs you must drink in', and commented that a visit to the pub was a 'lifetime experience'. The chefs at the time of Road Trip's visit were Larry Pender and Wotjek Durzynski. The food was locally sourced fresh produce, and included obligatory venison.

M is for Mason

Richard Mason first rented the merchant's house, and then bought it. He lived there from 1615 to 1662. He was a shoemaker, but just like Samuel Fawconer or Firmin Potto, this doesn't mean that he was lowly; He bought the whole house from Robert Holmes. John Chandler's book *Endless Street* contains an isometric drawing of the house at this time, with furniture and goods drawn in, based on a room-by-room inventory taken at the time. The hall (the upper dining room), has a long dining table, six stools and a cupboard listed. Henry Mason inherited the merchant's house in the late 17th century. He divided the house into two for his family.

M is for Medarts

Curious to relate, but a copy of the Haunch of Venison pub features as part of Medarts famous restaurant in St Louis, Missouri, USA, 'The Cheshire Inn'.

Bill and Blossom Medart were a pair of American entrepreneurs who had become wealthy, having started with just a hamburger stand, at a time when 'Californian Hamburgers' were a new thing. Bill Medart had been a lowly salesman, although a successful golfer, and had married the Cecil B. De Mille silent movie actress 'Rose Blossom' in 1928. The pair were successful from the start – although their hard-nosed business practices meant that they are now famous for a waitress strike and picket line, which even saw a bomb lobbed through the roof of their restaurant. The waitresses won.

In 1938 the Medarts visited the south of England for a holiday, passing through Salisbury, and took plenty of snapshots. After the War had ended, they decided to enlarge their premises and build an 'English street' to house a row of buildings standing shoulder to shoulder, and they used their holiday snapshots for inspiration. The row begins with a 'Batchelor's Bar' with an interior based on the Rose and Crown hotel, Salisbury. The next building was 'the Olde Cheshire' (actually the first to be constructed), based on the

Medarts - The Cheshire Inn Missouri USA © Medarts

Old Post Office in Tintagel, Cornwall (the original now belongs to the National Trust), and used as an Inn. The name is from 'Ye Old Cheshire Cheese' pub in London. 'The Olde Cheshire bar' enlarged the black and white beamed 'Olde Cheshire' and, on the other side of the white stuccoed Haunch section, 'The Rose and Crown' was a beamed gourmet restaurant for epicureans. It sat next to a quaint low cottage housing a hamburger stand, or 'sandwich shop'. The two beamed buildings, with bowed beams, were inspired by the 'Ye Olde Hostel of God Begot', in Winchester – and perhaps the Spreadeagle, in Midhurst.

The middle building, based on the Haunch of Venison, was the kitchens, and valet service, and was originally billed as being 'ultra-modern' inside, with stainless steel and freezers and fridges. However, the Missouri Valley Chapter of the Society of Architectural Historians describes the interior as being 'swathed in oak panelling' and having a banqueting room upstairs – which corresponds to the merchant's house restaurant.

The building is listed in the National Register of Historic Places, but is now part of a large St Louis hotel complex called the Cheshire Inn and sits, forlornly, on a car park. The hotel, which dwarfs it, has continued the theme, and has a black and white beamed look, dark wood interiors with stained glass windows, and cosy fireplaces.

M is for Medicinal Brandy
Brandy was once considered a medicine, as it was not looked upon in the same light as other spirits. It was thought to increase blood circulation, fortify the body, and calm down those who had become hysterical. For this reason, there are even newspaper reports of

Medicinal brandy bottle © Rod Poynting

19th-century doctors feeding brandy to children dying of malnutrition, or those in shock, wounded, or expiring.

Since brandy was recommended by qualified medical men, it was not forbidden by the temperance movement, but doctors were warned to treat it as other addictive drugs. According to an academic paper by Henry Guly on medicinal brandy, it could be administered 'rectally and even intravenously', if the patient could not be revived to drink it. It was, according to the *British Pharmacopoeia*, a medical dictionary, useful in cases of 'severe flatulence'. It was also recommended as a 'sedative for infants and young children'. The use of medicinal brandy declined in the first part of the 20th century.

Haunch of Venison
SALISBURY.

PURE COGNAC BRANDY.

FOR

MEDICINAL PURPOSES,
may be obtained on production of a

DOCTOR'S CERTIFICATE,
at 3/-, 3/3, 3/6, 3/9, 4/- per qr. pint,

and at

14/6, 15/-, 15/6, 16/6, 17/6 per bot.

No BRITISH (IMITATION) BRANDY IS SOLD AT
THIS ESTABLISHMENT.

FIRMIN S. BRADBEER,
Proprietor.

The smaller quantities of brandy in the medicinal bottles made them affordable to housewives, who could buy them openly and keep their respectability, and have a quiet tipple at home; therefore Mr Bradbeer demanded a medical certificate before he would sell them.

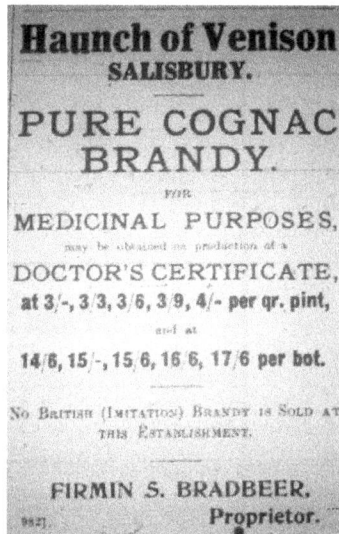

M is for menus

Here is an indication of the menus served by Firmin Bradbeer. The first one is evidently festive.

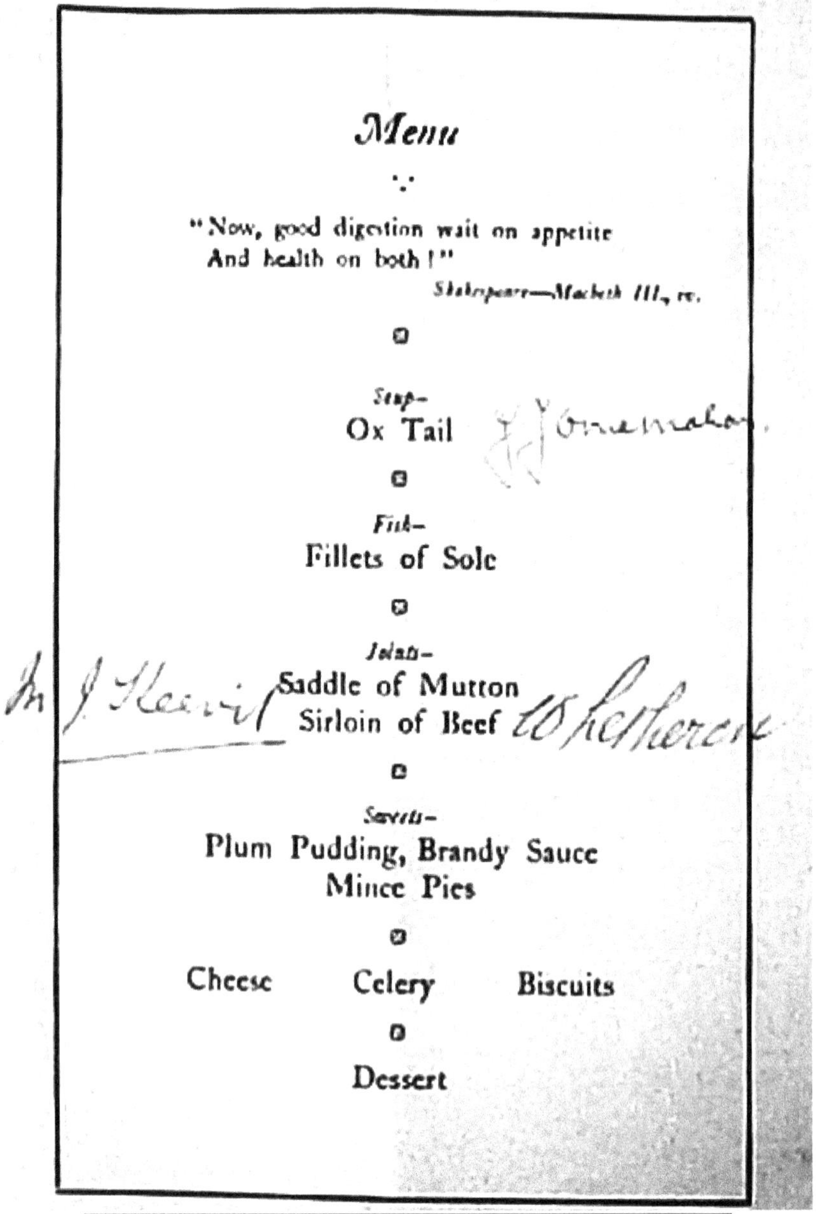

Menu

∴

"Now, good digestion wait on appetite
And health on both!"

Shakespeare—Macbeth III., re.

▣

Soup—
Ox Tail

▣

Fish—
Fillets of Sole

▣

Joints—
Saddle of Mutton
Sirloin of Beef

▣

Sweets—
Plum Pudding, Brandy Sauce
Mince Pies

▣

Cheese   Celery   Biscuits

▣

Dessert

In 1920 there was the ancient Coffee House called The Haunch of Venison that offered meals for epicures and lovers of good living. I remember being taken there for lunch and being enchanted by the sight of a large man in a white apron carving an enormous joint in one corner of the dining-room.

From the windows of the Haunch you looked out onto what is perhaps the oldest monument in Salisbury, the 14th century Poultry Cross under whose shelter markets have been held for six hundred years.

Three Haunch of Venison menus © Salisbury Museum

M is for Merchants Mark

Above the doorway of the merchant's house, which leads into the large dining room (once the hall) when you approach from the Cloisters Bar side, is the mark of the merchant for whom the house was originally built.

In the middle-ages most wealthy middle-class people were originally not allowed a heraldic shield like the nobility. Tradesmen, artisans and farmers would have an identifying mark, or symbol, which they might put on their property; brands (marks) on sheep and cattle still exist. Merchants had their marks put on their bundles of goods which were sent off to different buyers as an identifier. Eventually the trade companies to which they belonged came to have 'marks' or 'brands' – and so we end up with the 'mark' of Nike or McDonalds in 2022. It is interesting that the music artist, Prince, chose to change his identifier from a first name to a 'mark' which resembles somewhat the merchants' marks of the middle-ages.

Whilst Prince's 'love' symbol/mark was based on the symbols for male and female, the marks of the middle ages have a more

Merchants Mark in the merchants side of the Haunch
© Baptiste Vitotino (with drawing of the same mark)

complicated history. F A Girling, (*English Merchants Marks*, published by Oxford University Press in 1964), says that they are derived from a Scandinavian and Germanic tradition of putting runic symbols above houses for magical protection; runes are magical symbols. (Perhaps, we are looking at a Viking tradition). Merchants' marks have many stylistic similarities with runes, and, interestingly, the marks which this author has seen in buildings in Salisbury are all above chimneys; above a doorway, and in a stained-glass window (entrances into a house to be guarded by anti-witch protection measures by putting a potent symbol).

Merchants' marks evolved to have a Christian 'protection' magical side: the top of the one found in the Haunch of Venison has a deformed version of the magical four sign, or 'staff of mercury', based on a Roman-Christian symbol for Christ. Here the triangular part of the four has become a semi-circle, finished with a runic streamer, but

the horizontal part of the four is still finished with a cross, as was common in merchants' marks.

Also common in medieval merchants' marks is to finish the bottom with strokes resembling more or less a letter 'W'. Girling thinks this is runic, although two Vs came to mean 'Virgin of Virgins' and were another Christian symbol, known as the 'Marion mark'. However, as merchants' marks evolved, they also might incorporate the merchant's Initial(s). So, this might mean that the merchants name began with W.

F A Girling states, as a matter of fact, that the merchants' mark in the Haunch of Venison is that of William Warmwell. Sadly, the only example of 'Warmwell's' mark that he gives, is that of the Haunch, and so I don't know how he arrived at this conclusion. Warmwell died in 1423, and the house in Minster Street was built around forty years after his death. Warmwell's residence is also known to have been in Castle Street. He had no sons. It is often stated that the Mark is that of a wealthy woollen merchant, but this is speculation, and as I write, we have yet to know. The mark is now used by Carters, the jewellers, who own the house.

M is for Merryweather
Oustis Merryweather was the landlord of the Haunch of Venison in the latter part of the 18th century, leasing the Inn from the Fawconers. Oustis had been born near Bedford, around 1740, to a large family of farm labourers, of which many generations of Merryweathers had been christened with the colourful name of Eustace – surely denoting French ancestors. His name has been incorrectly cited as 'Austin', in some places.

Oustis's country accent comes down to us clearly across the centuries when we read the name 'Badford' as near his place of birth (it was 'Bedford'). He'd joined the army, and served with 'General Sheppard's Regiment' (on the Parish Register entry for his first marriage), or the '14th foot', according to his military records. The 14th foot was the Buckinghamshire Regiment (just over one of his county borders), which later became the Bedfordshire Regiment.

How Oustis arrived in Salisbury is not known (it was logically with the army, on Salisbury Plain, but there were plenty of Merryweathers in the area, and he might have had a Salisbury connection). Whatever the reason, he married Sarah Street in St Martin's Church, Salisbury, on the 16th of May 1766, while still in the army. Sarah had to sign the register with an 'X'.

Since Oustis does not appear to have left the army until the 1770s, he would have gone with his regiment to fight in the American War of Independence, and then to the Caribbean. At any rate, in 1779, he was an Army pensioner being nursed at the pensioner's hospital in Chelsea for 'Rheumaticks'.

Oustis came back to Salisbury – probably because his wife was still alive, and living in the city – and he evidently needed to find a new occupation, invalided out of the army as he was. Why he was able to set himself up as a publican is anybody's guess, but most probably he – or Sarah – had connections in the licensed victualler's trade. He also had an Army pension.

He would have been wearing breeches, stockings, a cutaway coat, and a tricorn hat. He would have been used to candlelight, and superstition. After fighting a war, and an army life, he would have been a hard man, whose rheumatism made all the stairs in the Haunch, difficult.

By 1784 he was definitely ensconced at the Haunch of Venison, because a later landlord, Firmin Bradbeer, recounted in his own history of the pub, a story which he had found in the *Journal* (22 November):

A man, John Lamb, stole from a bureau belonging to Mr Merryweather 70 pounds, but was caught the next day. The cash was worth over £6,000 in today's money, and gives an idea that the Haunch of Venison was a successful concern, and we can see that the inn was renting rooms to paying guests. However, one interesting fact is that John Lamb is described as a 'negroeman', and that he had a servant (although he might have hired him in Salisbury with the 70 pounds).

Lamb was heading to Liverpool. According to an English Heritage site on the black population in the late 18th century, there were only 5,000 black people (outside London), across the country, but there were mixed communities in ports such as Liverpool. Mr Lamb was sentenced to death, but was reprieved.

Fascinatingly, Mr Bradbeer then goes on to say that he discovered 'an earthenware mug' embossed with 'Merryweather Sarum', in the lower restaurant, 'during the renovations. Since Crewes, Drakes, Cheaters and Pottos had all run the Haunch in the intervening years between himself and Oustis Merryweather, the mug must have been well hidden. But why?

In 1789, Oustis remarried in St Thomas's Church. He is on the register as a 'widower'. Intriguingly, his new wife has the same name as his old – 'Sarah Street'. I presume that she was a relative of his first wife. He made his will the same year, leaving all his debts and expenses for her to sort out – he clearly didn't think that there would be much over. He described himself as a 'Victualler', and not an Army Veteran.

By 1791, the Merryweathers had disappeared into the mists, and Thomas Crewe had taken over the lease of the Haunch of Venison.

M is for Miller

Justyna Nugent was unmarried when she ran the Haunch of Venison for Tony Leroy in the late noughties. Back then, she was known by her maiden name of Justyna Miller. 'I had my name over the door', she explains, 'because I had the licence to authorise the sale of alcohol at the Haunch, even though Tony was the Tenant and had the licence for the premises, and was responsible for the pub to Enterprise, who owned it'.

Justyna is Polish by nationality, and first visited Salisbury while in England on holiday; she naturally made a beeline for the Haunch of

Justyna Miller

Venison. 'It was at the Haunch that I met Swarva, who is also Polish, and we became friends. Swarva's husband was David Prodger, who was in charge of the fixtures and fittings at the Haunch. I came back a couple of times on holiday, and in the end Swarva asked me to come back to stay. I said, 'I will if you get me a job!' -and she got me a job at the Haunch.' It was 2005. 'I ended up staying 7 years at the Haunch'

Tony and Vicky Leroy had already moved to France by then, and Arnauld Rochette was managing the pub for them. The restaurant was being run by Rupert Wilcocks as 'No 1, Minster Street', and was very popular in Salisbury. Says Justyna, 'The first year that I was there, we would often do 100 covers in the evening, in different sittings. Rupert was very talented, and very helpful and kind; everybody loved him, and people would come in to eat, just because it was him. It was his own business, because Tony sublet the restaurant to him'.

In fact, Rupert was Partner-Manager of the restaurant at the Haunch of Venison. He had trained at the Carlton Hotel, Cannes, after leaving Bristol Technical College, and had worked at various restaurants in Wiltshire, before Tony invited him to join the Haunch.

Justyna goes on, 'The restaurant was hung with modern paintings then, because Rupert used to get paintings by young artists from the Arts Centre'. This must have been the era that Cecil/Horace was relegated to the attic. 'I found the stag's head in the store-room', she'd told me previously, 'and I put him over the fireplace'. It was, of course, where he had hung before, although she hadn't known that at the time. Justyna only worked in the restaurant, and not behind the bar at this time. 'Rupert was like a 'dad' he said, 'watch everything that goes on here, and learn it all' – So, I did.'

Tony would visit the Haunch of Venison regularly, and I hit it off with him', although she never met Vicky. 'I would speak to her on the 'phone sometimes, but I think that she was just happy with her animals in France. She would ring straight away though, if there was a problem. She was still involved.'

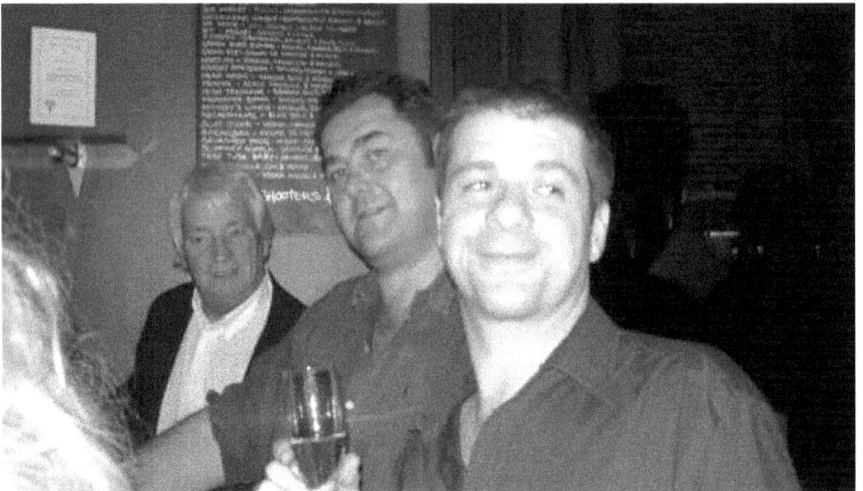

Tony Leroy, Rupert Willcox and Arnauld Rochette © Justyna Nugent

Justyna became Manageress a year after starting. 'Arnauld Rochette left to take over the Pheasant pub, and Tony asked me to take over from him. I think that he knew before that Arnaud would go, because he sent me to college to study for the qualification to get a personal licence.' It was 2006, and the date sticks in her mind, for another reason as well:

Tony was over from France, and he and Rupert went over for a morning coffee on the market place. 'The coffee shop was where La Piazza is now.' It was a cold morning in February. 'They went out together, and Tony came running back shouting 'He's gone!'. He told me, when he'd calmed down, that Rupert had suddenly clutched his forehead and dropped down dead.' Rupert had had a brain haemorrhage. He was only 46.

Such was the Chef's popularity that over 1,000 people attended his funeral at Salisbury Cathedral. Tony and Vicky and Justyna didn't forget him, but placed moving tributes in the paper on the anniversary of his death.

Justyna moved into the Haunch of Venison to live. 'Tony wanted me to live on the premises, because he was petrified of the building being empty, in case it caught fire, and there was nobody to raise the alarm. Once a Salisbury pub did catch fire, and Tony knew about it before me. He rang me about 5am to ask, 'is it us?'. I don't know how he knew, when he was in France!'

She had many ghostly experiences whilst living and working at the Haunch, as well as having the 'hand' stolen − but these are recounted in different chapters.

'Tony was very good to work for', says Justyna, who has stayed friends with him. 'I absolutely loved working there. The pub was so busy that people were packed in like sardines, and there were often two or three people serving behind the bar, even at lunchtimes. I loved the busy times! There was so much adrenalin! There were happy people!'. She goes on, 'There was never ever any trouble. We were in Pub Watch, and had walkie-talkies, and we knew if there were problem people in town, and didn't let them in. The Regulars were wonderful people, and they often used to sing spontaneously'.

'All the Haunch is full of music', had written Firmin Bradbeer, back in 1920!

'At Christmas, the carol singers would come in from St Thomas's Church, through the back door, and sing.' It is, perhaps, only at the

Haunch of Venison, that the beautiful image of a choir raising the rafters with Christmas hymns, necessarily begins with them traipsing through the Gents loos,

Justyna remembers. 'There were all different types of people who came to the Haunch. There were some wealthy foreigners who would holiday in Salisbury, just to come to the Haunch. They'd come in every single evening, when they were here. There were famous people who would come in – I saw the american actress, Diane Keaton. And Pete Docherty. Graham Norton.'

'All of us at the Haunch were friendly with the New Inn' (another ancient pub),' and we would help each other out, if we were short staffed.'

Justyna met all her best friends, while working at the Haunch of Venison, 'There's Sophie; there's Maggie – we looked like twins – there is Diana. They all worked at the Haunch; we were a family.'

Of course, there was also David Prodger, husband of her friend, Swarva. He was a great friend of Tony Leroy, – and of Justyna. 'Dave loved the Haunch of Venison so much', says Justyna. 'I remember him standing in the kitchen and looking at the churchyard, and all he ever wanted was to be buried there'. Dave got his wish, and his ashes are buried behind the Haunch.

It was in 2012, that Tony Leroy finally decided to retire, and relinquish the licence. 'The Brewery (Enterprise) offered the pub

Photograph of Dave Prodger. © *Justyna Nugent*

to me'. But Justyna didn't want to take it. By then, she had met her husband, Gary Nugent (known as Rugbi). 'I was behind the bar, and he spotted me through the window, and persuaded his mate to come in for a drink. He came up to the bar and asked for "two pints of bitter and your 'phone number, please". I didn't give it to him, but he was persistent, and I suggested that I take his, and call him if I were ever out with my friends. I found the number in my pocket sometime after, and my girlfriends suggested that I call him, and that we all go out with his friends, in a big group.' The rest is history, and the couple are now married with three young children.

'We discussed taking the Haunch of Venison, but we thought that it would swallow us up and take up all our lives, and we wanted time to ourselves, and to start a family.'

Reluctantly, Justyna walked away, when Tony did. It would be Alex Marshall who would take on the licence for the Premises, and Tracey Thorne who would become Manageress.

N is for Navy
The Glengorm Castle had been a hospital ship during World War I, and in the early 1920s (when this postcard was sent), it was a troop ship in the Far East.

The ship in the picture on the wall of the lower dining room is SS Kenilworth Castle. She was a steam ship built as a mail ship in

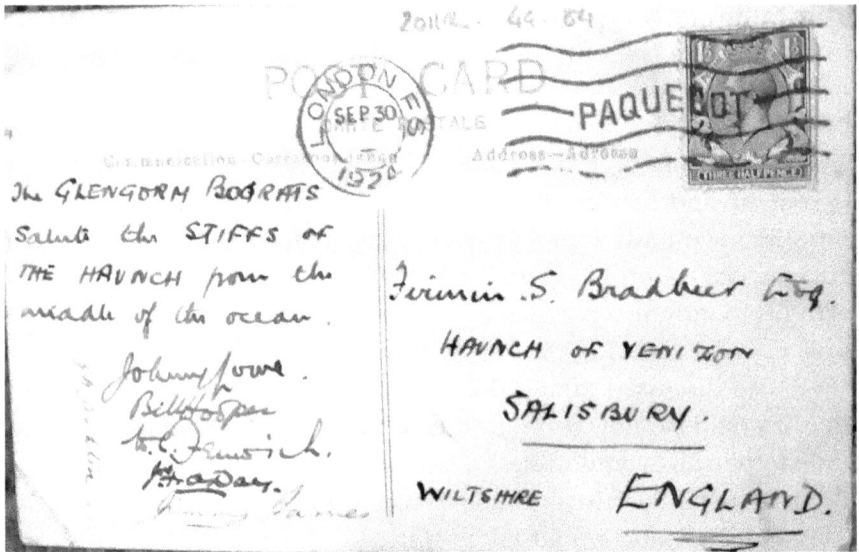

Front and back of 'The Glengorm Castle' postcard © Salisbury Museum

1904, carrying mail between Southampton and Cape Town. During World War I she was a troop ship, but unfortunately collided with another British ship in the Channel, in the pitch black, drowning 15 people.

If you google the Kenilworth Castle Incident 1918 then you will see that it was a horrendous incident for those concerned, even if they survived. It was 1918, and many of those who died were young nurses, whose lifeboats capsized. Kenilworth Castle was repaired and went back to commercial use in peacetime, and was broken up in 1936.

Why is there a picture of SS Kenilworth Castle on the wall of the Haunch of Venison? One can only imagine that it was given to the Bradbeers by sailors who had come up from Southampton on day trips. Or maybe some nurses were friends of Dolly's, from Salisbury. It might be written on the reverse of the picture, but as it is framed, we may never know. The picture was found in an attic at the

The Kenilworth Castle
© The Haunch of Venison

Haunch by the present landlords 2022. It must have been important to the Bradbeer family.

O is for Operatic Society

Salisbury Amateur Operatic Society was, according to the history printed to coincide with its Platinum Jubilee, formed in 1908. 'The idea was mooted in a small room in The Haunch of Venison during one of the pleasant gossips that nightly took place there. They used to call this room 'The House of Lords'. Well, the users of the room called a meeting at the Old Orderly Chambers, in the Market House Chambers on Thursday, July 23rd of that year'.

Salisbury Operatic Society opening night playbill   © Frogg Moody

The idea was to perform 'Pirates of Penzance' for two nights in aid of Salisbury Infirmary, and members would have to pay for their own clothes if they didn't make enough money to cover costs. The Gilbert and Sullivan operetta was so popular when it was performed the following year at the County Hall, in Endless Street, that two extra nights were put on. 100 guineas were donated to the Infirmary, and £64 went to form the treasury for the creation of a permanent Amateur Operatic Society.

Firmin Bradbeer would go on to write several librettos, with his friend, George Sand, writing the music. W.H. Jackson was an enthusiastic baritone.

P is for Photograph

This photograph is of the three Potto brothers, and dates from before 1868, when William's wife Sophia Cassey died, and after Thomas had married Anne Rooke. Firmin was a widower.

Thomas Potto   Firmin Potto   William Potto

Misses Potto

Firmin Potto
©Anthony Hamber Collection

(left) The three Potto brothers with Thomas and William's wives. ©
Salisbury Museum

The picture was probably taken by Edward Macy, who had a photographic studio in Mill House, St Thomas's Churchyard, a stone's throw from the Haunch – which then had a back door open onto the churchyard.

The picture next to it, taken by Macy, shows Firmin Potto, taken on or around the same date. If one were to compare the shape of face, protruding lower lip, width of mouth, thin upper lip, thin bridge of nose, long nose, baggy eyes, forehead, facial hair, shirt collar, jacket lapel, and white waistcoat – it is indeed Mr Firmin Potto of the Haunch of Venison!

In his will, made in 1874, Firmin Potto wrote 'I bequeath to my niece, Eliza Perry Johnson all my pictures, photographs and likenesses', showing that he must have had an interest in collecting images. It is likely that early photographs of Salisbury ended up in Suffolk.

P is for Potto, Firmin
See Appendix five for a family tree of the Potto family
Firmin Potto was Tenant, and then owner, of the Haunch of Venison from 1833 to 1875. He was born in 1804, in the reign of George III, lived through the Regency and then reign of George IV, and it was in the reign of William IV that he arrived in Salisbury and took over the Haunch of Venison. He died in the reign of Victoria.

Firmin Potto was the third of four children of a currier and leather cutter from Witham, on the Essex/ Suffolk border. He was born close by, at Nayland in Suffolk. His Father was William Marrows Potto, and the mother of all four children was Mary Pitts Perry, who was a local Essex woman from Matching. Mary died shortly after the birth of Thomas Pitts Potto, Firmin's younger brother. Thomas would later reside with Firmin at the Haunch of Venison.

A currier was somebody who finished tanned leather, and it was a specialist job. William Marrows Potto moved from Witham to Nayland when he took a large shop dealing in leather goods. This is almost certainly where young Firmin learnt to make shoes and boots from the finished hides. His brother Thomas could also make boots and shoes. William Marrows Potto sold or rented out the premises in 1816, and appears to have then returned to Witham.

The first mention of a Potto in Salisbury is when William Potto, Firmin's eldest brother, married the landlady's daughter, at the Wheatsheaf Inn in 1827 (see Appendix six for William Potto). It is unclear how William arrived in Salisbury, but I would speculate that it is due to the proximity of Salisbury Racecourse.

By 1831, Firmin Potto was living in Salisbury and was a boot and shoe maker. He married Maria Cheater, daughter of the landlord of the Haunch of Venison in April 1832 (emulating his older brother, who had also gained a public house of standing, by marriage). His father, Thomas Marrows Potto was a witness, as was Mary Arney, surely related to John Arney who had a boot and shoe makers in Minster Street, near the Haunch of Venison, 31 Minster Street (the street was numbered differently to now). It is probable that Firmin worked for the Arneys. As it happens, Mary Arney would later become the widowed Firmin Potto's 'assistant' living, then dying, at the Haunch

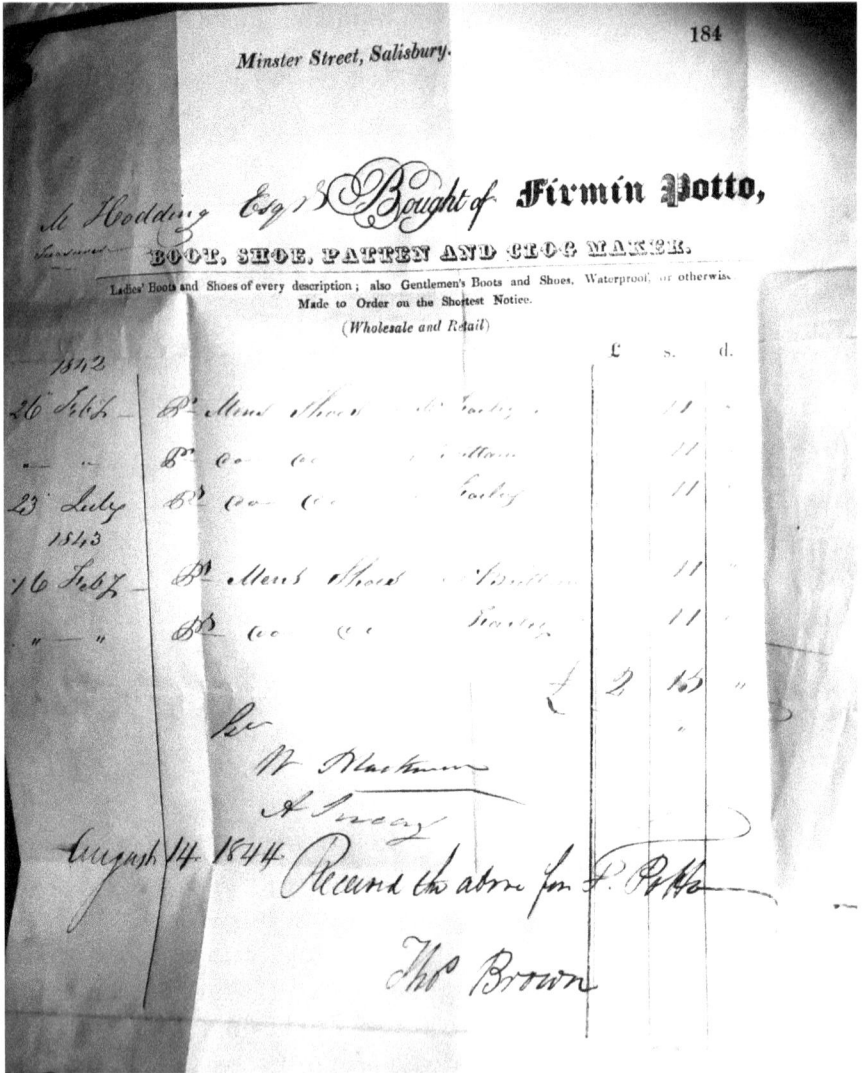

A receipt from Firmin Potto for boots and shoes © *Ruby Vitotino Moody*

of Venison, indicating that there was a close friendship between the Arneys and the Pottos.

Thomas Cheater died in 1833, and Firmin Potto became landlord of the Haunch of Venison – the same year that Salisbury got gas lighting – and so began his rise in the city to become one of Salisbury's leading citizens, and the source of wealth for a number of his family. The first thing that he did was announce that he had started an import/export wholesale wine and spirit business, to supply not only himself, but other businesses in the city.

In this *Journal* advertisement for 1833, his 'Wholesale and Retail Wine Vaults' are advertised as being at the Poultry Cross. The cellars at the Haunch of Venison are tiny, and hardly of a size to stock any quantity of wine and spirits, and furthermore he states, after advertising the Haunch of Venison Inn, 'N. B. in addition to the above...', which raises the possibility the 'Wine Vaults' are separate to the Haunch.

> **HAUNCH OF VENISON INN, SALISBURY.**
> **FIRMIN POTTO** begs most respect-
> fully to acknowledge the many favours so liberally
> bestowed on him since the death of his late Father-in-
> Law, THOMAS CHEATER, and hopes, by continued
> exertions in the same line of Business, to merit their
> future support.
>   N. B. In addition to the above, F. P. wishes to inform
> his Friends and the Public in general, that he has com-
> menced in the Wholesale WINE and SPIRIT Trades,
> and is determined to offer for Sale, *Foreign and British
> Spirits, and Foreign Wines,* of the best quality, at very
> moderate prices.
>   *F. Potto's Wholesale and Retail Wine Vaults,*
>   *Poultry Cross, Sarum.*   [2111]

An idea of what this wholesale business would eventually grow to be can be glimpsed by a newspaper snippet on the death of Louisa Potto in 1902 – Louisa was Firmin's second wife – who had continued the business – 'Very important sale of brandies, Irish and scotch whiskies, Port, and Tarragona. In all amounting to about 3,000 gallons'. The alcohol was imported into Bristol into a bonded warehouse. It is very likely that French wines and brandies were also imported through Southampton; this was the business that started in 1833, and grew.

Firmin Potto later rented cellars in Old George Yard, just off the High Street, but he perhaps at one time supplied a cellar in Fish Row, for his brother William who was running the Wheatsheaf. There is an indication that he was the first to rent the cellars in Culver Street later used by his nephew-by-marriage, Firmin Bradbeer.

However, Firmin Potto continued making and selling boots and shoes, buying Arneys business at 31 Minster Street in 1834. One imagines that he was supplied finished leather by his father, and that Maria did the daily management of the Haunch of Venison, something that she was very fitted to do, having grown up there.

Queen Victoria came to the throne in 1837, when Firmin was already aged 33, and an established business man; his second wife, Louisa, had yet to be born.

SALISBURY. *May 6, 1834.*

THE Creditors of JOHN ARNEY, BOOT and SHOE-MAKER, Minster-street, have disposed of the BUSINESS, STOCK in TRADE, &c., of the above, to FIRMIN POTTO, who intends to carry it on in all its branches ; and hopes, by keeping an extensive assortment of every Article connected with the Trade, to merit a share of public support.

In 1838 Firmin's father died aged 61, in Salisbury, after a 'long and painful illness', and was buried in St Thomas's churchyard; his widow (second wife), Sarah, returned to Nayland. Interestingly, the notice of his death says that William Marrows was the 'father of Messrs William and Firmin Potto 'of this city" – seemingly, younger brother, Thomas, had yet to join them. The freehold of the Haunch of Venison came up for sale in this year – apparently, Mr Potto could not yet afford to buy it – and although Firmin is described as being 'in occupation', as the tenant, he is still described as 'a shoemaker' (*Salisbury Journal* 1838).

Lot 2. All that Freehold MESSUAGE or DWELL-ING-HOUSE now in the occupation of Mr. Potto, shoemaker, most desirably situated for trade, between the Cheese-market and Poultry Cross, in Minster-street, Salisbury.

It appears that Firmin Potto was a pious man, and he was involved with St Thomas's Church, behind the Haunch of Venison (a back door then opened onto the churchyard). Perhaps it was due to his marriage at the church, and his father's burial there, but he donated the equivalent of £115 towards new seating in February 1838; his business was evidently thriving. It was somewhere around this time that he was elected as 'Overseer for the Board of Guardians', for the Parish of St Thomas's, because he is later noted in the *Salisbury and Winchester Journal* as volunteering for the position for a second term. An overseer was an administrator of relief to the poor. In 1842, he was still an overseer, publishing the yearly accounts. The accounts are often surprising, because as well as those things which one might expect the poor to receive, are included 'willow squares' (rush matting), vaccinations, wine and spirits, insurance, law expenses, examinations, gas fittings, gas, and 'regaling the inmates at the christening of the Prince of Wales'. It gives a glimpse into the life which Firmin Potto led. A bill for boots and shoes from Firmin Potto, dated 1843 (and owned by this author) shows that he made footwear for Mr Hodding's family. Generations of Hoddings were leading citizens of Salisbury, including solicitors, and town clerks, and so we see the standard of footwear that Mr Potto was producing. He was listed elsewhere as a 'clog and patten maker', but it would be entirely wrong to think that he was a simple shoemaker, serving beer. He was a business man; Mr Hodding would be someone that Firmin Potto would come to socialise with on an equal footing.

Firmin's younger brother, Thomas Pitts Potto, had arrived in Salisbury in this period, and was living with his relatives at the Haunch of Venison. He is also listed as a boot and shoe maker in a trade directory, working in Minster Street, in this period – so was probably working for Firmin.

By 1847 Firmin Potto had been elected the President of the Licensed Victualler's Association (a sort of publican's trade union, which had begun life as a friendly society for the relief of publicans). In this role he must have been at the centre of the Salisbury pub and hotel trade, and was overseeing the changing of hands of some Salisbury licensed premises. One pub which changed hands this year was the Butcher's Arms, on the Market Place (now known as the Market Inn). It was the same year that the railway arrived in the city.

> For further particulars, apply to Mr. F. Potto, Minster-street, Salisbury, or to Mr. Robert Futcher, at the Butchers' Arms.   [3278
> SALISBURY, *May* 8, 1847.

Luckily Mr and Mrs Potto survived Salisbury's cholera epidemic in 1849, but perhaps they didn't drink the water? Many people in this period drank 'small beer' instead of water, which was less dangerous in the short term. Maria (Cheater) Potto died, aged fifty, upstairs at the Haunch of Venison, in 1851; the cause of death was 'ascites' (a build-up of fluid in the abdominal cavities, which can be due to cirrhosis) and 'chronic nephritis' (kidney inflammation caused either by an infection, probably from the ascites, or an auto-immune disease). The couple had been married nearly twenty years, but had no children (although Firmin's 11-year-old niece, and heir, Eliza, is listed with them on the 1841 census). The death notice placed by Firmin Potto in the *Journal* read 'much respected and deeply lamented, Maria, beloved wife of Firmin Potto'. Although death notices often carried moving descriptions, Firmin's use of the four words goes a little further, and so appears very genuine. He would not remarry for over 20 years.

In 1854, He served on the Grand Jury at the city Quarter Sessions. The 'Grand Jury' were made up of the leading citizens of the town, and they made their own enquiries into a case, interviewing the witnesses in the presence of the accused, deciding on whether the evidence was strong enough to be a 'True Bill' and try the accused in front of a Petty Jury, or the case should be thrown out. This was the first date which I found, but Firmin would regularly serve on Grand Juries over the years.

In 1855, Firmin Potto was so comfortably off, that he evidently had pretentions, and he did a rather unforgivable thing. His niece, Elizabeth Potto, only daughter of his brother William, (and sole niece or nephew excepting Eliza Johnson – daughter of his sister, Mary, who lived in Suffolk) married a vet from Fisherton Street, called George Morton. According to their descendant, Kristi Summers, Firmin Potto was so angry that he tried to stop the wedding, and he accused Mr Morton of being

Elizabeth Potto Morton © Kristi Summers

'an adventurer' and only after HIS money. He threatened that if the marriage went ahead, then Mr Morton would not live to see a penny. The wedding **did** go ahead and the marriage was a long and happy one, with many children. Firmin Potto, however, changed his will so that some money would only be shared with his niece's family, decades after his death. This meant that Mr and Mrs Morton would probably be dead before they could inherit. In the event, there turned out to be so many Morton children and grandchildren, and what with inflation, each one only received a pittance. It must have been very awkward for Mr Morton living in Salisbury and suffering the wrath of the Pottos (because Thomas was evidently close to Firmin), and he finally took the opportunity to make a new life with his family in New Zealand, where he taught veterinary skills. Had he been embraced by the Pottos, and benefitted from Firmin's help, perhaps the Mortons would have stayed in the area. Their leaving removed William Potto's only child and all his grandchildren from him and Sophia, in his old age.

In 1856, Maria's brother, John Cheater died. He was a retired cheesemonger, living in New Street, and wealthy enough to have made a will in 1845, naming Maria and Firmin Potto executors and one of the beneficiaries of the will. Maria predeceasing John, the money now went to Firmin, as John did not change the bequest *(idavenport7 + Salisbury Journal 1856)*.

It was the same year as this bequest that Firmin Potto decided to sell on his shoe business. In a trade directory of 1851, I counted 56 shoemakers listed, so perhaps the competition had got too much. Salisbury, although technically a city due to its cathedral, was a market town after all (it had a population of less than 9,500).

In 1857 Firmin Potto advertised his shop in Minster Street to let. It is interesting that he was proposing to put in the plate glass front. At the Haunch of Venison, it is specified that the interior was the responsibility of the Tenant, but the exterior was the responsibility of the owner of the freehold. The 'house and shop' might be the same as the 'boot and shoe business' (once Arneys), or not, because the shoe business was taken on as such by George Bartlett in 1858. The 'lofty' shop might have been the original site of the wine and spirit wholesale business, which had grown too big. Note the 'capital cellar'.

Minster street has been renumbered over the years, so the shop was given as 31 Minster Street when Mr Bartlett took over, with the

TO BOOT AND SHOEMAKERS.

TO be DISPOSED OF,—A good and old-established BUSINESS in the above line, which has been successfully carried on by the present proprietor for the last 24 years. Stock and Fixtures to be taken at a fair valuation.   [10585

Apply to Mr. F. Potto, Minster-street, Salisbury.

TO be LET,—A HOUSE and SHOP, well situated for Business in MINSTER-STREET. The Shop is lofty, with Seven Yards' Frontage, good size Back Rooms, large airy Bed-rooms, capital Cellar, &c. &c. A new Plate Glass Front would be put in to accommodate a good Tenant.   [4858

Apply to Mr. Firmin Potto, Wine Merchant, Salisbury.

Haunch given as 36, and Carters as 35. It is given as 39 Minster Street in the 1871 census, with the Haunch at number 44 and Carter's at number 43. So perhaps it was here (picture, 2020s):

Trade directories listing Firmin Potto from the 1830s until the 1850s list next to Firmin Potto: *'Haunch of Venison'*, Wine & Spirit merchant, & Boot, Shoe, Patten & Clog Maker, Minster Street. Since

GEO. BARTLETT (many years Foreman to Mr. GEO. SYDENHAM, High-street), LADIES' AND GENTLEMEN'S FASHIONABLE BOOT AND SHOE MAKER, MINSTER STREET, SALISBURY, begs to return his sincere thanks to those who have so kindly favoured him with the honour of their patronage since his commencement in Business, and states that from the great extension and unexpected support he has received, he has taken the old-established Shop (lately in the occupation of Mr. POTTO), which he has entered on, and hopes to receive a continuance of those favours so liberally bestowed on him, and which it shall be his study to merit.

July 1, 1858.   [7706

F. POTTO begs to state he has disposed of the above Boot and Shoe Business to Mr. GEORGE BARTLETT, and trusts that the support he has so generally received may be extended to his Successor.

Minster-street, July 1, 1858.

The former shoe shop in Minster Street that belonged to Firmin Potto

there are no shop numbers, it is too easy to believe that all the businesses were carried out on the same premises in Minster Street, but I don't believe that they were.

In 1857, Mr Potto donated money to the Indian Mutiny Relief Fund. This was when there was a mutiny against the British East India Company, who then represented the Crown in India. It has been called the First War of Independence. One can only wonder at why Mr Potto felt strongly enough about the rebellion in such a far-flung place to dig into his pockets, and it begs the question as to whether he was merely being patriotic – which helps illustrate his character, in itself – or whether he and his co-contributors had shares in the British East India Company, which I feel is more likely.

Firmin Potto also gave £1 10s. (over £100 in today's money) in subscription to the Royal Agricultural Society in October of the same year (1857), which appears curious for a publican, but perhaps not so much for somebody buying hides to stitch into boots. It should also be noted that a large amount of custom came from farmers on Salisbury market day, when all the inns close to the Market Square, and the market crosses, were heaving.

There is another element that should reinforce the success and social assent of Firmin Potto in Wiltshire society, and also his interest in rural life, and probably horses. In 1858 Sir Thomas Assheton Smith died, and Firmin Potto was one of the subscribers for a print of Sir Thomas on his favourite Hunter, King Dan, with some of his staunchest hounds; it cost him £2 2s. The print almost certainly hung somewhere in the Haunch of Venison at one time. All the subscribers had their names 'engrossed in a volume handsomely bound in scarlet morocco, and presented to Mrs Assheton Smith, in testimony of the

A print of Thomas Assheton Smith © Getty Collection

high estimation in which Mr Smith was held'. Assheton Smith lived at Tedworth House, Tidworth, and was a Tory M.P. and a famous fox hunter. Of course, he was also famous as an outstanding cricketer, and Firmin Potto also played cricket (according to the newspaper), and so had a different reason to admire him. Nevertheless, there are several advertisements placed in the *Journal* by Mr Potto over the years, searching for the owners of lost hunting dogs (greyhounds, which were used to hunt hare), so it appears that he had some connection to the hunting world, and might well have ridden with Assheton Smith's pack. It is indisputable that Assheton Smith was somebody that Firmin Potto admired.

Other people subscribing to the print were the Rt Hon Sidney Herbert M.P. of Wilton House; E. Studd of Netheravon House; Thomas Baring M.P.; Vice Admiral Montague; A.F. Paxton of Cholderton House – but also two other inn keepers: Mr James Carter of the Ailesbury Arms, Marlborough, and Mr E. Davies of the George Hotel, Amesbury. The rest were farmers.

In 1859, Firmin Potto attended the opening of the new Market House building (where Salisbury's precious library is in 2022) with the shareholders. Although 286 people attended the opening, on

Salisbury Market House © Salisbury Museum

Queen Victoria's birthday, and were given a 'cold collation', only some of the people were named. Firmin Potto's name appears alongside the Mayor, Lord Thynne, a clutch of M.P.s and the architect of the building, as well as notable merchants of the city. He was almost certainly also a shareholder in the Market Company − all the money for the building, and the railway line leading to it, was raised by selling shares at £105 each, the 'council offering no assistance' (although the mayor did contribute personally). The new covered building was 'the same size as Westminster Hall' and increased the size of Salisbury Market, as well as keeping the corn and cheeses dry (it was in the cheese market). It was close to the Haunch of Venison, and doubtlessly increased custom.

In 1864, Mr Potto donated ten shillings to Salisbury and South Wiltshire Museum to help with the fitting up of the museum and cataloguing. The museum had been created in 1860, in St Ann Street. It can hardly be doubted that he was interested in history and wanted to help conserve interesting things of historical interest. He was evidently wealthy enough to buy or rent a worthy modern house, but he preferred to live at the Haunch of Venison.

Firmin Potto subscribed £1 10s. to the Bath and West of England Society in 1867. The Society (which is still going) was founded in 1777, according to their website, and is and was an agricultural Charity, 'for the development of Agriculture, Arts, Manufactures and Commerce', and it sought to 'improve rural life, and the rural economy'. Once again, it illustrates that Firmin Potto felt himself as close to currying and boot-making and Salisbury market trading – and hunting – as he did to the wine and spirit trade.

Firmin Potto certainly had shares in the White Hart Hotel Company, and a *Salisbury Journal* report on a share-holders meeting in 1869 shows him actively participating in the meeting. There is some evidence that he actually lived at the White Hart at one time (there was an advert placed in the *Journal* telling people to address themselves to Mr Firmin Potto at the White Hart Hotel). The White Hart was doing very well in 1869, and the report to shareholders was that after all expenses had been deducted, it had made a profit of £848 14s. 1d. (this was over £53,000 in today's money). The shareholders received a dividend of 10% on their investment, paid each half year. One wonders whether Firmin Potto also supplied wine and spirits to the White Hart? The hotel company was putting money aside and had ambitions to 'enlarge the business', without the shareholders being called upon for a 'heavy' contribution.

Remarkably, elections to elect members of Parliament were not by secret ballot, but the names of voters were published in the newspapers, together with the way they had voted, so we know that Firmin (and William) Potto both voted for the Tory candidate, Granville Ryder, in 1869; Ryder later became M.P. for Salisbury. Thomas Potto decided not to vote.

In 1871, a sad but intriguing notice was placed in the *Devizes and Wiltshire Gazette*. A five-month-old baby died in Trowbridge, the beloved first son of a young couple – William Butler and Eliza Annie Ponting (the couple already had two daughters). William Butler Ponting was a draper in Trowbridge, seven years older than Eliza, and the couple employed two assistants and two servants. What is intriguing is the baby's name – Alfred Firmin Potto Ponting, who can only be named for the landlord of the Haunch of Venison pub, in Salisbury.

The baby's grandmother was Eliza Howell (born Compton, in Kingston Devrill), who on the census of 1851 is a widow, with her three-year-old daughter, also Eliza, and running the Bull Hotel – which stood next to Salisbury Infirmary (to the right, as you face it), in Fisherton street. Eliza Howell was only twenty-five, and Firmin

Potto was 47 at the time of this census.

John Howell, Eliza Ponting's father, had been a builder, who had presumably taken the license of the Bull before he died in 1849, around the time of Eliza's birth, and so Firmin Potto is extremely unlikely to have been her genetic father. One can see that her mother, a very young widow, can hardly have had much experience in running an hotel such as the Bull, before she was left to manage it alone. The Bull was in a prime location on a busy shopping street on a direct route from Salisbury station, and is described in various publicity as having extensive stabling, gardens, and large light-filled rooms. Eliza Howell made a success of the business alone, before later remarrying to Adolpheus Hatcher – who played cricket with Firmin Potto (*SWJ 1862*).

In order for Eliza Ponting to have named her firstborn son after Firmin Potto, we have to deduce that Mr Potto had been a very important person to the Howells, at the Bull. This is most likely in his capacity as a Chairman and President of the Licensed Victuallers Association, and a wholesaler and supplier of wine and spirits, and somebody who had sound business advice. He may have been kind and paternal to the fatherless Eliza. Of course, by 1871, Firmin Potto was elderly, rich, and childless, and so Eliza might also have been angling for a bequest for his young namesake. At any rate, the Pontings went on to have other sons after Firmin had married Louisa, but none were given the names Firmin or Potto. We have seen what Firmin Potto thought of people after his money.

> Feb. 24, at Silver-street, Trowbridge, Alfred Firmin Potto, the beloved and only son of William Butler, and Eliza Annie Ponting, aged 5 months.

It was in the same year that little Alfred Firmin Potto Ponting died, that Firmin Potto attended the Mayor's Banquet with the full Council and 'the leading citizens and gentlemen of the surrounding neighbourhood'. The banquet was held at the Guildhall, which was decorated with banners and flags. The food was served 'a la Russe', and catered by the White Hart Hotel Company – of which Firmin Potto was a shareholder.

It was also the same year, 1871, that Firmin Potto is on the census living alone in the Haunch of Venison with his 30-year-old housekeeper, Louisa Bradbeer. He was 66. He doubtlessly knew

Louisa's father, Francis, as both men had been very involved with St Thomas's church, at the same time. Although 66 is not old, even in a photograph taken with his brothers and their wives before 1868, Firmin Potto looks ill, and is obliged to steady himself on his sister-in-law's shoulder. I believe that he was suffering from an undiagnosed illness (from his shaky writing, this might be Parkinsons disease – but that is pure speculation).

In 1873 he married Louisa Potto, and I believe that he trusted her to be able to look after his business for his family. Perhaps he thought to try for an heir (Louisa was young enough), or perhaps it was simply so that Louisa, as his widow, would be able to continue the licence.

> Lot 2.—All that old-established and well-accustomed FREEHOLD INN, known as the "HAUNCH OF VENISON," situate in Minster-street, opposite the Poultry-cross, now and for many years past in the occupation of Mr. Firmin Potto, on a Lease expiring at Lady Day, 1876, at a rental of £26 per annum—Tenant doing inside and the Landlord outside repairs.—Land Tax £1 6s. 3d. per annum.

In 1874 Henry Cooper, the owner of the freehold of the Haunch of Venison died, and his executors put the Inn up for sale. It is possible that Firmin Potto already knew in advance that this was going to happen, because Cooper was old with no children. At any rate, he went to the auction and bought the freehold, making a new will. In it he left the Haunch of Venison and the wholesale business to Louisa for her lifetime, and then to his niece Eliza Perry Johnson, for her lifetime, and then to her son Samuel Potto Johnson. Samuel would write to Firmin Bradbeer later, 'it was my uncle's intention that the Haunch of Venison should stay forever in our family' – which is certainly an indication of how much he had loved the place, and that he had been happy living there. One feels that he knew that Louisa appreciated it too, and would look after it.

Firmin Potto died in 1875, just two years after his wedding, and a year after buying the Haunch. His death certificate states that he died of 'general decay'. He was buried in St Thomas's churchyard. He left £100 to Salisbury Infirmary.

In support of the theories that the marriage between Louisa Bradbeer was to do with continuing the business, rather than passion, and was also a last minute attempt to produce an heir – both are borne out by Mr Potto's will. On the one hand he left practical things to Louisa (and £500 cash), but sentimental and personal things like 'watches, rings, jewellery, chains, trinkets and books', together with photographs and likenesses, went to his niece. However, the relationship was sexual because Firmin made provision for any children that the couple might have. He made his will in October, and was dead the following January.

Louisa had to pay an annual peppercorn rent of £2 per year for the Haunch of Venison, to Eliza, whose property it would become. Eliza Perry Johnson was also to receive the freehold of the shoe shop in Minster Street – then occupied by Bartlett (which would go to William Potto's eldest granddaughter, Rose Morton, after her death.) Eliza received freehold 'messuage, tenement and cottages in Nayland Suffolk'. Two freehold pieces of land in Boxted, Essex were to go to Eliza's mother, Mary Stow, even though they were occupied by Eliza's husband, Charles – but then to Eliza.

Firmin Potto also left 'hereditaments and freehold premises at Winsor, Eling, Hampshire (near Southampton) to his friend William Davies, in trust for his son Charles Davies. it is interesting to see that besides his brother, Thomas, and cousin Firmin, he left money to Dr Edward Young (then, Salisbury's coroner), and to 'my friend, Charles Cheater', a relation of his first wife.

Curiously, Firmin left sums of money to three women and their granddaughter and daughters. One, Mary Lock, was a widow who ran the Rifleman's Arms in London Road. Mary had grown up on the Clarendon estate, married a labourer and was later housekeeper at the Manor House, and there is nothing to suggest that her husband ran a pub. Another woman was Emily Deller, daughter of a man who was once the beadle for the corporation of St Thomas's. Emily had never married, but is on the 1871 census at the Queens Arms in Ivy Street, as a visitor, 'in charge of inn', for which the Hibberd family held the licence – but Emily was still there four years later. Normally, single women would not be granted a licence to sell alcohol unless they carried on the business from a husband or father, but Firmin Potto was the chairman of Salisbury's Licenced Victuallers Association, and it is my opinion that he helped these ladies, who were each around ten years younger than him. Alas, the third woman's name is illegible on the transcript of the will. It also puts a question mark over how the young widow, Eliza Howell, really became landlady of the Bull, in Fisherton Street. Since Eliza had remarried, she didn't receive a bequest, and neither did her daughter, Eliza Ponting.

The rest of Firmin Potto's wealth was to be invested by the trustees in shares, stocks, and securities in Britain, Ireland, India and the colonies, to produce an income. If there were no last-minute children for Mr Potto, then £500 of the money invested was to be earmarked for Elizabeth Morten, but she could not cash it in. The money was eventually shared between her descendants, but they were then so numerous that the money was paltry."

P is for Potto, Thomas

Thomas Pitts Potto was born in 1806 in Nayland, Suffolk, the youngest son of William Marrows Potto, a currier from Witham, Essex, and Mary Pitts Perry, from the same place. He was born in the reign of George III, lived through the Regency, and the reigns of George IV, and William IV, before arriving in Salisbury at the beginning of the Victorian era.

Thomas had an elder sister, Mary who married a Henry Stow, and stayed in the Essex/Suffolk area, and whose daughter, Eliza Perry Stow, and grandson, Samuel Potto Johnson, would each eventually inherit the Haunch of Venison pub. His elder brothers were William, who ran various Salisbury inns, and Firmin, who was a wine and spirit dealer based at the Haunch of Venison of which he was first Tennant, and then owner.

William Marrows Potto's job was the specialist finishing of leather, after it had been tanned, which meant that he had to make sure that it was a uniform thickness, supple, waterproof, coloured, and matt or shiny as required. He had had a shop in Nayland selling finished leather goods, but returned to Witham, and then followed his son William to Salisbury, where William had become very successful after marrying the daughter of the landlady of the Wheatsheaf, in Fish Row.

In 1838, William Marrows Potto died, and the announcement in the *Salisbury Journal* mentions that he was the father of only 'William and Firmin Potto of this city', indicating that Thomas had yet to move to Salisbury, and that he followed his brothers to Wiltshire only after his father had died. Like his brother, Firmin, Thomas began life in Salisbury as a boot and shoe maker – a trade that they had almost certainly learned at their father's shop.

It is tempting to speculate on the reason that Firmin Potto might have persuaded Thomas to relocate to Salisbury, and that is so that he might marry a suitable woman of whom Firmin approved, and produce a Potto heir. Brother William had gone bankrupt the same year, and there is evidence that Firmin did not trust his elder brother, nor his daughter, with money.

Thomas appears on the 1841 census, aged 30, living at the Haunch of Venison with his brother Firmin, and sister-in-law Maria – and their niece, Eliza Perry Stow, who was then only 11. Firmin and Maria had no children of their own. Thomas's occupation isn't given, but he is in a Trade Directory for 1842, as a boot and shoe maker in Minster Street. Since Firmin Potto had bought Arneys Boot and shoe business in Minster Street back in 1832, one imagines that Thomas is trading out of that address.

Thomas evidently didn't like the boot and shoe business, and he soon set himself up as a grocer in Salisbury High Street, although Firmin kept the shoe business on until 1856. The grocer's shop stood on the corner of High Street and New Street, and opposite Mitre House, which was a corset shop when Thomas was there (*Salisbury Journal*, 1847), run by Mr Naish, who moved out in 1855. In trade directories Thomas is sometimes 'Grocer and Cheesemonger'. He lived above the shop.

Thomas Potto married Anne Rooke in 1847. She was the daughter of a local draper, and the pair were both 41 by then, and never had children. Neither William nor Firmin Potto signed the Wedding Certificate as witnesses.

In 1855, along with other shopkeepers in the city, he placed a joint plea to the mayor, to have all shops closed on Boxing Day.

In January 1859, and 1862, Thomas Pitts Potto (he seems to have often used the 'Pitts'), served on the Grand Jury at the Quarter

Sessions before the Wiltshire Assizes in the Guildhall (his brothers also served on Grand Juries). The qualifications to serve on the Grand Jury have been described as generally consisting of 'gentlemen of high standing in the County'. The Grand Jury, who could be 'no less than 14 and no more than 23', had to do their own enquiry to decide whether there were sufficient grounds to put the accused on trial before a Petty Jury, or not – returning a verdict of 'True Bill' if so, or throwing the case out, if not. It was a big responsibility at the time, since the death penalty was still used. The Grand Jury was abolished in England in 1948.

Incidentally, the Court, whilst lamenting the recent death of Prince Albert, were most concerned as to how Queen

Thomas Potto and Anne Rooke
© Salisbury Museum

Victoria was going to cope as a single mother, given that her eldest son (the future Edward VII) was about to inherit a good deal of wealth when he was 'just at an age when he might either go right or go wrong'; the Court's concerns with teenage delinquents evidently didn't exclude the highest in the land.

22, HIGH-STREET, SALISBURY.

T. P. POTTO, in returning thanks to his numerous Friends for the very liberal support he has received during the last three years, takes this opportunity to inform them, that he has now a full supply of the NEW SEASON'S TEAS, of the choicest description, which will be found worthy of notice. 3 lb. Bags at wholesale prices, for cash.

A well-selected Stock of prime CHEDDAR and other CHEESE constantly on sale.   [3081]

Salisbury Cheese Market – is this Thomas Potto? © *Salisbury Museum*

Thomas donated 10s to the fund for a new school in St Thomas's ward, in 1860. His grocer's shop is still listed as being in the High Street in 1863, and Thomas and Anne were still living above it.

The photograph on the opposite page was taken in the 1860s, and before 1868. The whole picture shows the three Potto brothers with two of their wives.

Like William and Firmin, Thomas was a member of the Modern Order of Foresters, a Friendly Society whose parent lodge was at the Ship, whilst William Potto had it, but then moved with him to the King's Arms in St John's Street. William was the Treasurer.

Thomas decided not to vote in the by-election of 1869. Both his brothers were listed in the newspaper as voting Tory; M.P.s were not voted by secret ballot. It would be lovely to know why Thomas didn't think that any of the candidates were good enough.

By 1871, the Pottos were comfortably enough off to have moved to a house in Harcourt Terrace, where they lived with a servant, until their deaths in 1886. The houses were fairly grand, and very comfortable, being new at the time. By now in their 60s, the stairs at the Grocery shop must have been getting rather much. Having no children, the contents of their home were auctioned off at their death, and the newspaper description of the sale contents gives an idea of just how comfortably the Pottos lived. However, one shouldn't imagine that this lifestyle came from only the grocer's shop; Firmin Potto had become wealthy by buying shares and owning property, as well as his successful wholesale business. It is highly probable that he advised Thomas Potto on investing money as well.

Here are two advertisements for the Sale. The second advertisement has blurred ink, but I think that it is worth me copying it out as it gives us a glimpse of the Pottos tastes and lifestyle. I believe that Anne's relative, 'Miss Rooke' mentioned in the cutting, had a Music Shop in Catherine Street.

38, HARCOURT-TERRACE, SALISBURY.
THURSDAY, SEPTEMBER 2nd, 1886.

DEAR & WOOLLEY are instructed by the Exors, of the late Mr. T. P. Potto, deceased, to SELL by AUCTION, on the Premises, on THURSDAY, September 2nd, 1886, the HOUSEHOLD FURNITURE AND EFFECTS, comprising the Furnish of DINING, DRAWING, and Four BEDROOMS, and the usual Kitchen Requisites, together with a few MUSICAL INSTRUMENTS, late the property of Miss Rooke, deceased.   [2454

38, Harcourt terrace, Fisherton, Salisbury
Thursday, September 2nd, 1886

Dear & Wooley are instructed by the Excors. Of the late Mrs T. P. Potto, deceased, to SELL by Auction, on the premises, on Thursday September 2nd 1886, the whole of the

HOUSEHOLD FURNITURE, SILVER AND ELECTROPLATE, CHINA, GLASS, LINEN, AND OTHER EFFECTS, comprising:

In the DINING ROOM – Tapestry Carpet, Mahogany Sideboard, three-corner Whatnots, Mahogany Chiffonier, mahogany-framed Easy Chair, cane Chairs, mahogany two-flap table, Work Table, Mantel Glass in gilt frames, Piano in rosewood case by Ward, Oil Paintings, and engravings including
7 PROOF ENGRAVINGS BY HOGARTH

In the DRAWING ROOM – Brussels Carpet, skin Hearthrug, walnut inlaid centre table on carved pillar and claws, Fender and Fire Irons. Walnut framed Easy Chairs. Couch and six chairs to match covered in maroon Rep. Walnut Davenport Mantel Glass in gilt frame. Handsome Ormolu Timepiece under glass dome. Occasional table. China and Terra-cotta ornaments. five Tier mahogany Whatnot. ENGRAVINGS AND OIL PAINTINGS.

The SILVER consists of Gravy, Table, Tea and Salt spoons, Sugar tongs, Fish Carver, etc. The Plated Goods – salver, Teapot and German Silver Forks.

Did this stags head come from the sale at Harcourt Terrace? © Baptiste Vitorino

In the Bedrooms – Painted and mahogany half tester Bedsteads, Feather Beds, Bolsters and Pillows, Straw Paillasses, Flock Mattresses, Carpets, Fenders, cane-seat and rush seat chairs, Mahogany and painted Washstands and Drawing Tables. Mahogany and marble top washstands. mahogany and painted Chests of Drawers. Mahogany swing glasses, mahogany Night Commode. Walnut framed Easy Chair, Mantel Glass, Pictures, Blankets, and the Linen.

In the HALL and LANDING – Hall Clock in Oak case, Stair Carpet, cocoa mats, Iron Umbrella Stand, **Two pairs of Antlers, Two Stags Heads,** Weather Glass by Hyde, etc., together with the usual KITCHEN UTENSILS and a few OUTDOOR EFFECTS. Also, the Property of the late Miss Rooke, a few MUSICAL INSTRUMENTS Including violins, Flageolets, Flutes, Brass Trombone, Harmonium in Walnut Case by Hillier.

Sale to commence at 12.30 o'clock
Catalogue at the Auctioneers, Market Place, Salisbury

That was the life of Thomas and Anne Potto sold up in an afternoon. The pair died both aged 77, with Anne following Thomas by only a few months. But I can't help wondering . . . Did their sister-in law Louisa Potto, landlady of the Haunch of Venison, carry off those Antlers and Stags Heads back to the Haunch, where they can still be seen? It would be lovely to think so.

P is for Potto Johnson

Samuel Potto Johnson was an Ipswich cattle dealer who inherited the Haunch of Venison from his mother, Eliza, who was the daughter of Firmin Potto's elder sister, Mary. He was the owner of the Haunch of Venison for most of the time that Firmin Bradbeer was landlord, eventually selling it in old age to Simonds Brewery (who bought it at auction), who already held the licence for the premises.

Samuel had a cordial relationship with Firmin Bradbeer, by letter, and they would exchange family photos. He probably only came once to Salisbury, to see his property (he employed an agent, in Salisbury Close) but he liked to remind Firmin Bradbeer that various friends of his from Suffolk would visit the Haunch anonymously, when in Salisbury, and report back to him.

P is for Poultry Cross

The Poultry Cross was built around 1450, and the monument and the old Inn have therefore always known each other. The Poultry cross

19ᵗʰ Century engraving of the Poultry Cross

was one of four market crosses, and fruit and vegetables were sold there as well as poultry (it was at the end of Butchers Row, so selling a type of meat appears logical). The Poultry Cross is also known as Green Crosse, and Butter Crosse in the Parish Rates books.

The image in the picture shows the Poultry Cross in the early 19th century, when Mr Potto was landlord. It had been greatly altered in the 18th century – like the frontage of the Haunch of Venison. It was restored to its present gothic looking appearance in 1852/54. In 2022, as I write, the Poultry Cross is braced by scaffolding after a drunk driver pursued by Police drove into it, causing structural damage.

P is for Powell

John Powell (the elder) bought the building which is now the Haunch of Venison, from Walter and Katherine Hammond in 1685. They had changed their minds about selling to him, initially, and Powell was obliged to take them to court for a breach of promise concerning the building. The Hammonds did not live in Salisbury, and presumably had leased the building; Powell told the Court that he was being kept out of the building which he considered legally his by contract, although he had not yet paid for it.

This branch of the Powell family had moved to Salisbury from Wales not long before buying the Haunch. They were very wealthy and set about amassing a good deal of land and property in Wiltshire, although their town house was in Castle Street.

John Powell (the younger) left the Haunch of Venison in his will to his wife, for her life, and then to his own son, Alexander, 'all my messuage with appurtenances near or against the Poultry Cross expectant upon a term of years determinable upon the death of

Memorial to Sir Alexander Powell

John Godfrey, (Cook?)'. The rent from it was to be saved and £100 of it paid to Alexander's sister, Catherine, within two months of Alexander inheriting the building. Two of John's other tenements, in Brown Street, were in the occupation of members of the Fawconer family. The will is dated 1712 (and is available on Ancestry).

John died in 1735, and is buried inside St Thomas's Church, and Alexander inherited numerous estates and property. Alexander was knighted. He married three times, probably because his wives died in childbirth, which was common at the time. He was 'Deputy Recorder of the Borough', according to the History of Parliament website, and stood unsuccessfully as M.P. for Salisbury (his grandson would become the M.P. for Downton). Besides the house in Castle Street, he also had Hurdcott House, at Barford St Martin, near Wilton.

It was Sir Alexander Powell who sold the freehold of the Haunch to Samuel Fawconer (before 1741), according to a later letter to the Fawconers' solicitor (with the Haunch of Venison records at the Wiltshire History Centre). The writer asserts that it was only the intention of Alexander to let Samuel Fawconer have the building 'commonly known or called by the name of the Haunch of Venison' for his lifetime, and Alexander had made his will in 1765, leaving it to his wife and heirs. Sir Alexander's will can also be read on the Ancestry site, but he had so much property that he didn't list it individually.   More about the dispute between the Powells and Fawconers is under F.

The author outside the Haunch of Venison to commemorate the Platinum Jubilee of Queen Elizabeth II

Q is for Queen

2022 saw the Platinum Jubilee of Queen Elizabeth II. On Thursday June the 2nd (the first day of the celebrations), I went to Haunch of Venison to record the day. Above me flies the Union Jack, and behind me the flag for the Armed Forces. It's moving to think on how many Kings and Queens the Haunch has seen come and go.

R is for RAF

During World War I, Firmin Bradbeer was a member of the RFC and then the RAF, and the Haunch of Venison became a pub frequented by those brave lads, who had a romantic aura around them due to the newness of flying and the high death rate (even in the 1920s, there is scarcely a year where the *Salisbury Journal* doesn't report a flying accident at local airfields such as Old Sarum, with the victims all in their early 20s).

The Visitors Book of the Haunch of Venison (in Salisbury Museum) has many entries during World War I for members of the RFC, and then the RAF.

Firmin Bradbeer became a member of the RFC and then RAF, service number 283350. He was a 'Disciplinarian', and finished the war based in Hampshire. This would begin a tradition of the Haunch of Venison linked to the RAF, which would last decades. A Discipinarian was an older man who was assigned to the RAF to keep discipline, take drills, impose punishments etc. The

Firmin Bradbeer in uniform
© Salisbury Museum

reason was that most of the pilots were very young (many of those who risked their lives were too young to vote), and officers became increasingly younger as the war progressed and they replaced men who were killed. Therefore, older men were drafted in from the Army (and Firmin was a member of the Territorial Army, as the Volunteers had become). He would stay on an extra year after the war was ended.

Mr Bradbeer must have been well liked by the young men, because they would not have flocked to his pub had they not appreciated him. They continued to drink in the Haunch of Venison between the wars, because in his song, the 'Firm Inn', written circa 1920, he mentions that they affected french expressions "Every 'R.A.F'. boy speaketh Francais | Little Mick, | Every 'night night' always 'bon soir', |Little Mick.'

The RAF lads evidently became the social set of Dolly Bradbeer (according to a letter written by Marjorie Bradbeer, now in Salisbury Museum archives). Marjorie was ten years younger than Dolly, but when she got her first job, at the Orchard Hotel near Ruislip, it was a mile from RAF Northolt, and frequented by the pilots (which may, or may not, be a coincidence).

The Haunch's association with the RAF continued into World War II, when Dolly married Captain Jack Edwardes (he was actually part of Coastal Command, stationed in Bristol). Jack eventually became Landlord of the Haunch of Venison, although Dolly held the Licence. They ran the RAF Benevolent Association in Salisbury (Jack was also on the National Committee, and later toured the Country, organising and performing in fundraising events).

Dolly Bradbeer was Chairman of the Ladies section of the RAF Benevolent fund, and organised a children's party at the Assembly Rooms in Salisbury for children of RAF war veterans, and those who had lost their fathers. She helped Jack organise the 1st Battle of Britain commemorations in Salisbury.

Although the Bradbeers had left the Haunch of Venison by the 1950s, an ex-RAF officer from Portsmouth had arrived in Salisbury and headed to the Haunch of Venison to borrow money from the landlord, Mr Bennett, in a scam. He probably headed to the Haunch as he thought that it would be the very place to receive a welcome and sympathy.

R is for Rayner
Louise Rayner was a Victorian female artist working in the late 19th century. She visited, and did a series of pictures of, Salisbury. In one of the pictures, we can recognise the merchant's house and the Haunch of Venison. The picture is not accurate however, because far from being a hairdresser, the next door was already Carters the watchmakers. The Haunch of Venison was in the hands of the Potto family, and would not have clothes hanging from the frontage. There are no traces of a pub called the Sun in Minster Street (although there was one at the other end of Castle Street).

Despite the inaccuracies though, the picture gives a good idea of the cobbled street, the buildings, and clothes worn.

The Haunch of Venison by Louise Rayner

R is for Redgrave

The Haunch of Venison was always a favourite pub for performers to visit, not only because of its antiquity and fine dining, but its proximity to Salisbury Playhouse and the City Hall. 'We got so used to seeing famous faces that nobody took any notice,' says Les Mitchell, 'and they liked that'. Consequently, there aren't many photographs of celebrities at the Haunch, but Sir Michael Redgrave's visit did make the newspapers, as he was very famous at the time, and the Haunch had a high reputation.

R is for rooms

In 1911 Eliza Johnson was dead (Firmin Potto's niece) and her son, Samuel Potto Johnson, became the owner of the Haunch of Venison. Firmin Bradbeer had to furnish Mr Johnson with an

Sir Michael Redgrave photographed at the "Haunch of Venison" in Salisbury, with the Manager, Mr. Ian Bennett, after he had lunched and dined there recently

Sir Michael Redgrave with landlord Ian Bennett ©The Simmonds Family

inventory of fixtures and fittings at the Haunch, which is illuminating – or not – because much of the inventory details the gas lighting (which was still in place) and the electric lighting. Firmin Bradbeer was obliged to regularly paint the building, inside and outside with oil and white lead paint.

In 1930 Firmin Bradbeer signed an agreement for Simonds brewery to take over the licence for the premises. Together with Frederick Simonds, Mr Bradbeer visited each room to make an inventory of the landlord's fixtures and fittings, which went with the pub. The 1911 inventory is in Wiltshire & Swindon History Centre and the 1930 inventory is in Salisbury Museum. Let's take a look at the different rooms in the Haunch, and both inventories, and pull out some interesting bits:

Smoke Room (House of Lords):

In 1911 there were '3 antique lantern shaped electric pendant lights' (with three switches controlling them, remotely, from the bar). There was a 'stained glass dwarf lettered blind to window'. There was a 'perforated gauze short blind'. Most astonishingly there was a 'striped canvas outside blind'. It might be because of the outside yard, which the Haunch then had.

In 1930 The room is described without the furniture or pictures, and is almost exactly as today. However, there were '4 electric bell pushes with brass plates. It would seem that customers could summon a waiter without leaving the room, or having to wait. There were folding shutters to the window.

The Grill Room (lower restaurant)
In 1911 there were three bevelled glass panels above the overmantel, and eight enamelled white picture rails. The room then had curtains and two wooden shelves. There were two wooden benches, one of which is clearly the one now in the Lords, and the other still in place.

Second Floor (now private)
Store cupboard.

Dining Room
A smaller dining room was actually on the second floor (the upper dining room was not part of the Haunch at this time, and was part of the Bradbeers' private living accommodation, rented independently from Carters. The connecting door was not opened until 1950). The small dining room had two folding metal screens. It had a gas fire with a circular mirror above it. Like the Lords, it had a bell push to call the

The room that was once used as a small dining room on the second floor
© Salisbury Museum

waiter. There was a 'service shelf', from where to serve the food carried up from below. The room was previously advertised as a 'private' dining room, and had been part of previous landlords' living accommodation.

Bedroom

The bedrooms still had brass gas brackets (with incandescent burners and smoke consumers, and engraved globes) as well as electric brackets, in 1911. There were figured spring roller sun blinds in every room.

There was a bedroom on this floor which was rented to guests as an hotel room. It had obviously also been living accommodation for the previous landlords. It had a moulded picture rail, and a large cupboard (the word 'sheets' is written in pencil).

Bathroom

This had a 'body bath' and a pedestal toilet (the pan cracked in two places, has a line through it, suggesting that it was repaired). It had a wooden towel roller, and a plated towel airer, for two towels. 'Hot linen cupboard' is crossed out. There was a 4' 6' white painted wardrobe with sliding doors, and two drawers under it. It had almost certainly been another bedroom, when houses did not have bathrooms, but rather wash stands in the bedrooms.

Landing and stairs to first floor

Brass plate on bathroom door is crossed out. The stair to the dining room has a 'brass nose'.

Landing and stairs to Ground Floor
The Passage top of stairs adjoining smoking room

'Antique oak door opening onto right of way'. I have been told that, when the Gents toilets were built, skeletons were discovered in the foundations (I have not been able to verify this), indicating that the graveyard came right up to the back of the Haunch, and one could walk over to St Thomas's church from there. There was an outside urinal at this time, and nothing for the ladies! They would have needed to go to the second floor. Brass nosings to well mat. 5 iron nosings to stair to bar. Iron extending gate with fitting. The stairs to the bar (and thence to the cellar) could be locked. Perhaps the Landlord did not trust those hotel guests not to nip down for a nightcap after dark!

Office

This was where the Ladies' loos are today. It contained a '3 ft. 6 ins. front fall oak desk' (a 'bureau'?). It had a 2 ft. cupboard under it, with folding doors. There was also a 3 ft. chair under the window, with drawers under it. There was a 'stained oak matchboard dado'. It must have been from here that the Haunch of Venison business was conducted.

Service Room First Floor (the Kitchen)

In 1911 this was known as the 'grill room'. It had a 'new Silver Grill' which had green glazed tiles around it and a hot plate. A portable boiler by Wiltons of Salisbury with piping to the chimney. There was also hot water piping to the bath, the scullery, the bar, and backyard. A Eureka gas stove on a stone platform, with brass taps and fittings. An iron corner bracket support for a stock pot, and a 4 ft. 6 ins. painted dresser. There was a scullery leading off the kitchen, with another dresser, a pot shelf, and a deal plate rack.

This is the kitchen in 1930, and is perhaps the most interesting: 4ft 2 tier gas griller by John Wright & Co, Birmingham; 3ft New Eureka Gas Cooker, seven taps; 2ft 4' Wrights Eureka New World Gas Cooker, seven taps; White rose Domestic Boiler and fittings in recess. It had two sinks (one of them stained), and both an electric fan and extractor. There were iron hoods over the cookers and grill. There was a service hatch, and a wooden towel roller on the door.

The Bar

The bar would appear to be almost exactly as it is today, except there was part of a 'smoke jack' conserved on the wall. Alas! Where did it go?

Ladies Bar

This is the Horse Box. It was almost the same, except that it had a 'glazed cupboard'.

Back of Bar

In 1911 the bar was new, and the description is too long to put here in its entirety. What leaps out as being different, are the white glazed tile flooring behind the bar, and the white glazed tiles to the surround of a gas stove, which had a detachable white tile top. The counter next to the Horse Box also had a pewter top with the sides and floor being lined with white glazed tiles. There were pewter drainers and beer drips, and taps were of brass or china. There were sliding mirrored drawers and mirrored backs to the shelves, and a white glazed sink. There was a 'pillar burner'. The cellar had a panelled door, leading to it, although the sides were detachable. There were two telescopic wrought iron gates to enclose the bar.

S is for Salisbury & Districts Trades Union Council

The research for this book has repeatedly thrown up the fact that the Haunch of Venison has always been part of the social history of Salisbury, and, in the early part of the 20th century at least, part of Salisbury's political history (bearing in mind that its two main bars are nicknamed the 'House of Commons' and 'House of Lords'). I am indebted to our Mayor of Salisbury (2022), Tom Corbin, for the following information: 'It is believed that the decision to create "Salisbury and District Trades and Labour Council" had come about following a meeting of like-minded workers in the Haunch of Venison. (Sleeping on it and looking at the carefully written pages that form the preliminary meeting 31st March 1914 there would most likely to have been a few such informal meetings to get to this point).'

The Mayor of Salisbury Tom Corbin in 2022 © Salisbury Newspapers

According to Alan Clinton, and his work *Trade Councils During the First World War*, it was during this period that the Labour Movement gained significance, and was consulted with, as never before. In fact, one might say that different political sides pulled together when faced with a common enemy in 1914. (The first local Labour Party was set up in Salisbury in 1922, from Tom Corbin's research).

There were four bodies represented at the first meeting of

the Trades and Labour Council in Salisbury. It is very interesting to consider that the landlord of the Haunch of Venison was that arch-Conservative Firmin Bradbeer, in 1914, and to realise that the pub was surely an inclusive place of lively political debate − continuing more formal discussions from Salisbury Parliament debating society.

Tom Corbin says: 'We celebrated our 100th anniversary with a march through Salisbury led by Casa-de-Samba with Union banners and flags flying, members and family paraded from the Boat House down Castle Street through Blue Boar Row, Brown Street, the Canal and onto Fisherton Street, culminating in ending at the Fisherton Street Working Men's Club for drink, food speeches and a look back at 100 years.

However before setting off on the march and constrained by venue size, the main active members of S&DTUC along with special guests South West TUC Regional Organiser Nigel Costly, ASLEF National Organiser Simon Weller, and South West MEP Clare Moody joined in a celebratory drink at the Haunch of Venison, November 2014. We occupied the largest room upstairs. Having shuffled tables and chairs to sit as a large round table we all felt the effect of the extremely uneven floor!'

S is for Samoilova

Anastasia Samoilova, her husband Ilya Klekovkin, and Anastasia's sister, Anna Samoilova took over the tenancy of the Haunch of Venison, from Alex Marshall, in the summer of 2015.

Says Anastasia, 'I met Ilya in school whilst training to be a journalist − we were both on the same course. He followed me to the USA, and then to Ireland where I was studying Business and Marketing. Any spare time that we had was visiting old places − castles, and old houses and pubs. We loved the historical places'.

Anastasia continues, 'I am very close to my sister, and she has been living in the West of England since she was 17. We moved to the area to be closer to her. We were looking for a pub to run − we searched for over a year − and it was Ilya who first visited the Haunch of Venison, and he loved it straight away. He came back excited and told me 'You have to see this place!' He knew I would love it! It has so much history'.

I was having lunch with Anastasia in the House of Lords on a quiet Wednesday in May 2022. Outside, the sun had come out after the rain, and lit up the graveyard behind us; the light looked blinding from inside the darkened – wood – panelled, tiny, smoking room. Anastasia was remembering her first days at the Haunch: 'I was seven months pregnant, so it was Anna and Ilya who were Front of House. We said, 'whatever happens we will always be all three of us to hold this licence'.

Anastasia and Ilya decided not to move into the building, 'We can live there, if we want, but we personally think that to live above the work is not a good thing. We want a break. We don't want to be tired of the place, we want to be inspired' (Anna already had a home).

Anna was popular with customers straight away, but had a break to have a baby 'She still comes back, at least once a week.' (Said one local – actually, my husband – 'Anna is a cracker!').

'The place is very surprising. Customers find it surprising – especially foreign customers. A lot of places look old from the outside, but then you go in the furniture is modern. Here it is old. We want to keep it like that. We look at old pictures (of the Haunch) and we try and source things to put it back as it was. We found things in the attic – we found the sign in the downstairs bar pointing to the restaurant? We didn't know where it went. Then a lady was so kind to send us a photo in the post – we don't know her name – we saw where the sign hung, and we put it back where it used to be'. She gave a tinkling laugh, 'That is the first thing we did.'

Some noise floated up from the House of Commons – I could hear Tallulah serving some customers from behind the bar; the clink of pint glasses on the pewter bar top, and regular, Vince, regaling an innocent tourist with tall stories about the old pub.

Anastasia went on, 'If we see pictures, of the chairs that used to be upstairs, for example, I send them to an antique specialist. If he finds any matching, for sale, he calls us up, and I buy them straight away. I'm slowly replacing all the chairs – there are still some modern ones left upstairs, but not many'.

I could sense the ghosts of generations of Pottos and Bradbeers nodding their heads in approval. Perhaps that's why Anastasia feels only peacefulness in the old building, 'I love being alone here', she'd told me on a previous visit, 'My favourite time is early in the morning, before the staff arrive. It is so quiet. Tranquil.' We'd commented, then, that the building seems to love the people who love it. 'If the staff don't like it and find it too spooky and creaky, they don't stay long.'

The current staff do call the staffroom upstairs 'the Spooky Room'. One of them told me, good humouredly, 'We tidy it, but the next day it is always messy the same'.

I was appreciative of how much Anastasia, Ilya, and Anna love the Haunch of Venison; It is not just a pub to them, 'We felt really sad when we saw the photos of the things that belonged to the Haunch and now everything is gone?' She was getting heated, 'We didn't want to buy new chairs that came from the factory – they just don't belong here!'. They're making an inventory and writing down everything that is in the pub, to go with the lease, so that the contents will always stay part of the building. 'It's a heritage! We gave the list of everything here to the heritage people so that it cannot be removed' She is worried about changeovers between pub companies and breweries, as much as future landlords and managers changing things.

'There is a candelabra which we found upstairs, and we have it to show people who are interested'. I wondered who had dined by its candle light in the past – flickering flames casting shadows in a draughty room.

Of course, it is the antiquated look to the interiors that ensure that visitors to Salisbury will always seek out the Haunch of Venison, so Anastasia is far seeing. And for all that, the place doesn't feel like a museum when it's heaving on a Saturday night, and the Lords is filled with lively conversation between locals and tourists coming together – and even having a sing song!

Richard popped in to say something to Anastasia, whilst I was with her, and it was nice to see a familiar face from a few years ago. Richard shares Front of House with Nick. Richard has just returned to the Haunch, replacing Albert Paz, who is from Barcelona, and did the job between 2019-2022 (Albert left to complete his Masters). Richard

Albert Paz

and Nick, like Albert, are used to coping with the high spirits of some of their customers. Albert had told me:

'One evening, about ten came in, all together; a small place, and a big group. They were in the House of Commons. They saw the 'Horse Box', started chatting with the locals, and they got up a bet about 'how many drinkers could you fit into the 'Horse Box'? Well, the ten people went in – and then they started gesturing and inviting in visiting tourists – there were so many that glasses were being smashed. There were 27 in the end! It was hysterical! It was so funny! – but it was people drinking in a 'happy' way. The tourists were mixing with locals and it was a happy time'.

You have to go through the bar to reach the restaurant upstairs, something that has always been, although at different periods the entrance through the secret bar has been used.

'It's a difficult balance getting both the bar and the restaurant to work together', says Anastasia. 'Sometimes people who have booked and don't know the place, come in and they are very surprised at the atmosphere downstairs . . . they don't know what to expect for the restaurant . . .'

My mind went back to Frogg Moody's mother visiting, dressed up, for special occasions, many decades ago, and much later making a comment to me about the restaurant and the bar being 'two different worlds'; to my mind, it has always added to the quirkiness of the place – it's folkloric.

'We'd like to open the other entrance – with the small bar – to the restaurant', said Anastasia, 'it's a lot of work; but we've planned it for a long time. Things got in the way, but hopefully we can still do it'.

In the meantime, diners who arrive early for their bookings can always have a pre-lunch tipple with the pub's locals, who enjoy telling them all about Churchill meeting with Eisenhower, the Hand, and the resident ghosts. However, tourists should be warned: 'The locals love spinning stories: "The beam you see there was once part of the Titanic," Bob and Dennis tell passing foreign visitors (which, of course, it wasn't)', Albert once told me.

I always drink in the House of Lords, so I was asking Albert about the regulars who sit, where the regulars have always sat, lined up on Death Row; it has never worried most of them (although you would not catch Les Mitchell sitting there).

'One of the regulars is called Florida. He is proud to say that

Regulars Dennis and Nigel

he is the only person named Florida in the UK – he's a plaster boarder. He was there all the time that I was there. Then there is John – 'Long John' – an ex-RAF man.'

One of the locals, Nigel, popped his head around the door of the Lords to greet Anastasia, whilst we were there; Everybody knows her, although she's usually upstairs in the office, and doesn't serve behind the bar. I was sorry not to see Jez.

'There were loads of American tourists before Covid struck Salisbury in 2020. They are interested in Eisenhower and Churchill, every time. It was all really, really, funny…we could all have a good laugh together,' Albert had said.

It seems that if you are a tourist and enjoy meeting Salisbury residents, then the Haunch of Venison is the place for you. I mused on the fact that, if I were visiting another country, I should love to find a friendly local hostelry where the regulars would soon give me a welcome and get chatting. It has conserved, along with its antique décor, the atmosphere of a good old fashioned English boozer that is rare in our day – and which is probably like marmite to some visitors who have come to dine. The pub is listed as a 'Community Asset', so that the building cannot be used for a different purpose.

Whisky lovers are in for a treat; Ilya is a specialist and has whisky from the 'four corners' of Scotland: Highland (Clynelish), Lowland (GlenKinchie), Speyside (Cardhu) and Isle of Islay (Caol Ila). There are 130 different types of Malt according to the CAMRA website. Ilya collects whisky from all over the world, 'We even have Japanese whisky. People come to the Haunch just to try the whiskies.' And there was me thinking that it was for the beers from Hopback and Downton Brewery.

By now, Anastasia was looking askance as I dipped my chunky chips into the remains of my duck liver pate. The chips are my favourite, by the way, and are hand-cut from flavoursome potatoes. She was eating calamari and sweet potatoes.

She told me about the floors in the dining room. They currently have bare boards (which is the fashion in 2022) 'The lower dining room is flat enough, but the boards in the big room are totally uneven. That is why light chairs are not good, it needs heavy chairs'.

I remembered Bill Jakeman's sadness that the red Wilton carpets had gone, which had made it such a luxurious place, and Val Gainsford's shock at arriving at work one day (she worked for Tony Leroy, and Rupert Wilcox had just taken over the restaurant), to find that the carpet had been removed.

'Most of the people we talk to are against the carpet, because they would like to see the original wooden floors', says Anastasia 'here, we would have to have to get permission to put a carpet down.' It would make for an interesting discussion with a conservationist, because this author would guess that none of the former inhabitants lived with bare floorboards (they might have had tiles or rugs) upstairs until the 1990s, when that look became fashionable. I worry that the constant footsteps will eventually wear the floorboards out. 'It is the original floor and we cannot do anything about it', was the reply, and the majority of diners would doubtlessly agree.

The big restaurant room does not belong to the Haunch of Venison (as part of the merchant's house, it is part of Carters), and is leased. 'The agreement is between them and the Brewery' says Anastasia, 'and we cannot see what Carters and the Brewery have agreed about that room – they are separate from us. It is really a third-party agreement'. It is an agreement begun in the time of Firmin Bradbeer with Carters, and taken over by Simonds.

One of the toughest challenges for Anastasia, Ilya and Anna, when they first took over, was to get the restaurant up and working again. 'We had regulars drinking, and tourists coming in for a picture, but that was about it,' she said. I recalled a time, just before she arrived, when I went to the Haunch for a birthday lunch; it was raining outside, and my husband and I sat alone in an empty, cold, room. I can't remember what we ate. 'I think that they wanted to do fine dining, because there were white tablecloths and everything, but actually when you ate the food, it doesn't match the surroundings?'

Something had clearly happened since 'Road Trip's' (website Road Trip, A Sales Guys Guide) visit to the Haunch in 2014. It is a well-known fact that restaurants are only as good as their chefs, and perhaps the restaurant staff had changed? Something had happened, and happened fast.

Anastasia had another theory, 'Another problem was probably because times change, and we noticed that there were a lot of people who were coming upstairs, and when they saw the tables dressed in a certain way, like with the white tablecloths and napkins in the glasses, they went out again. I think that its ok for a special celebration, but people are more laid back now, and they would turn round and walk out. They wanted something cosy and nice'.

Two thoughts struck me here: The first was that, together with my husband, we had walked out of a rather grand and formal Pizzeria in Rome which had white linen table cloths, in favour of a gaily ochre painted trattoria with wrought iron and fake flowers – even though price was not a problem – for the very reasons that Anastasia was suggesting; it was not relaxing and convivial. Secondly, I thought of Tony Leroy's comment about the chef Rupert Wilcox, 'Rupert, had he lived, would have taken the restaurant in a completely new direction – and quite rightly so'.

Anastasia said 'The way the restaurant was, was not for us. We took off the white tablecloths, and we started to put flowers, candles everywhere, to make it cosy and welcoming. We started to light the log fires, because they had done that only on specific days. We brought a warmness to the place, and it started to pick up.' She went on, 'Anna – she started to work in the kitchen. None of us, not her, not Ilya, not me, had ever worked in the kitchen. She worked as a kitchen porter – and Ilya as 'Front of House' – for around a year without any weekend off. I was pregnant, but I was sitting down working out 'profit and losses', because they were working so hard that they didn't have time to think.'

Anastasia is admiring of her sister, and is keen to document her contribution to their joint successes. 'Anna worked in the kitchen to make sure that the food was coming up to our expectations. She

Staff members Patrick left and Nick

worked beside the chefs – even washing up the dishes.' They were, all three, understanding of the problems which staff might have, working in such a small kitchen, and running up and down the stairs.

They have worked hard and have turned the restaurant around by also sourcing top quality meat and fresh vegetables, and serving traditional English dishes, cooked well. Of course, venison is always on the menu. I love the Sunday Roast – the gammon is not the horrible pink stuff that you usually get in other places, but tender, pale, and tasty.

The youngsters waiting at table always go further to be smiley and friendly, too. Fianna knows that I like the chocolate mints that come with the bill, and always gives me some extra ones (but forget that you read that). We missed Patrick. 'He has come back and is working in the Kitchen now', Anastasia said.

It's always special sitting in the restaurant of the Haunch of Venison and dreaming of the past. There are so many things that have hardly changed; how many occupants of the merchant's house or the Haunch of Venison must have gazed out of the windows at the Church of St Thomas? How many times did they glance out and see the gravediggers at work? Or see the place where their loved ones lay, knowing that one day they would be joining them, and some other occupant would be gazing from the window at THEM? Of course, they couldn't guess that one day it would be a table of American tourists tucking into fish n' chips, and sipping pints of bitter looking out. Most of the gravestones have gone now, but the ghostly smell of freshly turned earth sometimes hangs in the air of the Haunch, it is said. At the other end of the dining room, you can eat your venison sausage and mash and look out at the Poultry Cross, which was built around the same time as the Haunch. On Tuesdays and Saturdays, you can see the traders, and watch people scurrying back and forth with their purchases, just as they have always done for centuries. To paraphrase John Chandler who wrote about the Haunch in his excellent book, *Endless Street* – 'And in that dining-room we find the link that binds together the history of Salisbury'.

Anastasia told me, 'We didn't want to find just a job, we wanted to find somewhere that we could love. We were always interested in old buildings, and antique furniture, but this place gave us everything that we needed, all together. We think that is ridiculous money that we need to put into the place, but we are ready to do that for the Haunch.'

Anastasia then said something very important 'We feel that we're not just working, but doing something for the generations to come.' She went on, 'Because to keep this place up to – life – is very difficult.' She has something to compare the pub with, 'we were caretaking the

'Bell and Crown' (opposite the White Hart Hotel), but it had been refurbished, and although it did need upkeep, here (the Haunch) it is every day; you could take all your money, but it would never be enough'. I thought of Dave Prodger, who upkept the building for Tony Leroy, and loved it as well as anyone, and Firmin Bradbeer using the song 'Ours is a nice 'Ouse' (an affectionate tribute to a happy household in a broken-down old house) as a subtitle for his song 'The Firm Inn'. keeping up with repairs has always been a daily job; it's a labour of love 'We can always do regular work, but here it is endless. It is more and more difficult – for example, when we installed CCTV – which is very important for the business, for safety – we were waiting around for months just for approval.' The building is listed and she told me, 'Something that might cost £5,000 to do somewhere else, costs £30,000 to £40,000 here – Do you see the difference? – Builders turn up, but when they see the complexities of the job, they just go away.'

Landlords who take on the Haunch of Venison have to have broad shoulders. The terms of the lease (full obligation) are that it is the Tenant who has to do the repairs and not the Pub Company (currently Stonegate), who own it. We should have some sympathy for previous tenant, Alex Marshall; Anastasia certainly has: 'If the restaurant is not working, and the pub is not working, and you are not a builder who knows about the renovations needed, then you have no chance. You are responsible and you have to pay out more than anywhere else.'

Anastasia, Ilya and Anna have had some tremendous bad luck as well. It was not many years after they had taken over, that the infamous Salisbury poisonings took place, when a Russian ex-spy and his daughter were victims of an attempted assassination using the nerve agent Novichok. The pair collapsed in the Maltings, which is not too far from the Haunch. From one day to the next, the streets of Salisbury emptied (except for dozens of reporters), as the public became aware that some Novichok that might fit on a pinhead could kill them, and that Mr Skripal and his daughter Yulia had wandered around the area with Novichok on their hands. I remembered the disastrous effect on the takings at the business where I worked at the time. Still, things could have been far, far, worse for the Haunch of Venison, had the pair dropped in for a drink and a meal in the restaurant: The Bishop's Mill pub, and Zizi's restaurant, where they had gone, were sealed off for months whilst they were completely gutted.

Then came the Covid 19 pandemic, which saw hospitality venues forced to close. When they could reopen, it was firstly only those with outside seating who could serve people, and the Haunch doesn't have a garden. Then there were strict rules on social distancing to be obeyed, and the Haunch is tiny. The numbers who could be served were severely curtailed by the distancing.

The Haunch had hardly reopened when the kitchen was forced to close because the gas system broke down. 'It was complicated to replace, because it is a listed building', Anastasia said. She also had a problem finding a very good chef, after their long-term chef died. 'Chefs are hard to find in Salisbury. Good ones already have jobs. The kitchen at the Haunch is so small that it puts a lot of pressure on them, and chefs who are used to working in big modern kitchens don't like it'. Luckily, she has sorted out all the problems, and the food is now well worth a detour. But it's all cost them money.

Salisbury owes Anastasia, Ilya, and Anna a big debt for their care of the Haunch of Venison, and the money that they have poured into it.

Let's pray that Anastasia, Ilya, and Anna continue at the Haunch of Venison for a very long time, because it is hard to see how anybody else would have so much love for it as to invest their personal savings in it, as they have done.

S is for secret bar

The 'Secret Bar' (AKA the Cloisters Bar) is situated in the merchant's house, and is so called because few people know that it is there. It is situated on a landing between the entrance in Minster Street (on the other side of Carters the Jewellers), and the first floor, which holds the coffee machine, and crockery. From there is a doorway into the main restaurant, and a room which was once an extension into the Cloisters Bar. From the other side of the stairs is a door, and on the other side more stairs lead up to three rooms and the cocklofts. In the time of Firmin Bradbeer, all this side of the building was the Bradbeers' private apartments, and rented from Carters.

It was after World War One that permission was granted to make the Hall into a large restaurant room, and open a door into it from the Haunch of Venison proper. The entrance was to be the stairs from

The Secret Bar © Courage

the street that meant that customers no longer had to pass through the pub to dine. The landing was made into a little bar, with stools at the counter, and a table and chairs, where customers could enjoy a cocktail while awaiting a table. It has been opened on and off over the years, but was never really big enough to warrant blocking a member of staff, and there was a problem then, of keeping the beer cool. It has often been a private place where favoured customers could find a quite place when the pub has been packed, if they are not nervous in the spooky atmosphere – it is said to be particularly haunted. At the moment it is only opened on special occasions, that may change in the future!

S is for shield

Painted above the bench known as Death Row, upon the panelling, is what looks like a heraldry shield with a Latin inscription. The shield was painted by Roy Spring above the place where 'regular', Norman Bryant used to sit. His pewter tankard still hangs behind the bar.

'Uncle Norman used to practically live in the Haunch of Venison', says his niece. 'He worked at an Estate Agents around the back of the Church, and he'd be in the pub every lunchtime and evening'. The shield shows some banana sandwiches, for which Norman had a fondness, a tankard of foaming beer, a pipe, and the motto 'Mine's in'. It is amazing that Roy was able to paint on the oak panelling of the listed building, but somehow the shield adds to the history and quaintness of the old pub, and Norman Bryant will always have his seat near the fire.

The shield made for Norman Bryant

Roy Spring (with hat) & some of the former Haunch locals © Nick Spring

S is for Smoke Jack

When Firmin Bradbeer renovated the Bar, a 'quaint old smoke jack, consisting of pulleys to drive the spit in the chimney were found between two old storey posts'. This was still on display in the bar in 1930, since it is on the inventory which he completed for Simonds.

The smoke Jack works using a wheel which is turned using the ascending gases rising in the chimney. There would either be a pulley like figures D and E (see image) each side, which turns the spit, or the meat, such as a Haunch of Venison might hang straight down and rotate.

The arrangement drawn above is of a smoke jack from the 1600s, but the design was very similar in the 1800s. Where did

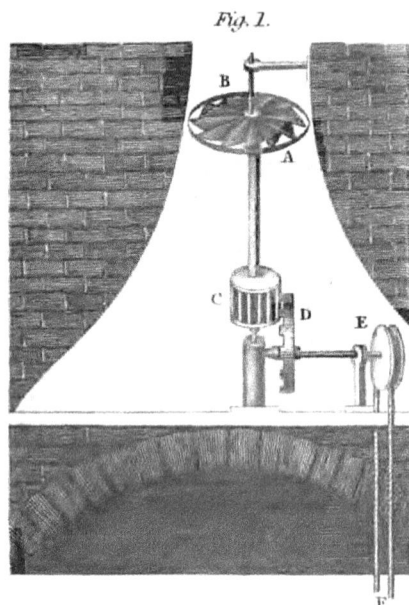

Engraving of a Smoke Jack

the smoke jack from the Haunch disappear to? Perhaps it will one day be found in Salisbury Museum!

S is for St Edmund's Church

In 1458, Agnes Wynchester, widow of barber surgeon John Wynchester, left the corner building next door to the Haunch of Venison to Trinity Hospital. In the description of the emplacement of the building, we can see that the building which would become the Haunch of Venison was then in the possession of the Provost of St Edmund's Church (the church is now Salisbury Arts Centre).

In 1458, the provost was John Sax. St Edmund's church had been founded as a collegiate church in 1269, and the provost was its head. At its creation, the college had 13 priests who also served the parish of St Edmund's, and they were then lodged on the site of what is now the registry office and council buildings (2022). Over the next centuries the college suffered from insufficient income and mismanagement, and rarely had many priests. However, in 1447, at the time of the Provost John Pyeville, the Tailors Guild of Salisbury founded a fraternity which provided for one chaplain to celebrate at the altar in the chapel of St John, attached to the college. In 1449, the fraternity was moved from the college at St Edmund's to St

Thomas's church. The coincidence in the dates of the construction of the Haunch of Venison building, belonging to the provost, and the transfer of the fraternity to St Thomas's might be simply a coincidence – or it might not.

In 1535, most of the income for St Edmund's church was coming from rents from property in Salisbury, of which the Haunch might be one. At any rate, in 1546 – so 100 years after the Haunch building was constructed – any remaining property still in possession of the college was forfeited to King Henry VIII, and sold. This would correspond to the time period where the Hammond family were living in the Haunch building, which they had bought, since they transferred it by wills.

S is for St Thomas's Church
The church of St Thomas of Canterbury stands behind the Haunch of Venison and the two have very strong links, particularly since the back door of the Haunch led into the path which ran around one side of the churchyard.

The Church is first mentioned as existing in 1248 (although a chapel stood on that spot in 1238). It was rebuilt after 1448, because part of the church collapsed at that date. Interestingly, it is in 1449, the fraternity of the Tailors Guild, which was founded at St Edmund's College, was moved to St Thomas's, when the church was rebuilt. The Haunch of Venison was built in 1450 as a church house, belonging to the Provost of St Edmund's. Whether there is a link between these dates and events is only a theory.

When researching the landlords and landladies of the Haunch of Venison, it is striking how their histories are linked to the church. Sometimes the only trace of them is through births, deaths and marriages celebrated or lamented in St Thomas's, and pews rented, and the churchyard has received the bodies of many of their families. On Sundays, they worshipped there, and at least three of them were churchwardens or were on the board of governors. They could never escape the church, since it is visible from every back window of the Haunch; they could hear the bells ringing out, and the thud of earth as graves were dug.

St. Thomas' Church © Baptiste Vitorino

There are some other strange ties. Whilst the Haunch of Venison hid a cache of probable apotropaic objects, so St Thomas's hid a mummified cat, and supposed crucibles in a wall.

And what of the medieval doom painting? When it wasn't covered up with whitewash, those ladies of the Haunch of Venison must have gazed up at the cheating alewife and felt at least a twinge of something bad; Alewives were generally thought to be sexually promiscuous swindlers and portrayed as such in medieval art.

Yet no doubt, after church on Sunday morning, many of the gentlemen would have come out of St Thomas's in their Sunday best, and marched straight over to the Haunch.

S is for Sweetapple

Although Solomon and Joseph Sweetapple didn't have the hall (upper dining room) of the merchant's house, I have included them because of their ties to Butcher's Row, which I feel is important to the Haunch, and reflected in its name. It's also another example of the standing of people involved in the building, which is not immediately apparent from their trade.

Solomon Sweetapple (1737-1816?) lived in the northern half of the merchant's house for a while. He was born in St Martin's Ward and married Laetitia Biggs from Hampshire. He was probably living in the merchant's house in 1772, because his daughter Elizabeth was christened at St Thomas's Church in that year. The most interesting thing about Solomon is that he was a successful butcher by trade, working for himself (judging by his will, probate granted 1817) and the Haunch of Venison, and merchant's house, stand close to Butchers Row.

On Solomon's death, his son Joseph is listed as living in the merchant's house (according to John Chandler, citing the Rates Book 1817). Joseph was also a butcher, and is listed in *Pigots Directory* of 1830 in Butchers Row. Joseph's will (1832/1834) describes himself as 'gentleman', living in a house in the market place, of which he owns the freehold. He also owned a building in Butchers Row, which was leased out. Joseph was not just a butcher, but he appears to have raised animals, presumably for meat, since his will mentions several meadows at Milford, as well as the Lady Meadows by Salisbury cathedral, held from the Dean and Chapter. Joseph didn't have children but his will mentions a brother and a nephew, both called William Sweetapple.

There is some indication, given the rare name, that Sweetapples lived at Tidworth Down Farm, in the 1860s.

T is for tunnels

A rumour has long persisted that there exist tunnels that lead to the Haunch of Venison from St Thomas's church, to make a discreet entrance for the clergy to have visited at a time when the pub was supposedly a brothel. Sadly, it cannot be true: the main reason for this is that the water table around the church is extremely high – and is the reason that the cellar at the Haunch of Venison is not sunk low. An illustration of this is that when digging graves behind the Haunch, the hole would fill with water, depending on the time of year. When this happened, the gravediggers would ask the miller at the Town (Bishops) Mill to shut the mill head. (Incidentally, it was then discovered that the water in the drinking wells around the churchyard rose and fell at the same time as that in the graves, and that people were made ill from water which had clearly passed through rotting corpses in the severely over buried graveyard). Moreover, catholic clergy visiting brothels was tolerated, and a punishment might be the donation of a small sum to the Church funds, and a few Hail Marys. Salisbury's red-light district was around the Love Lane area, and not Minster Street.

However, there is a good reason why stories of tunnels abound in Salisbury, and that is because there are some. They were originally part of Salisbury's water system and a map of them can be found in the book on Salisbury by the Royal Commission on Historical Monuments. Most of the waterways which used to run through Salisbury streets were shallow, and were filled in, but there are two much deeper waterways – now drained – which crossed Salisbury from the river Avon to re-join the river at Bugmore. One such tunnel

The Haunch of Venison © Austin Underwood

can still be accessed by steps under Trinity Hospital, and another part of it is supposedly under what was Trinity Bakery.

U is for Underwood
Austin Underwood was a teacher at Bishop Wordsworth school who took around 50,000 photographs, in the middle of the 20th century, the negatives of which were bequeathed to Salisbury Museum. Together, they form an important historical record of the local area.

V is for Venison
Above the fireplace in the merchant's house hangs a stag's head, which has become the logo of the Haunch of Venison. An article in the *Salisbury Times,* January 1972, informs us 'Mrs Jakeman arranges the flowers herself, and the Deer's head reposing over the fireplace is known as Cecil'.

Cecil or Horace? © Baptiste Vitorino

'He was always Horace to us', says ex-waitress Val Gainsford.

Cecil/Horace had a brief stay in the attic when the restaurant became '1 Minster Street' and was brought up to date in the 1990s. 'I found him in the attic when I was managing the Pub,' says Justyna Nugent, 'and hung him over the fireplace. I had no idea that was his home'.

Hopefully Cecil/Horace will stay put now, the symbol of the House.

It's very fitting that the deer's head should hang in the restaurant because not only does he reflect the name of the pub, but venison is naturally the speciality of the Haunch. A snippet from a wartime *Salisbury Journal* shows that Dolly Bradbeer/Edwardes/Lemon had venison on the menu in 1941.

Ian Bennett, the Wards, Bill and Kate Jakeman, Tony and Vicky Leroy, and Anastasia Samoilova all served venison, and perhaps if you were only ever to order one thing in the Merchant's Hall, then venison is what it naturally should be.

W is for Ward

Peter and Celia Ward were brought in by Simonds Brewery to manage the Haunch of Venison after Ian Bennett had left, as caretaker landlords. The Haunch of Venison already had a very high reputation for food, and the brewery wanted to take their time to find the right people who would keep up the standards (as Bill Jakeman, who met the Wards, explained to me). As the brewery in Reading was close to where they lived in Berkshire, the pair were probably known personally to Simonds. The Wards were at the Haunch from around 1967 to 1971. They lived above the pub.

Peter Ward and Celia Ward returned to Berkshire in 1971 to take over the St George and Dragon pub at Wargrave, which sits in a stunning location on the river. The George and Dragon was also

Peter and Celia Ward © Simmonds Family

an historic pub, popular with celebrities. It was announced in the *Hop Leaf* that the couple had just come from 'the famous Haunch of Venison in Salisbury' and would be serving 'really good English food using locally purchased fresh meat and vegetables, with game and venison in season'. This gives a good idea of what menu they must have been serving in Salisbury, and which the Brewery obliged the Jakemans to continue.

W is for Wine Butler

The Haunch's restaurant under Ian Roy Bennett, in the 1950s, was so sophisticated that, not only were the waiters in tail coats and hand tied bowties, and the food presentation was silver service, but the Restaurant Manager was an expert Wine Butler, and the only local member of the Guild of Sommeliers, of which there were only 500 members all told. Not only that, but the Belgian sommelier, Charles Dabomprez, was one of 20 administrators of the guild.

Charles Dabomprez
© Salisbury Newspapers

Charles Dabomprez was a much-decorated war hero, having earned five British medals, and having been decorated by both the Belgians and the French. He was in the Special Service Branch of the Commandos and so, alas! the details of his war record are top secret (he was a Lance Corporal in 10 Commando Nominal D-H).

He had some sage advice for readers of the *Salisbury Journal*, 'young before old, sweet before dry, light before heavy'. He recommended drinking sherry with your soup, and something sparkling with your chicken. He is, presumably, giving the glass of red in the photograph, a good sniff, before swilling it around his mouth, and spitting it out. Wine tasting is deadly serious business.

W is for Witchcraft
In the past, people were (arguably) far more superstitious than they are today. It is innate in human nature to want to make sense of life; for us to try to influence 'luck', and protect ourselves from 'evil'. Our ancestors thought that this could be done, not only by prayer, but by the use of amulets and symbols and special objects. In this way, they could ward off the Devil and witches, and attract good luck to a house. Counter-witchcraft objects and symbols are known as 'apotropaic'.

There are a number of objects which have been found hidden in the Haunch of Venison, which may, or may not, be apotropaic. Here is a list:

Two single shoes were found 'behind the panelling', upstairs (Salisbury Museum labe)l. The shoes are 17th century. Of course, the Haunch of Venison was associated with shoemakers, and it is situated in an area of Salisbury where shoemakers worked, so it is possible that the shoes got there by accident (although it is hard to see how).

Hiding shoes near places that 'witches' (evil) might enter (roofs, chimneys, doors, windows) was incredibly common both in England and on the continent, between the medieval period and the early 20th century. The shoe tradition supposedly came about when a Buckinghamshire rector with a reputation for piety and working miracles, named John Schorne, died in 1313 – and became venerated as a Saint after his death. (Nevertheless, a concealed shoe, said to date from 1308 was found behind the choir stalls in Winchester Cathedral, suggesting perhaps an earlier root).

One of the important 'miraculous' things which John Shorne did, was to discover a well by 'divining' (using a rod), during a period of drought, whose waters turned out to be supposedly medicinally miraculous. After his death, his tomb at Great Marston became a place of popular pilgrimage. It is said that one of the ailments that the water of Schorne's Well was said to cure was gout (or corns or

*Shoes found in the Haunch of
Venison
© Salisbury Museum*

bunions!), because a series of medieval paintings show Schorne inducing a devil OUT of a boot or shoe. This quickly became interpreted as Schorne forcing a devil INTO a shoe, and there were a lucrative number of visitors to the tomb; In the medieval period, popular pilgrimages were the birth of modern tourism. There were so many 'tourists' to Great Marston, that Edward IV had Schorne's body moved to Windsor. In the meantime the 'catching the devil in a shoe' idea had caught on (or so goes the popular story).

It therefore became a very common 'folk' habit to conceal a *single* shoe in a building to ward off evil, and as protection. The shoe was singular so that the witch, putting in a foot, could not run off because he/she did not have the pair. It was also practical, because shoes were expensive, and the owner had evidently worn out, or lost, the other shoe (most hidden shoes are worn). Superstitions can be very powerful, and perhaps the people who originally hid the shoes in the Haunch (if they are apotropaic) did believe that they might trap witches, but perhaps they were simply to ward off bad luck from the building.

China or brass shoes were a popular Victorian ornament, and boot charms on charm bracelet, or shoes tied to wedding cars, are all said to bring luck.

Also found hidden behind the panelling was a 17th century Sack bottle. Sack was the name given to Spanish white fortified wines, of which Sherry is the most famous. The question is, how did a bottle come to be walled up in the Haunch of Venison, and why? It would seem to be almost impossible that it should get there by accident. It is probable that it is a 'witch bottle'.

Witch Bottles also had different uses. They might be used to trap witches with a mixture such as urine – thought to attract them – and bent pins and nails to hook them. Other common ingredients are fingernail clippings, teeth, written spells, and plants. Witch Bottles have also been found with medicinal plants, and they were said to protect the health of those in the house. Witch Bottles are in any case a 'protection' for the building.

The Sack bottle found in the Haunch of Venison is bigger than the traditional 'bellarmine' bottles often used for Witch Bottles between the 15th and 18th centuries – (because of the ugly face imprinted on the neck by the German manufacturers, and said to resemble the hated

Sack Bottle © Salisbury Museum

Cardinal Bellarmino, who wanted to ban alcohol). It has a cork in it, and is translucent, and so it can be seen that the bottle is empty. However, the archaeologist Brian Hoggard, a specialist of apotropaic charms, laments that the reaction of most people if they find a witch bottle is to clean it out, not recognising it for what it is. It could be that Firmin Bradbeer had managed to get the cork out, and to replace it (he was equipped for that), being curious about the contents, and washed out any noxious sludge before showing the bottle to the museum.

Another small 17th century bottle, described as a stoneware flagon with three hearts imprinted, was found in a cache with the hand and the playing cards; Firmin Bradbeer thought that it was probably Flemish. It was hopefully taken to the museum.

Another item found walled up, was a wooden rat trap. The academic website, The Conversation, has an interesting article called 'The spellbinding history of cheese and witchcraft'. It would appear that cheese has long been held to have magical and seductive properties, and witches like to steal milk and cheese. It could be that the trap was set to attract – not rats – but witches! Elizabeth Turner (working at Salisbury Museum 2022), says 'sharp objects do turn up occasionally in mixed-item caches, and Brian Hoggard's suggestion that dried cats were used as a form of 'spiritual pest control', both feed into why the rat trap might have been selected as another way of trapping malevolent spirits.'   It is very interesting to note, given the links between the occupants of the Haunch of Venison and St Thomas's church, that a mummified cat was found hidden in St Thomas's church.

It would seem that the rat trap would not have been placed in a handy spot for killing rats, because had a rat died in a walled-up spot, it would have stunk the house out, and surely frightened off customers.

Elizabeth Turner, who did her thesis on apotropaic charms, is of the opinion that the assortment of objects is unlikely to be the result of accident, as they could hardly all fall behind the panelling. Said Elizabeth, in an email to this author: 'I am 98% confident that the cache is an apotropaic concealment. The presence of the two shoes, the bottle, and the rat trap and the location of the cache are all suggestive of deliberate concealment. Likewise, the contents can all be seen in other concealments that have received academic attention and are widely accepted as apotropaic.'

There can be little doubt but that the mummified hand, found in its location walled up in the fireplace, is a counter-witchcraft 'hand

Drawing of objects found at the Haunch of Venison © Salisbury Museum

of glory', and this author is of the opinion that they were deliberately walled up for luck in card games. I also suggest that the Elizabethan groat in the ceiling of the House of Commons might have been put there to attract money to the house.

These are some of the items which Firmin Bradbeer found hidden around the house during renovations. He does not mention the larger jugs, and so I imagine that they have no great age, but are more likely to be Firmin Potto's, kept by Louisa.

W is for Wogan

It was in March 2015 that Irish radio and TV 'national treasure', Sir Terry Wogan visited Salisbury, along with London Cabbie, Mason McQueen. They were filming a TV series called 'Terry and Mason's Great Food Trip', where Wogan and McQueen followed in the footsteps of Samuel Chamberlain, and his 1963 book for the Gourmet Distributing Corporation called 'British Bouquet. An Epicurean Tour of Britain'. Alex Marshall was the Landlord, and Tracey Thorne his manageress.

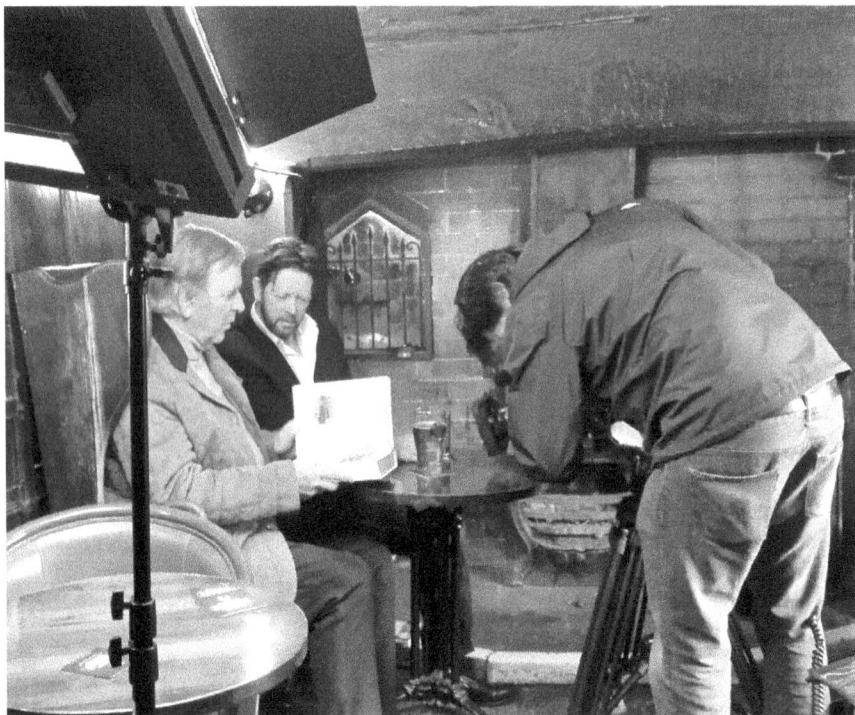

Terry Wogan with Frogg Moody © Matt Pike

Samuel Chamberlain had visited the Haunch of Venison on his original trip, and so Sir Terry was keen to enjoy a pint in the picturesque old pub. Curve Media, the production company behind the series, and BBC2, knew what they were after – 'personal anecdotes, and surprising historical facts, recounted by local people', according to the *Salisbury Journal*. The severed hand and cheating card player story were gold dust to them, and they soon found co-author of *Haunted Salisbury*, Frogg Moody, to meet Sir Terry on camera, to tell him the tale.

Frogg got to the Haunch early, and bought a pint of cider, and installed himself in the House of Lords, on the bench closest to the hand. 'I knew when Terry walked into the pub', Frogg says, 'because there was a bit of a commotion downstairs, and I peered down at him through the little window. He came in and started chatting to the locals.' Frogg watched him buy a pint of Summer Lightning. 'I could tell straight away that he was ill. He looked thinner and drawn'. Sir Terry was secretly suffering from cancer, and would be dead within less than a year.

'He walked in and he was all smiles, asking me if I were nervous, putting me at my ease, and explaining what was going to happen. We had no script at all. We just chatted naturally, and it took only one take', says Frogg. 'I told him the tale of the card player, and he advised me 'never let the facts get in the way of a good story'. He was very good humoured. I was surprised when he downed his pint – and I offered to buy him another drink. He ordered a whisky – I said 'are you a whisky man, Terry?', 'he said – I'm a red wine man, really. I was shocked when he died.'

X is for Xmas

Christmas has long been a special time at the Haunch of Venison, as menus going back to the time of the Bradbeers show. The following menu is from the time of Tony and Vicky Leroy. Justyna Nugent remembers, especially, the choir coming in from St Thomas's Church, to sing carols in the Haunch. A customer from an earlier date (who wishes to be known as just 'Terry'), told me that carol singers came from the Cathedral and sang the Whiffenpoof Song.

Simonds Brewery also made a big thing of Christmas, in their hotels, and the Haunch of Venison was one of them. The *Hop Leaf*, Simonds' in-house magazine, explained in a 1950s edition, that more

Tony and Vicky Leroy would wish to extend their season's greetings for Christmas 1990 to you the Everyman Bookshop customer. The Haunch of Venison is very much part of the fabric of Salisbury, built c.1320, it is one of the oldest pubs in the city. We are renowned for the quality of our beer, we have one of the best selections of whiskies and brandies in the South of England - over 90 varieties of malt and blended whisky - and a superb wine list

Why not have a Christmas drink in front of our open fires in one of the bars where Pepys once sat? Or, better still, come and enjoy our

Christmas Dinner
£11.50*

Homemade Soup of the Day
Fresh Crab Paté & Toast
Mushrooms French Style (with brie & garlic)
Melon Perles with ginger & orange

* * * *

Roast Turkey (with cranberry sauce, chipolatas & bacon rolls)
Roast Haunch of Venison Montmorency (with apple & redcurrant jelly)
Sirloin Steak with anchovies & olives
Sole Florentine (on a bed of spinach with cheese sauce)

All served with fresh vegetables or salad

* * * *

Sweets from the buffet table
or
a selection of ice cream or sorbets

* * * *

people were going away to hotels for a Christmas break, and thus avoiding all the hard work that goes with the festivities. Their catering manager explained that their different hotels offered different styles of Christmases; some were frivolous with 'plenty of dancing, games, entertainment and parties'. Others were different. The *Hop Leaf* went on, 'Some people like to spend the holiday quietly, to recapture the spirit of Yuletide – churchgoing, logs on the fire, dim lights and ghost stories told quietly over the nuts and port.' That the latter included the Haunch of Venison is certain, because the magazine chose to print a photograph of the Haunch as an illustration.

Other activities were gathering around the radio to listen to the Queen's Speech, and drinking from a punchbowl in the evening, but most interesting to this author is that on the day following Boxing Day, the staff would sit down to a Christmas Feast – and be waited upon by the guests!

This does not seem a likely attraction for prospective paying hotel guests today, but it is a festive tradition that, perhaps, goes back to antiquity. In Catholic England, up until the protestant Eizabethan period, a 'Lord of Misrule' would be appointed for a 'Feast of Fools' – the culmination of the 12 days of Christmas, during which time of 'drunken revelry', normal life would be turned 'topsy-turvy'. That is to say, people might wear their clothes backwards, masters wait on servants, and everybody stopped work. There are some historians who have suggested that this tradition came from the Roman 'Saturnalia' – festivities around the god Saturn, when

Christmas at Haunch 2016 - the author with her husband © Spencer Mulholland

the stupidest person would be chosen to represent Saturn, and be treated like a God during days of drunken parties, until being made a human sacrifice to Saturn.

It is lovely to be able to note that the present landlords have carried on the 'topsy turvey' tradition in a small way. On Christmas morning they opened the Haunch of Venison for regulars, and I walked down with my husband, on a crisp winter morning, through the deserted streets. The Haunch felt almost Dickensian, with the decorations draped around the fireplaces, the log fires lit, and the smell of mulled wine in the air. The bells of St Thomas's rang. Anastasia and Ilya were both behind the bar themselves, and they served their staff, who one by one dropped in for a drink on the house.

Y is for 'Ye Olde Inn of Goodwill'
In 1930 Salisbury Infirmary built a new hospital ward, called the Carnival Ward, financed by a week-long carnival. The Licensed Victuallers Association came third with their float, which was dressed

The Carnival Float 1930 © Salisbury Museum

as a 17th-century inn, which had, as the *Salisbury Journal* put it, 'no thought of puritanical interference'.

Firmin Bradbeer is dressed as a cavalier, sitting in the centre and holding his feathered hat. The furniture was 'authentic antiques', and the inn was apparently inspired by the Haunch of Venison. Mr Bradbeer was long time Treasurer, and sometime President, of the Licensed Victuallers Association – as Firmin Potto had been long before. He belonged to so many Salisbury clubs that it must have been difficult for him to choose which organisation to represent. One assumes that the other men riding on the float, are other Salisbury Licensed Victuallers of the time.

Firmin Bradbeer wrote a libretto about a fictitious Inn, set at this period, and described like this float – but called the Swan Inn. The heroine was Dorothy (as his daughter, Florence – or Dolly – liked to call herself). The libretto is in Salisbury Museum.

Z is for Zeppelin (Led!)

On Tuesday, 21 December 1971, rock band Led Zeppelin played at Salisbury City Hall. Frogg Moody who covered the Salisbury Music scene for two books, co-written with Richard Nash (*Hold Tight*, and

Endless Beat), told me: 'Whilst I was researching the book, *Endless Beat,* I was told that at some point during the evening Jimmy Page rolled up at the Haunch of Venison – perhaps Jimmy's love of history got the better of him. I was also told that he wanted to play a gig at Old Sarum. I think that Led Zeppelin went to the Provencal French restaurant in the market square, near the Poultry Cross.'

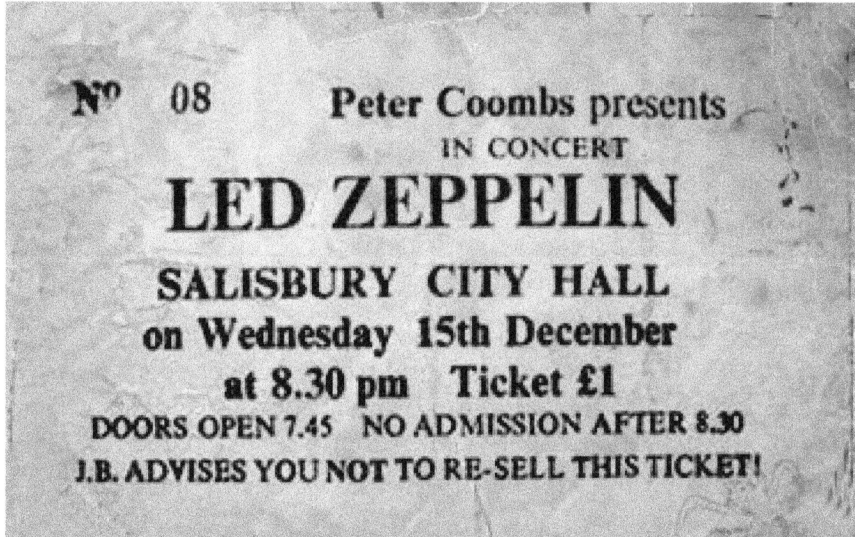

The Salisbury Led Zeppelin ticket

Appendices

Appendix 1.
The Bradbeer Family Tree (see opposite page)

Appendix 2.
Francis Bradbeer
The name Bradbeer is from the West Country, and Francis was born in Charmouth, Dorset. When he was young his family moved to Charlton, in Kent (Woolwich, London).

His wife, Sarah Richards, appears to have been slightly better off, and the Bradbeer children would remain close to their Richards cousins. The Bradbeers were a close family.

Francis Bradbeer arrived in Salisbury in 1826, and opened a tailor's shop in New Canal. His brother Joseph William Bradbeer was already a successful tailor and breeches maker in Salisbury (with shops, at various times, in Exeter Street, New Canal, and Catherine Street, before he moved back to Kent).

Contemporary adverts from Francis Bradbeer in the *Salisbury Journal* show that he tailored for the fashionable and well to do, since he boasts of going regularly to London keep abreast of the latest trends. He was an active member of St Thomas's Church, like his contemporary, Firmin Potto (landlord of the Haunch of Venison), and he was both a churchwarden and an 'overseer of the poor'.

It is impossible to guess why Francis went bankrupt in 1835, but it must have damaged his reputation to some extent, and his standing with the Church. The Bankruptcy evidently led to the Bradbeers having to leave their dwelling house, as well as the shop.

But then tragedy struck for the second time, when Francis lost his wife, and his seven children were left motherless. Four of his children, Sarah, Emma, Louisa, and Alfred, went on to live and work at the Haunch of Venison and so have been dealt with in the main text. The others are as follows.

His eldest daughter was Elizabeth Richards Bradbeer, born

BRADBEER FAMILY TREE

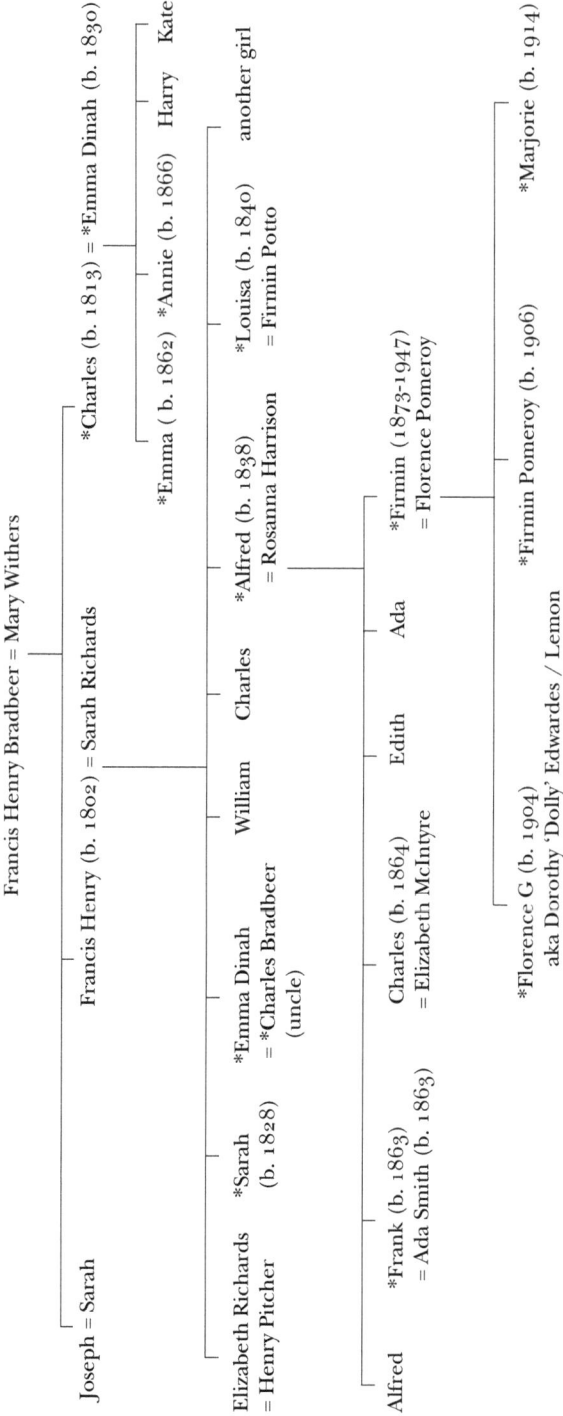

Francis Henry Bradbeer = Mary Withers

Francis Henry (b. 1802) = Sarah Richards

*Charles (b. 1813) = *Emma Dinah (b. 1830)

Joseph = Sarah

Elizabeth Richards = Henry Pitcher

*Sarah (b. 1828)

*Emma Dinah = *Charles Bradbeer (uncle)

William

Charles

*Alfred (b. 1838) = Rosanna Harrison

*Firmin (1873-1947) = Florence Pomeroy

*Emma (b. 1862)   *Annie (b. 1866)   Harry   Kate

*Louisa (b. 1840) = Firmin Potto

another girl

Alfred

*Frank (b. 1863) = Ada Smith (b. 1863)

Charles (b. 1864) = Elizabeth McIntyre

Edith

Ada

*Florence G (b. 1904) aka Dorothy 'Dolly' Edwardes / Lemon

*Firmin Pomeroy (b. 1906)

*Marjorie (b. 1914)

All marked * lived or worked at the Haunch of Venison. A more complete family tree can be found under 'Haunch of Venison' on Ancestry.com, created by the author with the help of Helen Lederer.

in 1826, who became a dressmaker, before marrying a solicitor's general clerk and moving to London. Two of his sons were William and Charles. William Bradbeer was born in 1832, and baptised at St Thomas's. He became a tailor, still in Brown Street, Salisbury. William appears to have worked alongside his father and siblings until one by one they died or married. He then appears still in Brown Street as a 'cutler' (cutlery maker), in *Kelly's Directory*, 1895. This is not entirely strange, since his brother Charles (the same one who would move to 69 London Road), was a cutler and had been living with him on the 1881 census. William never married, and died at 54 Brown Street in 1901. Charles Bradbeer was born in 1836. By 1851, he was a cutler's apprentice to Thomas Neesham, and living with Neesham's family at 34 New Canal (although just around the corner from his own family). Charles never married, but set his horizons wider than Salisbury, lodging with families around the country. He eventually retired to 69 London Road, Salisbury, to live with his sister and nieces as 'a boarder' (as he had been all his life), living on his own means, as a 'retired working cutler'. One can only surmise that he took charge of the cutlery at the Haunch of Venison! Charles died in 1923.

Francis Bradbeer died in 1880, so he lived long enough to know that his family in Salisbury were taken care of.

Appendix 3.
Alfred Bradbeer
Firmin Bradbeer's eldest brother, Alfred Harrison Bradbeer, trained to become a teacher, and became Head Master of the National School in Codicote, Hertfordshire, between 1895 and 1896. He then left to be Head Teacher in Weston until he retired. Alfred's daughter, Edith, went on to become Headmistress of nearby Cowbridge School until 1953. The Bradbeers were so well loved and remembered by their local community in Hertfordshire, that they are the subject of a local history project, and he can be read about by googling 'Bradbeer Codicote'.

Appendix 4.
Charles Bradbeer
Charles Bradbeer was another brother of Firmin Bradbeer, born just a year after Frank, in 1864, and by aged 16 he was living in London with his father's eldest sister, Aunt Elizabeth, who was a solicitor's clerk. Charles was put to train as the clerk of an auctioneer. By 25,

he was back in Southampton, and married to the daughter of the Quartermaster of the 60th Rifles. By the time that he was executor of Louisa's will, he was a mercantile clerk working for a shipping agent at the port of Southampton. He died in 1925.

Appendix 5.
The Potto Family Tree (see next page)

Appendix 6.
William Potto
Like Firmin Potto, and Thomas Pitts Potto – his younger brothers – William was born, and grew up, in Nayland, Suffolk. The Potto family were proud to be related to John Firmin of Watertown, Massachusetts, who had left Suffolk in the same period as the Pilgrim Fathers (John Firmin was a hero of Nayland). Unlike Firmin Potto, there is no suggestion that William made shoes or boots or other leather goods (but he probably could). However, like his brothers, he was born in the reign of George III, who died when William was 19. He lived through the reign of William IV, and was already in his thirties when Victoria came to the throne. He is the first of the Potto family to be mentioned in the *Salisbury and Winchester Journal*, and possibly preceded his father and brothers to Salisbury.

The only hint as to why the Pottos left the region where they were born can be found in the *Essex Herald*, 14 March 1843, which shows that there was a major family falling-out over money. This was between William's uncles, and resulted in two court cases, Potto v Potto. Although the date of the court case is over ten years later than our Pottos moving to Salisbury, it is evident from the trial account that the family had been feuding over a curriers shop, belonging to a grandfather, for a long time. It is impossible to know for sure why William chose to come to Salisbury, but there are a few clues that this may have been to do with Salisbury racecourse. It could be that William had been employed looking after horses in Suffolk, where the relative proximity to Newmarket, and flat racing, was the source of much employment (Wikipedia says that today one in three jobs in the Newmarket area are generated by horseracing). Salisbury has one of the oldest flat racing courses in the country. At any rate, William appears to have owned racehorses, and have competed at racecourses around our area, employing jockeys.

POTTO FAMILY TREE

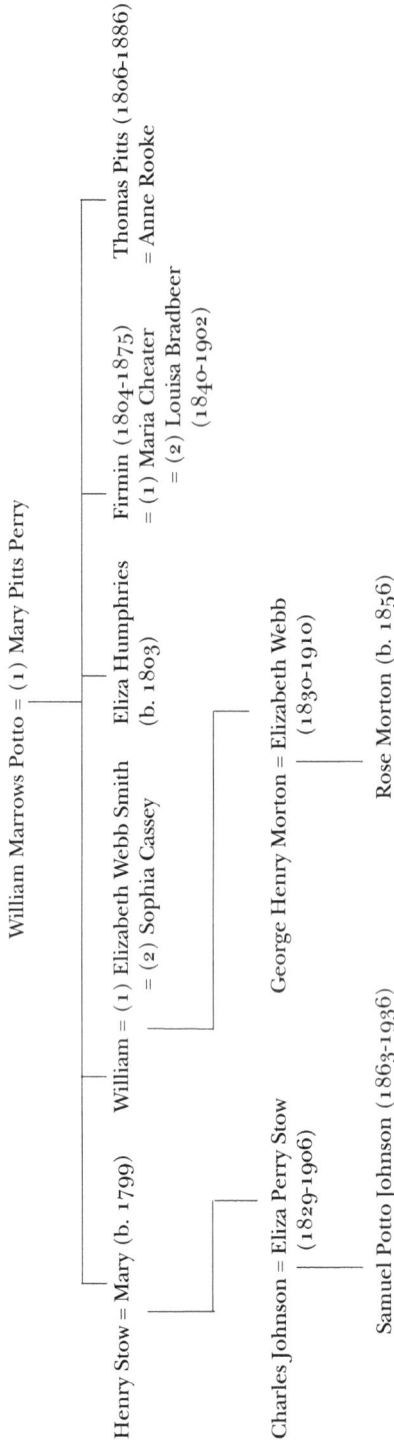

William Marrows Potto = (1) Mary Pitts Perry

Henry Stow = Mary (b. 1799)

William = (1) Elizabeth Webb Smith
= (2) Sophia Cassey

Eliza Humphries
(b. 1803)

Firmin (1804-1875)
= (1) Maria Cheater
= (2) Louisa Bradbeer
(1840-1902)

Thomas Pitts (1806-1886)
= Anne Rooke

Charles Johnson = Eliza Perry Stow
(1829-1906)

George Henry Morton = Elizabeth Webb
(1830-1910)

Samuel Potto Johnson (1863-1936)

Rose Morton (b. 1856)

A more complete family tree can be found under 'Haunch of Venison' on Ancestry.com, created by the author with the help of Helen Lederer.

William first appears in local newspapers when he married Elizabeth Webb Smith, daughter of the landlady of the Wheatsheaf Inn, Anne Richards. Anne had been born Webb, and was the widow of Henry Smith, before marrying Thomas Richards, being widowed a second time. Webbs had run the City Arms (Ox Row), at the end of the 18th century. and the Cross Keys, and Anne was probably from the same family, since Salisbury publican's families were very often inter-related.

It was not long before Anne Richards retired, leaving the Wheatsheaf to her daughter and son-in-law. The stables, which gave onto the Canal, included 'loose boxes for racehorses' (*SWJ*. 1828)

William and his wife Elizabeth, had a son, William Firmin, born at Christmas, the same year as he took the Wheatsheaf, but sadly the infant survived only nine months; it must have been a bitter blow. Elizabeth was soon 'with child' again, and Elizabeth Webb Potto was born in 1830; this time it was the baby's mother who died.

William recovered enough to remarry in 1831. Widow Sophia Cassey – or Cossey – (née Frost) was eight years older than him at 38, and so it does not appear that William was eager for a large family, as Sophia would have been considered already quite old at this date. What is more, Sophia had previously been married nine years to William Cassey of the City Arms (now the Ox Row), but had no children (although William already had a son).

Horse dealing was William Potto's speciality, and Mr Potto continued horse dealing from all the pubs which he ran. Advertisements are a regular occurrence in the local newspaper from his time at the Wheatsheaf, to the King's Arms (several decades). He also advertised his services for Market days, with 'well aired beds' and 'excellent stabling'. Tuesdays and Saturdays, when Salisbury Market was on, were the most important days for trading (this author, having worked in a jewellers' near the market place, can attest that it is still the case, for shops in that area).

It would seem, that when the following accident occurred at the race track, then the jockey was taken to the Wheatsheaf, although whether he was riding Mr Potto's horse, or his horse was ordinarily stabled at the Wheatsheaf, is not known (*SWJ* 1830). William Potto did race his own horses. It is, I think, worth reproducing a description of Salisbury Races from the same day in 1830 as the accident. This was the world which William Potto inhabited. The   thimbles   and garters were the 'three-cup swindle' and the 'fast and loose' swindle, practised by sharpers.

At Christmas, 1832, the *Salisbury Journal* announced for Mr Potto, that he had 'in conjunction with his old established business, opened a wine and spirit vault in the Fish Market', behind Salisbury Guildhall. This is the same time that his brother Firmin Potto began a wholesale wine and spirit import business, and one imagines that Firmin became William's supplier during this time, as there is no suggestion that the pair were ever in partnership. Pub historian Edwin Garman considers that the vault might be at no. 7, which became part of the Wheatsheaf. An advertisement for the cellars in 1833, offers 'a good article at small profit', and makes clear that his 'Hunters and Hacks for sale' can be seen at his livery stables on the Canal. He was serving bottled and draft porter, and cider.

In January 1833, a prize Dorsetshire ox was raffled in the Market Place, and William Potto arranged to hold a dinner for all those who had bought a ticket, to be paid for by the winner who would spend £10. The man raffling the ox would contribute a further £5 to the dinner. According to a study called *Rural Queries*, by the Poor Law Commissioners, in 1834, a farm labourer was earning around 10-*12s.* a week at this time, and so this gives an indication of what the ox was worth, and how expensive the raffle tickets were – and how rich the participating farmers were, since presumably everybody was happy with this arrangement.

In 1834 William Potto moved to the Cross Keys Inn, which stood near the entrance to the present (2022) Cross Keys Shopping Mall, and can be seen in an engraving of the old council house. Numbers 13 and 14 Queen Street were probably part of this old inn. From a description of the clientele in newspaper articles, it was agricultural and commercial, and so obviously still linked to the market. A clue as to why William might have made the move is the extensive work which he did to the stables, and the position directly onto the front of the Guildhall Square. The stables catered for 'gentlemen of the turf', with looseboxes for racehorses, 'stalled stabling' and 'diligent ostlers'. The Inn had a fine reputation, and was a step up from the Wheatsheaf. On 18 September 1834 the opening dinner was held, at a price of 10*s.* 6*d.* for dinner and dessert.

The Wheatsheaf was taken over by a veterinary surgeon called Mr Kite (who moved from the Butcher's Arms), who promptly also took over the building next door to the Wheatsheaf to start a horse-shoeing business, and started selling medicines for horses, cattle and dogs, alongside the drink.

By 1835 William was serving annual oyster suppers at the Cross Keys. This wasn't as 'posh' as it sounds, because oysters were a cheap food at the time, 'sold on almost every street corner in London' (simply oysters.com), and 'oyster pie' was a poor dish. However, Salisbury was rather further from the oyster beds, and the shellfish needed to be kept in ice, without the benefit of fridges, and so perhaps it was a treat for the diners. William continued placing regular advertisements in the newspaper selling horses.

However, although Mr Potto no doubt had a favourable deal for spirits, the fact that he had such a large, and prestigious, premises, meant that he was paying higher taxes (*SWJ* 1835) than he had been at the 'Wheatsheaf'. It's worth printing the following announcement, because it gives a list of contemporary innkeepers. Firmin Potto, at the Haunch of Venison, did not sign it.

The Royal Wiltshire Yeomanry Cavalry, Salisbury Troop, used the Cross Keys Inn, when in the city, and were provided with a substantial dinner there, the year that William Potto arrived, in 1834.

In 1837, 'Walker' a bay gelding owned by William Potto was racing at Bridgwater Races. And in 1838 William's horse 'Walker' was racing in the Hurdle Race sweepstakes at Salisbury races.

In September 1839, William was providing the dinner for the Salisbury and West of England Royal Dahlia Society's Grand Annual Show, which was held in the Guildhall. The *Salisbury Journal* announcement gives a list of the patrons, president, and vice-presidents, which is headed up by William IV's widow, Queen Adelaide (Victoria had just been crowned in 1837). Local important people included the Countess Radnor and the Dowager Countess Pembroke, Wadham Wyndham M.P., the Honourable Sydney Herbert M.P, Dr Finch (of the Asylum), and the mayor – as well as a host of other prominent figures. The fact that Mr Potto and the Cross Keys are cited in the advertisement, placed by the Society, shows the standing which the Inn had in Salisbury, and how far William had risen in a little over a decade. 'Each competitor in the show is expected to take a ticket' (to the dinner), the Society ordered, and one imagines that some, if not all, of the big-wigs attending were there to give the toast. The Cross Keys had rooms big enough, and grand enough, to hold balls.

In June 1840 William was racing his chestnut hack at Plaitford Races, near Romsey. The horse ran in the Hack stakes (it was not a real racehorse), meaning that Mr Potto put up part of the prize, and the results for him were 3 2.

In 1840 William went bankrupt. The reasons for this can only be guessed at, but horse racing is probably the first place to start. Racing horses is an expensive sport, but there must have also been the temptation to gamble when at the racetrack. There are no more newspaper, racecourse run-downs, mentioning William Potto's race horses, after this date (that I have found). The following snippet from the *Journal* is also interesting because it shows that William's wine supplier wasn't his brother, Firmin Potto, at this date, but a London wine merchant called Valentine Morris. Perhaps the canny Firmin did not trust his brother to pay up? And with good reason it seems. On the other hand, William had only got the Cross Keys because the previous landlord, John Perry, had gone bankrupt before him, so perhaps the costs of running the Cross Keys were far too high. In December 1841, William Potto was one of the insolvents discharged from bankruptcy in Salisbury.

Mr Potto gave up his beer tent at Weyhill Fair in 1841. Weyhill Fair was a very ancient fair in Hampshire, at the crossroads of numerous drover's tracks, near Andover. It was an important sheep fair, but also dealt in other livestock. It was also a place for hiring workers, and Thomas Hardy based the wife-selling incident in the *Mayor of Casterbridge* on true events at Weyhill Fair. There was also a very strange custom called 'horning the colts', where newcomers had to wear some silver horns with a full glass between them. A rhyme was recited which begins 'as fleet runs the hare, as cunning runs the fox, why should not this live calf grow to a noble ox? ...' before the 'colt' had to drain the glass. The fair was declining steadily by 1815, and so by 1841 William probably decided that it no longer merited all the work involved, and he was reining in his expenditure.

In March 1842, William Potto announced that he had moved to the Ship Inn, which had undergone extensive repairs, and he advertised that, as well a selling wine and spirits, he was brewing his own beer. This might also have been the aftermath of the bankruptcy, because the Ship was cheaper to run. It was situated in Winchester Street near the corner of Pennyfarthing Street. Although the Ship was later on considered to be 'rough' (probably because it was near

Churchill's Lodging House), it was very respectable under William Potto.

Of particular interest is the following notice (*SWJ* 1845). The Modern Order of Foresters was a Friendly Society, like the Ancient Order of Foresters, which was democratically run and whose aims are explained in the notice. The Modern Order had 'lodges' whilst the Ancient Order had 'courts'. The Ship Inn was clearly the parent lodge of the Modern Order. The Modern Foresters followed William Potto from the Ship, and thence to the King's Arms, because he was the treasurer. Both of William's brothers were also Foresters. The *Forester's Heritage Trust* alleges that the Salisbury Unity was formed in 1845, but 'took three years then to secede', because it was run by a central committee who were too autocratic (the fault deemed with the Ancient Order). I like that they wanted to raise the moral character of mankind; they didn't want much.

In 1849, William Potto served on a Grand Jury at Salisbury City Sessions, at the Guildhall. The Grand Jury was made up of 'leading citizens' of the County, who decided whether there was enough evidence (a True Bill) to send an accused for trial. Clearly his recent bankruptcy did not hinder his standing in Salisbury.

One can see from the above, that the Ship Inn was not on the corner of Winchester street and Pennyfarthing street at this date, although Mr Potto did occupy a room there.

William Potto left the Ship Inn in 1852, and as can be seen by the advertisement placed by his successor (John Rumbold), he had installed loose boxes for racehorses. Mr Rumbold fast tried to take charge of the Modern Foresters, advertising their anniversary dinner, and a row developed that certainly was about democracy of the organisation. Rumbold not only advertised the following (1852), but 'lodge' had been replaced by 'court' elsewhere in the advertisement. (Rumbold does not appear to have lasted long at the Ship, because Caleb Newman was advertising himself as the new proprietor, the following year).

William Potto was obliged to tell the *Salisbury Journal* (1853) that the Parent Lodge of the Modern Foresters was now at the Kings Arms, and that those at the Ship were disgruntled former members who had created a schism. The Foresters continued to meet at the Kings Arms for many years after William Potto had gone. There is an 'all seeing eye' still to be seen in the Kings Arms; it was a symbol of the Foresters (ancient and modern), as much as the Freemasons. The King's Arms, like the Ship, had facilities for brewing beer.

When Caleb Newman left the Ship in 1855, he sold up the contents of the Inn. Since this was only three years after William Potto had moved on from the Ship, it is worth reading. Probably, a lot of the contents had recently been owned by Mr Potto, but anyway they give a unique insight into the life of the Ship Inn in Potto's era. There is no mention of the stabling, nor the arrangements for the wines and spirits which William was selling.

In February, 1852, William Potto had moved to the King's Arms in St John's Street. It was whilst living at the King's Arms in 1855, that William Potto's only child, Elizabeth, by his first wife, Anne, married George H. Morton, a veterinary surgeon of Fisherton Street (who had perhaps attended his horses, one could speculate). The marriage sparked a family row with the bride's uncle, Firmin Potto of the Haunch of Venison, who considered the bridegroom an 'adventurer', and tried to halt the marriage. The wedding went ahead, and Kristi Summers, a direct descendant of Elizabeth Potto (in an email to this author) does not believe that Mr Morton was anything other than a respectable man, who was not swayed by Firmin Potto's threats to disinherit his niece if the marriage went ahead. Elizabeth named her eldest son William, and her second daughter Elizabeth Sophia – (so Mrs Cassey did not turn out to be wicked step-mother) – and another son, Firmin. Nevertheless, there is an indication that there was a continuing unease between Mr Morton and the Potto family because after four children born in Fisherton between 1856 and 1861, George moved his family to New Zealand, where another five sons were born after 1864. This must have been a major sadness to William Potto, who was now left with no children in Salisbury to care for him in his old age; he was already around the age of 60, and his wife nearly 70. Given the time and cost of the passage to New Zealand, and his age, it must have been apparent to William that they were unlikely to see, nor hear the voices of, his daughter and grand-children, ever again.

It should be noted that from at least 1842, the New Zealand company had been actively searching, through the *Salisbury Journal*, for farmers and people of 'the industrious classes' to emigrate to New Zealand by offering free passage to those who qualified, or reduced fares. As a Vet – who ended up teaching veterinary skills – Mr Morton was no doubt sought after in New Zealand and saw the opportunities to 'get on'. Rejected, as he was, by the Potto family, he probably felt no urge to stay.

William voted for the Tory candidate, Granville Ryder in 1869 (ballots were not secret, and the names of voters were published under the candidate, in the newspapers). William Potto died in 1870. He is buried in London Road Cemetery.

Lightning Source UK Ltd.
Milton Keynes UK
UKHW020842230822
407709UK00006B/511